FOREIGN AND AMERICAN POCKET WATCH IDENTIFICATION AND PRICE GUIDE

BOOK 3

INTRODUCTION

This book contains carefully selected pages from original factory sales, jewelry supply house and parts catalogs, along with various advertisements and brochures dating back to 1865.

Included inside on fully illustrated pages are thousands of foreign imported and American watches that were offered to the American public.

The following information is given for each watch: The year it was offered for sale—the factory description—the price it sold for originally—and the PRESENT RETAIL VALUE.

You are holding a unique book. The original antique and historic material has not been altered. Long after the current retail prices no longer apply it will still be a valuable book for research and identification to anyone interested in pocket watches. It will always tell you the best and most desirable from the junk.

First Printing April 1976

ISBN 0-913902-16-0

Author — Roy Ehrhardt

HEART OF AMERICA PRESS
P.O. Box 9808, Kansas City, Mo. 64134

INDEX

IMPORTED WATCHES

AMERICAN WATCHES

AMERICAN CASES

ALL PRICES IN THIS BOOK ARE RETAIL

POCKET WATCH PRICE GUIDE - BOOK 1
EHRHARDT,1972, 164 8½x11 pages.$6.95

The first pocket watch price guide ever written. Fine book for beginners. Great for dealers to use as a buying reference. Investors use it to see what watches have shown the most improvement in value. Over 2600 watches priced with values from $5. to $16,000. with 95% being common every day watches you need to know the value of. Still a very popular, strong selling book. Lists of all major American & Foreign watches showing descriptions & retail prices. Charts of production dates, grading movements and cases, how to determine size, and other useful information.

AMERICAN POCKET WATCH IDENTIFICATION AND PRICE GUIDE-BOOK 2, EHRHARDT,1974,192 8½x11 P. $15

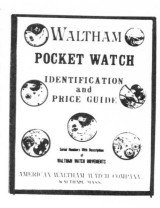

THE AMERICAN WATCH COLLECTOR'S BIBLE. This book was immediately accepted by everyone interested in watches who saw it. You can identify your watch, its age and retail value by comparing it with an original picture. It contains selected pages from original factory sales, supply house and parts catalogs, along with various advertisements and brochures dating back to 1865, the beginning of serious watchmaking in the U.S. Over 1900 pocket watches pictured & described. Completely new and different from the 1972 Edition of Book 1—nothing was duplicated. No collector, dealer, or anyone who has a good watch for sale can afford not to look up your watch in this book before acting if you have any doubts about what you are doing.

1976 POCKET WATCH PRICE INDICATOR
ROY EHRHARDT, 1975. 64 8½x11 P.$5.00

This is the first of a yearly "Price Indicator". Mr. Ehrhardt is using this means to make available to the watch collectors & dealers new information acquired during the year. This issue updates the watch prices shown in the 1974 Edition of Book 2 and 40 additional pages of pictures, advertisements and new material not shown in Book 2, i.e., 1875 Illinois brochure showing all keywinds with descriptions—4 pages of Illinois—Ben Franklin including 25 J—1877 watch cases—1877 Howard—1864 Waltham factory price list with descriptions—all Webb C. Ball serial numbers & production figures & dates—25 J. Columbus—more Hampdens, Walthams, 14 J. Seth Thomas, etc.—Elgin—New York Standard—Trenton—Elinvar Hamilton, etc.—13 page section on cases—and a 1975 summary of what's been happening to prices of American watches. This book will not make much sense if you don't have Book 2.

ROCKFORD GRADE AND SERIAL NUMBERS WITH PRODUCTION FIGURES. EHRHARDT,1976. 44 8½x11 Pages. $10.00

This Rockford book & all the other single company books contain specific information impossible to present in any other way. I have completely reproduced the 1907 Rockford serial number list & parts catalog with all serial numbers up to 824,000. Without a doubt the most important section is the breakdown of how many were produced of each grade. This enormous task was undertaken and completed by Roger Weiss, Jr. of Yorkville, Il. Most of you know the value of the 24 J, 18S Rockford. There are 50 grades with less production than the 24J open face. There are literally hundreds of sleepers out there waiting to be found. Without the proper method of identification, the one you are holding is just another old watch.

WALTHAM POCKET WATCH IDENTIFICATION AND PRICE GUIDE, EHRHARDT,1976. 172 8½x11 P. $10.

Waltham, being the first American watch factory beginning in the 1850's and continuing to the 1960's and manufacturing over 33 million watches, takes a book by itself to cover their production properly. This book is for the advanced collector or dealer who wants to get the most enjoyment out of his hobby or the most money for his watches. Partial material presented:Complete 1954 Waltham serial numbers with descriptions—selections from the following:1890 Waltham Prouts Catalog (watches & cases)—1874 Waltham Illustrated Price List—1901 Waltham Mainspring Catalog (giving model numbers to KW16, KW20, KW14, etc.) —1948 Waltham Watch & Clock Material Catalog—1952 E & J Swigart Co. Manual of Watch Movements. All of the important models, along with all of the grades in each model and a value for each, is given. This book does not leave many questions about Waltham unanswered.

ELGIN POCKET WATCH IDENTIFICATION & PRICE GUIDE. EHRHARDT, 1976. 65 8½x11 Pages. $10.00

At last—for the first time ever available—all of the Elgin pocket watch grades with the number of each produced. (A minor miracle in itself). With the help of John Miller of Springfield, Illinois and his computer, I am very proud of this work on Elgin. Partial material presented: All named & numbered grades with classification and description as originally made. Also shown for each grade: the total production—the number of runs—the first and last serial number—and the current value. In addition: the first & last serial number of all the runs for all grades with production of less than 10,000. The complete Elgin serial number list of 50 Million is also included—line drawings of the Elgin models & on and on with information that the advanced collector and dealer needs to know.

HAMILTON POCKET WATCH IDENTIFICATION & PRICE GUIDE. EHRHARDT,1976. 53 8½x11 P. $10.00

How much is my old pocket watch worth? How many were made, and when? Three questions very important to anyone interested in pocket watches. With this and the other single company books you first look up the serial number of your watch to find the grade, then look up how many were made & finally, how much is it worth. The complete Hamilton serial number list is included along with everything else you need to know.

1858 E. HOWARD & CO. REPRINT $3.00

This fine facsimile reprint is a great piece of watch and clock history. Issued by Howard the first year in business. Pictures their early clocks & talks at length about the new watch they were in the midst of producing. A very interesting little book.

* * * * * * * * * * * * *

All of the above books are available from the author-publisher on a money back satisfaction guarantee. All books will be kept in print as long as someone wants one. If you have bought this book from a dealer send in your name for my mailing list so I can notify you when new books are released. Dealer inquiries invited. Send 50 cents postage and handling with each order

**TO
ROY EHRHARDT
P.O. Box 9808
Kansas City, Mo. 64134**

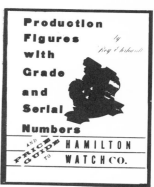

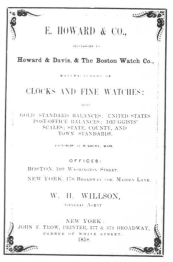

HOW TO USE THIS BOOK

I have tried to show in this Book 3 watches that were not included in any of my other books. There have been so many hundreds of different kinds of pocket watches produced in the last 150 years that it takes a series of books of this type to show them all.

I have tried with this book to show the hundreds of worthless imported watches that you see every day and also have included sections of American and foreign high grade watches and cases so you can compare one with the other. By studying the pages of this book and comparing your watch with a similar one you should be able to arrive at an approximate value of your watch.

"ALL PRICES ARE FOR WATCHES IN MINT CONDITION."

There isn't any way that I know of to make you an instant expert on pocket watches. No one knows all there is to know. The unlimited amount of different watches makes this impossible.

There is a great opportunity for anyone who is interested to make a great amount of money buying and selling pocket watches. No books had ever been written before my Book 1 in 1972 that would tell you anything about the current value of a watch. When the small number of people who have my books are compared with the over two million people in the U.S. who might have a watch for sale the possibilities are unlimited and you can find many sleeper watches. There is no other valuable collectible that is fairly readily available in varying amounts anywhere in the U.S. and the world for that matter that less is known about .

The biggest double thrill comes when you find a rare or scarce watch and then can buy it for nothing. My friends and I have found many sleepers in the past few years. Listed here are some examples with the buying and selling price. At a flea market in Kansas City, Mo., 11 Jewel 18 Size Hamilton $18.00 - $550.00; Pawn shop in Indianapolis, 23 Jewel 16 Size Premier Maximus in 18K white gold, $300.00 - $3,200.00; From a collector in Memphis, 23 Jewel 16 Size Howard made by Waltham, $150.00 - $450.00; Out of a show box in a repair shop in St. Louis another 11 Jewel 18 Size Hamilton marked "Constant", $40.00 - $950.00; From a watchmaker in Las Cruces, New Mexico, 21 Jewel 16 Size Model 72 Waltham, $60.00 - $950.00; Flea market in West Des Moines, Iowa, 18 Size San Francisco Cornell, $18.00 - $475.00; At an NAWCC show in Dearborn, Michigan an A. Lange one hour Tourbillion in 14K gold, $350.00 and in less than ten minutes sold for $2,500.00; and many others that we have doubled and tripled on.

Collecting, studying, buying or selling pocket watches is a great challenge. Anyone who has some time on their hands and are willing to study and have a little loose change can have a ball with never a dull moment.

I have tried to make each page or series of pages self-explanatory with comments and prices. I have left out many of the basics that you already know from Book 1 and Book 2. If you don't feel that you can afford your own copy of those books you can read them at your local library or they can buy them for you through my listing in PTLA.

If you have bought this book from anyone excpt me through mail order and you want to be notified of future books on watches, send me your name and address to be put on my mailing list

I included in this book, starting on Page 124, a complete reprint of Mr. William L. Scholnik's "CATALOG OF WATCHES". Combined here are his December 1975 and January 1976 actual catalogs of watches he has for sale with asking prices. This is an excellent selection of upper bracket antique and complicated foreign collector pieces.

EDITORS NOTE: Mr. Scolnik would be happy to buy a watch from you, sell you a watch, or appraise your collection for estate or insurance purposes. But please don't call or write him to either identify your watch or appraise it free. He is very busy and must devote his time to earning a living.

Beginning on Page 156 is a reprint of my January 1976 Watch List. By studying this list you can get the feel of case and watch descriptions and how the condition affects the value. Many people buy watches by mail for any number of reasons but the main one being they do not get to see many watches and they can build their collections faster and more reasonable this way.

SELF-ADDRESSED, STAMPED ENVELOPE

I get many letters from all kinds of people asking all kinds of questions. I am pleased to hear from you and will be happy to answer but you must supply a self-addressed, stamped envelope.

WATCH CASES
(Mostly American)

On many watches the case of the watch is of greater value than the movement inside. This was true when the watch was new, and so it is today. Therefore, in trying to determine the value of a watch it is important that you consider the case. Many things are to be regarded, such as the material used, the weight, workmanship, the subject of the engraving, the condition, originality and eye appeal. I will take each of these and try to explain their importance in determining watch value.

MATERIAL USED FOR CASES

The principal material used were base metal, chrome, brass, copper, stainless steel, silver, gold plate, rolled gold plate, gold filled, solid gold, platinum, and a specially made metal which consisted of approximately 45% nickel, 54% copper and 1% manganese. Cases of this material are usually marked with one of the following names: SILVEROID, SILVERODE, SILVERINE, SILVERORE, ALASKA SILVER, ORESILVER. etc. You can categorize these in three groups with some overlapping.

Take a case—say a new 16S open face—in each of the above materials. The lowest value group, or No. 1, would contain base metal, stainless steel, chrome, brass, copper, silveroid, and silverine. Group No. 2 would contain gold plate, rolled gold plate and silver. Group No. 3, and the most valuable, would contain gold filled, solid gold and platinum.

The silver from Group No. 2 and the gold and platinum Group No. 3 needs some additional explaining. Most silver cases are marked with the quality of silver, that is "925 Fine", "Coin", or "Sterling"; and foreign cases with a hallmark. As to the gold cases, the gold plated case is of least value and is usually worn through with the brass showing. Next is the gold filled, which is two sheets of gold on either side of a brass or base metal sheet, sweated or soldered together under pressure and high temperature. The sheets of gold varied in thickness according to how long the case was to wear. For instance, an 8 or 10 year case was thin and usually made of 8Kt to 10Kt gold. The 25 year case was thicker and usually made of 14Kt gold. These were made in grades of 5, 10, 15, 20 or 25 year cases. Most cases were so marked until the mid-1920's when the U.S. Government outlawed the use of the "5, 10, 15, 20 and 25" year terms. The American case companies then used such wording as "10K" and 14K gold filled", and "10KRGP" (rolled gold plate). Some case makers used the word "extra" and "permanent" to indicate a better grade of gold filled.

The solid gold cases ranged from 8K up to about 20K, with the majority of cases made in the 14K and 18K range. Most of the 20K cases were made in foreign countries. Watch the foreign cases marked 18K. Most are low karat—6 to 10. Only an acid test will tell you for sure.

To end this portion on cases, as far as material is concerned, the most valuable is the solid gold and platinum case.

WEIGHT

This applies mostly to the solid gold and silver cases. In other words, the heavier the gold or silver content the more valuable the case. Example: In an 1896 jewelry catalog a plain hunting case, 6S, 19 1/2 DWTS (20 DWTS to the ounce), 14K solid gold case retailed at $29.92 with this note—"Variations in weight will be added or deducted at the rate of $1.28 per DWT list." From this we can figure about $4.32 for workmanship and $25.60 for gold.

WORKMANSHIP

Most cases were very well made. Probably the worst fault here is that some were too thin and bent or dented easily.

SUBJECT OF THE ENGRAVING

Here we find collectors that collect certain scenes, subjects, etc. This affects the value of the watch greatly, especially historical (Liberty Bell, Independence Hall, battles, etc.), eagles, autos, trains, portraits and others. These cases are always worth extra money.

IS THE CASE ORIGINAL TO THE WATCH?

This is the age old question that is always thought and many times spoken aloud when a collector or buyer is examining an old watch. This is a very important factor on early watches, especially WALTHAM, and the rare early makers. Many times the case will be two to ten times the value of the movement.

MIS-MATCHED CASES

Many times and for many different reasons, cases and movements will be changed around. Keep a sharp eye out for cheap or non-collectible movements. Will often be found in a rare or special case that when put with the right movement would greatly increase the total value.

CONDITION

The condition of the case is very important. Examine the case for wear. Look for brass showing through gold plate or gold filled cases. In the hunter cases (spring-opened lid over face of watch) look for worn or bad hinges, broken or missing case springs, worn or missing bows, stems and crowns. Parts for watch cases are scarce and qualified repairmen are hard to find—and expensive. Collectors pay a premium for almost any kind of case in "new" or "like new" condition. A watch in new or mint condition may bring double or triple the price of one in fine condition. Any watch in mint condition is always much easier to sell.

EYE APPEAL

A watch to bring a premium price should look appealing to the man or woman who is buying it. Only the collector is very interested in the movement. A watch must be beautiful as well as a good time-keeper to bring a good price.

A note about the 14K and 18K markings on solid gold and gold filled cases. There are always a few rascals and shysters around. A few cases came from the factories marked "14K", etc. and were only gold filled. Others were marked by fakers after leaving the factory. A sure way to test the validity of the markings is by using a jewelers file and a touch of acid. If it is gold there will be no reaction. If it is not gold it will boil. Unmarked solid gold cases are much harder to sell than those with a gold mark. That is the reason for so many fake and misleading marks.

In conclusion I will say that almost any watch case in fair condition and with most of its parts has some value. Remember that during hard times in the 20's and 30's when wrist watches were gaining popularity, many watch cases were sold for their gold content and melted down. There have always been—and still are—movements that have no cases. Collectors, dealers and investors are always looking for cases.

Watch cases have been made in America since the mid 1850's, and a recent book lists over 200 case makers. For me to try and give you a definite value for a particular watch case would be impossible because of the many variables. Go to the pages in this book where cases are shown along with the descriptions to get a better idea of value.

PRICES GIVEN IN THIS PRICE GUIDE ARE RETAIL

6

GRADING OF MOVEMENTS AND CASES

The following grading system was first suggested in my first POCKET WATCH PRICE GUIDE published in 1972 with the suggestion that mail order dealers either adopt it or one of their own to give buyers some idea what they are getting. To some extent this has been done. This cuts down on watches having to be returned because the watch the buyer received was in worse shape than he thought it was going to be.

GRADING OF MOVEMENTS

FACTORY NEW: New, never been used, usually still in factory packaging.

MINT: Same as new but small and almost invisible scratches on movement. No wear marks showing on movement and keeps time at least as good as designed. That is, slightly used. No rust.

EXTREMELY FINE - NEAR MINT: Movement has been carried many years but has been properly cared for and repaired correctly, is running and keeping time. Just a slight indication of rust but has been removed.

FINE: Movement has been carried many years but has been repaired poorly. Plates are scratched or discolored or wrong parts used (botched jewels, etc.). Running and keeping time. Rust or fingerprints and pits easily removed - overcleaning evident.

GOOD: Movement is not keeping time but is running. Is complete but needs cleaning and/or adjusting. Rust and/or pitting prominent, not easily removed - repairable.

PARTS: Good for parts only.

A movement in any of the above grades with parts missing or a corrective condition may be listed with the grade plus the necessary exception, i.e. "Mint, staff broken."

GRADING OF CASES

FACTORY NEW: New, never been used, usually still in factory packaging.

MINT: Same as new but small and almost invisible scratches on case.

EXTREMELY FINE-NEAR MINT: Case has been in use and shows some slight wear.

FINE: Has been carried enough to show some brass wearing through on gold filled cases but is still solid and not dented.

GOOD: Case is showing wide areas of brass and/or dented, loose hinges, bows, etc. Explain.

FAIR: Case is in sorry condition, usually not worth restoring but will hold a movement with a crystal intact to make a watch.

PARTS: Good for parts only.

A case in any of the above grades with parts missing or a corrective condition may be listed with the grade and the necessary exception, i.e. "Extremely Fine, bow, stem and crown missing."

HOW TO DETERMINE THE SIZE OF A WATCH

Here is how to determine the size or approximately the size of your watch. Take off the cover holding the crystal. Be careful in doing this, some are screwed on - like most RR watches, some are hinged, some pop off - like most hunting cases and dollar watches. The dial in most instances covers about all of the pillar plate, of which you can usually just see the edge. Take a piece of paper and mark the width of the dial or plate if you can see it, then go to the next page and place it on the proper scale. This will tell you the size of the watch. If you remove the works from the case (only experienced people should do this) you can measure it more accurately. The plate to measure to determine the size is the one with the dial fastened to it.

I will write here mainly of the system used on American watches. The Lancashire Gauge for determining watch sizes is of English origin and is the standard commonly used by watch manufacturers of the United States. By this system one inch was taken as a basing figure and to this was added 5/30 of an inch for fall or drop (the extra width for the dial). English-made watches were usually hinged, swing-ring in the case similar to the swing-ring in modern (1923) swing-ring cases. The top plate was made enough smaller than the pillar plate to permit the movement falling or dropping into position without coming in contact with the case center. Thus, 1 and 5/30 of an inch from the base also forms a size smaller than naught size. Howard watches used letters instead (see Dennison System next page). Their A= 1 inch, B= 1 1/16 inch, C= 1 2/16 inch, etc. The above was taken from a 1923 Illinois Watch parts catalog. Most watch material houses have for sale for under $1.00 a small gauge showing all systems. On the following page I have drawn a gauge to scale.

LANCASHIRE SYSTEM - One inch is the base for a 6/0 size and 1/30 inch is added for the next higher size.

DENNISON SYSTEM - One inch is the base for the letter A size and 1/16 inch is added for each following letter.

SWISS SYSTEM - One ligne equals .088814 inches or 2.25583 millimeters. One ligne equals 1/12 of an inch of a Paris foot, which is slightly larger than an English foot.

LANCASHIRE SYSTEM			DENNISON SYSTEM			SWISS SYSTEM		
INCHES	MILLIMETERS	WATCH SIZE	HOWARD LETTER	INCHES	APPRX WATCH SIZE	LIGNES	INCHES DECIMALS	MILLIMETERS
					18-0	7	.622	15.79
					15-0	8	.710	18.05
					12-0	9	.799	20.30
					10-0	10	.888	22.56
1	25.40	6-0	A	1	6-0	11	.977	24.81
1 1/30	26.24	5-0						
1 2/30	27.08	4-0	B	1 1/16	4-0	12	1.066	27.07
1 3/30	27.94	3-0						
1 4/30	28.78	2-0	C	1 2/16	2-0	13	1.154	29.32
1 5/30	29.62	0	D	1 3/16	0	14	1.243	31.58
1 11/30	34.70	6	G	1 6/16	6	15	1.332	33.84
1 13/30	36.40	8	H	1 7/16	8	16	1.421	36.09
1 15/30	38.10	10	I	1 8/16	10	17	1.510	38.35
1 17/30	39.78	12	J	1 9/16	12			
1 19/30	41.48	14	K	1 10/16	14	18	1.599	40.60
1 21/30	43.18	16	L	1 11/16	16	19	1.687	42.86
1 22/30	44.02	17						
1 23/30	44.86	18	N	1 13/16	18	20	1.776	45.11
1 25/30	46.56	20				21	1.865	47.37

10,000 WATCHES

THE LARGEST PURCHASE EVER MADE BY A WHOLESALE JEWELRY HOUSE AT ONE TIME OF ANY ONE GRADE OF SWISS WATCHES

We have just purchased 10,000 open face gun metal watches from one of the largest importers in this country who states

<table>
<tr><td>THE LARGEST ORDER EVER GIVEN</td><td>WE HOLD THE RECORD</td><td>THEY WILL NOT LAST LONG AT THESE PRICES</td></tr>
</table>

By placing this immense order we secure a price so low that we can sell them lower than our competitors pay for the same watches. The greatest value ever offered the watch world. Order at once.

① MINT $45.00

16 Size Gun Metal Fancy Dial Watches

② MINT $40.00
FINE $15.00
GOOD — $2.00

These prices will keep competitors awake nights wondering how we do it

No. C723. Embossed Dial.

No. C726. Metallic Dial.

③ MINT $40.00
FINE $15.00
GOOD $2.00

$1.65 EACH

$1.65 EACH

No. C725. Frame Dial.

④ MINT $35.00

No. C724. Fancy Color Dial.

⑤ MINT $30.00

No. C727. Fancy Cream Dial.

0-Size Imitation Gold Filled Watches

HUNTING AND STEM-WIND

AN ASSORTMENT OF GOOD RUNNING MOVEMENTS

THESE CASES SHOW WEAR ON THE GOLD VERY FAST VERY LOW QUALITY WITH A LITTLE WEAR THESE CASES ARE NOT WORTH MUCH.

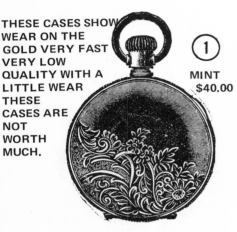

① MINT $40.00

No. 947.

M—$45.00
F—$20.00
G—$5.00

②

No. 948.

③

MINT $40.00

No. 949.

SAME CASES WITH ANTIQUE BOW 5c. MORE ON A WATCH

$10.00

MOVEMENT ONLY MINT AND RUNNING

④

No. B624. The Malton Special, 0 size, three-quarter plate, 11-jewels, exposed winding wheels, patent regulator, double sunk white enameled dial, black steel hands. Has the appearance of a 15-jewel movement, guaranteed to give satisfaction in every respect. Great seller. Complete, price, each.............$2.75

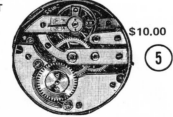

$10.00

⑤

No. B626. Wellington, 0 size, three-quarter plate, jeweled, exposed winding wheels, finely damaskeened plates, patent regulator, double sunk white enameled dials, black steel hands. A sister in every respect to the Malton Special. Complete, price, each.........................$2.75

$10.00

⑥

No. B628. 6 size Alpine, bridge model, jeweled nickel damaskeen plates, exposed winding wheels, patent regulator, assorted colored fancy dials and gilt hands. This movement is in a class by itself, and will give perfect satisfaction. Complete, price, each $2.30

$10.00

⑦

No. B680. The Mignon, 0 size, three-quarter plate cylinder escapement, bridge model, jeweled movement, exposed winding wheels, white enameled dial, gilt blue steel hands. Complete, price, each..........$2.25

$10.00

⑧

No. B632. The Malton, 0 size, three-quarter plate cylinder, screw set, jeweled, fancy damaskeen plates, assorted, fancy dial, gilt hands. Best movement of its grade on the market. Complete, price, each.....$2.00

No. B634. Same as above, with white dials, gilt or blue steel hands. Price $1.90

$10.00

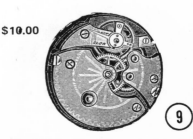

⑨

No. B636. The Diana, 0 size, three-quarter plate, exposed winding wheels, cylinder escapement, damaskeen plates, fancy dial, gilt hands, Complete, price, each..........$2.00

6 Size Imitation Gold Filled Watches

HUNTING, STEM-WIND

We have a large assortment of cases in very showy designs

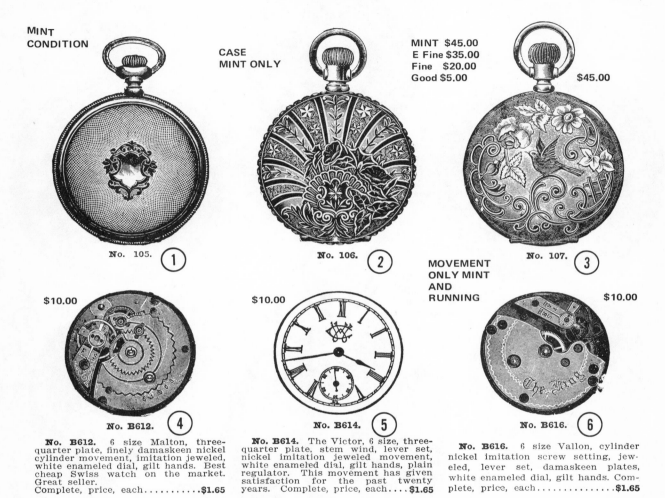

MINT
CONDITION

CASE
MINT ONLY

MINT $45.00
E Fine $35.00
Fine $20.00
Good $5.00

$45.00

No. 105. ①

No. 106. ②

No. 107. ③

MOVEMENT
ONLY MINT
AND
RUNNING

$10.00

$10.00

$10.00

No. B612. ④

No. B614. ⑤

No. B616. ⑥

No. B612. 6 size Malton, three-quarter plate, finely damaskeen nickel cylinder movement, imitation jeweled, white enameled dial, gilt hands. Best cheap Swiss watch on the market. Great seller.
Complete, price, each..........**$1.65**

No. B614. The Victor, 6 size, three-quarter plate, stem wind, lever set, nickel imitation jeweled movement, white enameled dial, gilt hands, plain regulator. This movement has given satisfaction for the past twenty years. Complete, price, each....**$1.65**

No. B616. 6 size Vallon, cylinder nickel imitation screw setting, jeweled, lever set, damaskeen plates, white enameled dial, gilt hands. Complete, price, each...............**$1.65**

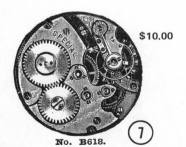

$10.00

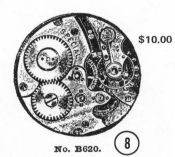

$10.00

$10.00

No. B618. ⑦

No. B620. ⑧

B622 ⑨

No. B618. The Algier, 6 size, three-quarter plate, stem wind, raised, red imitation jewels in setting, exposed winding wheels, patent regulator, assorted fancy colored dials, gilt hands. The leader of the 6-size watches, best seller on the market. Complete, price each **$2.00**

No. B620. Bradford Special, 6 size, nickel cylinder, lever set, imitation jeweled raised setting, patent regulator, exposed winding wheels, fancy damaskeen plates, assorted fancy dials and gilt hands. Complete, price, each **$1.95**

No. B622. 6 size Madison, ¾ plate cylinder imitation raised ruby jeweled exposed winding wheels, patent regulator, fancy damaskeen plates, white dial, gilt hands. Complete, price, each **$1.95**

THESE SWISS IMPORTED MOVEMENTS ARE OF LOW QUALITY AND CHEAPLY MADE UNLESS THEY ARE MINT AND RUNNING THEY ARE WORTH ABOUT $1.50, FOR USE IN COLLAGES AND PICTURES. BEAUTIFUL MINT DECORATED DIALS ON THESE MAKE THEM COLLECTABLE AND INCREASE THE VALUE. THE VALUE SHOWN FOR THE CASES ARE FOR MINT. WITH ANY BRASS SHOWING, THE VALUE DROPS 50% to 75%.

16 Size Imitation Gold Filled Watches
Hunting, Lever Set, Stem Wind
We here give you the best assortment of low price 16 size watches on the market

NOTE THESE PRICES   **ORDER TODAY**

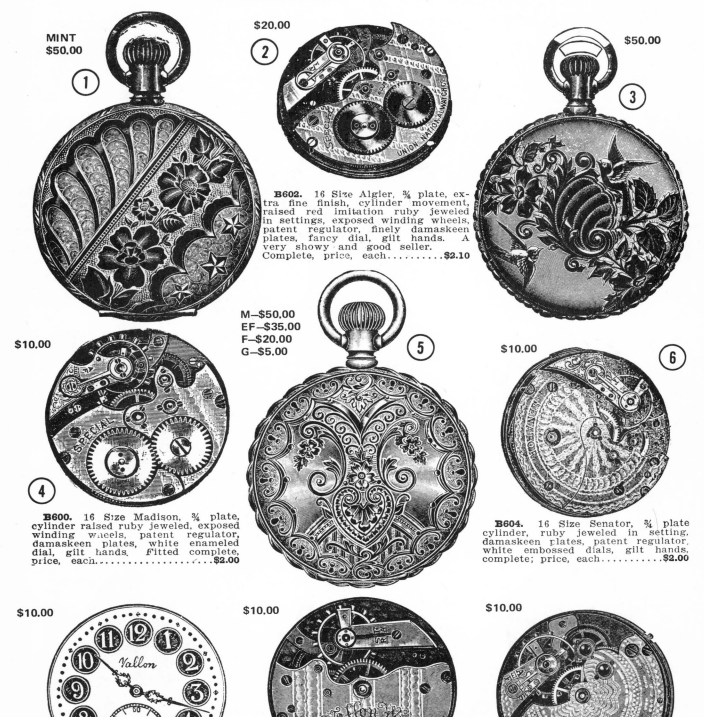

MINT
$50.00

①

$20.00

②

$50.00

③

B602. 16 Size Algier, ¾ plate, extra fine finish, cylinder movement, raised red imitation ruby jeweled in settings, exposed winding wheels, patent regulator, finely damaskeen plates, fancy dial, gilt hands. A very showy and good seller. Complete, price, each..........$2.10

$10.00

④

M—$50.00
EF—$35.00
F—$20.00
G—$5.00

⑤

$10.00

⑥

B600. 16 Size Madison, ¾ plate, cylinder raised ruby jeweled, exposed winding wheels, patent regulator, damaskeen plates, white enameled dial, gilt hands. Fitted complete, price, each..................$2.00

B604. 16 Size Senator, ¾ plate cylinder, ruby jeweled in setting, damaskeen plates, patent regulator, white embossed dials, gilt hands, complete; price, each..........$2.00

$10.00

⑦

$10.00

⑧

$10.00

⑨

B606. 16 Size Malton, ¾ plate, imitation jeweled, cylinder movement, finely nickel damaskeen plates, raised colored embossed dial, gilt hands; complete, price, each....$1.80

B608. 16 Size Malton, ¾ plate, imitation jeweled, cylinder movement, finely nickel damaskeen plates, white enamel dial, gilt hands, best plain cylinder movement on the market. Complete; price, each.....$1.75

B610. 16 Size B. W. Special, ¾ plate, cylinder movement with exposed winding wheels, raised imitation jeweled, patent regulator, nickel damaskeen plates, fancy dial, gilt hands. Complete; price, each..$2.10

18s Imitation Gold Filled Complete Watches

Stem-Wind, Hunting or Open Face.   Every One Guaranteed.

Prices Always The Lowest.   Order By Number.

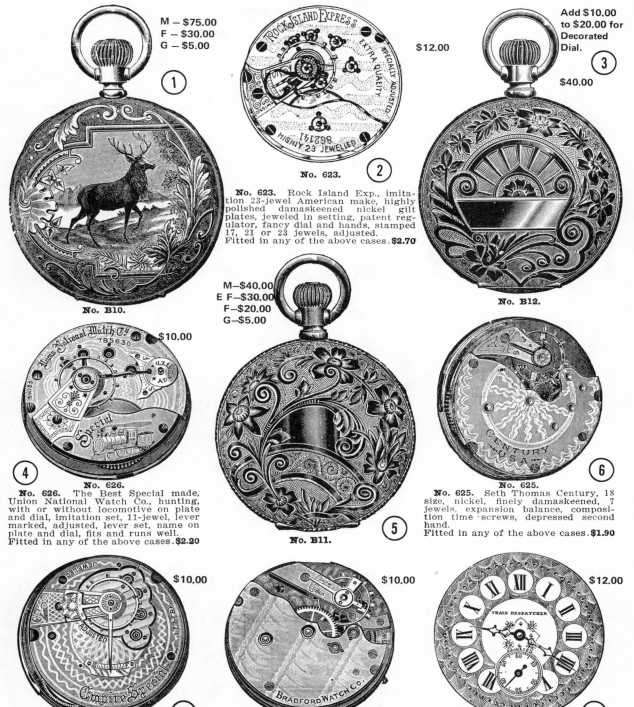

M – $75.00
F – $30.00
G – $5.00

① ②

$12.00

Add $10.00 to $20.00 for Decorated Dial.

③

$40.00

No. 623.

No. 623. Rock Island Exp., imitation 23-jewel American make, highly polished damaskeened nickel gilt plates, jeweled in setting, patent regulator, fancy dial and hands, stamped 17, 21 or 23 jewels, adjusted. Fitted in any of the above cases. **$2.70**

No. B10.

No. B12.

$10.00

M–$40.00
E F–$30.00
F–$20.00
G–$5.00

④ ⑤ ⑥

No. 626.

No. 626. The Best Special made, Union National Watch Co., hunting, with or without locomotive on plate and dial, imitation set, 11-jewel, lever marked, adjusted, lever set, name on plate and dial, fits and runs well. Fitted in any of the above cases. **$2.20**

No. B11.

No. 625.

No. 625. Seth Thomas Century, 18 size, nickel, finely damaskeened, 7 jewels, expansion balance, composition time screws, depressed second hand. Fitted in any of the above cases. **$1.90**

$10.00

$10.00

$12.00

⑦ ⑧ ⑨

No. 627.

No. 627. Empire Special, imitation 21 jewel American movement, highly polished damaskeened plates, sunk balance, 4 pair jewels in setting, patent bridge regulator, stamped 17 or 21 jewels and adjusted, white double sunk dial.
Fitted in any of above cases.... **$2.55**

No. 628.

No. 628. The Malton, three-quarter plate nickel damaskeened, cylinder escapement, white enameled dials, fancy hands.
Fitted in any of the above cases. **$1.65**
Same as above with fancy embossed dials **$1.75**

No. 624.

No. 624. Train Despatcher, imitation American Railroad movement, highly finished damaskeened lower plates, stamped, especially adjusted, extra quality, highly jeweled, patent regulator, fancy sash dial, assorted colors. Fitted in any of above cases **$2.70**

THE MOVEMENTS AND CASES ARE ALL VALUED INDIVIDUALLY. BOTH MUST BE MINT. ANY WEAR ON THESE CASES CAUSE THE VALUE TO DECREASE SHARPLY. THESE CASES USUALLY ARE NOT MARKED INSIDE AND IF IN GOOD CONDITION WILL BE BRIGHT & SHINEY INSIDE. THEY ARE BRASS WITH GOLD DIP OR PLATING ON THEM.

NEW ERA AND COLUMBIA WATCHES
ENOUGH SAID

They are known all over the world.   The best low price complete watch on the market.
Every one is a guaranteed time keeper, being fitted and timed at the factory.

FINE
MINT
CONDITION
RUNNING

$50.00 ①

THESE ARE AMERICAN
MADE NEW YORK Std.
MOVEMENTS AND
PRICES ARE FOR
COMPLETE WATCH
IN NEAR MINT
CONDITION

$50.00

②

2879

No. 2879. 18 size Perfection Imitation Gold Filled Hunting Case, in a variety of beautiful engraved patterns, fitted with the celebrated 7-jewel three-quarter plate New Era movement, which is a nickel damaskeened movement, in assorted white and colored dials. Price each...**$1.85**

$45.00 ③

2881

No. 2881. 6 size Perfection Imitation Gold Filled Hunting Case, in assorted engraved and engine turned, fitted with the celebrated Columbia nickel damaskeened three-quarter plate lever movement, which comes in assorted fancy and white dials. Price, each **$1.92**

2880

No. 2880. 18x16 Perfection Imitation Gold Filled Open Face Case, assorted designs, plain polished, engine turned and engraved, fitted with the celebrated 7-jewel New Era movement.   An up-to-date watch. Price **$1.85**

$25.00 ⑤

④

$25.00

2882

No. 2882. 18x16 S. B. & B. Condensed Model Nickel Case, antique crown and pendant, fitted with the celebrated New Era movement. Price, each **$1.90**
No. 2885. Same as above, with round bow. Price, each.......**$1.85**

2883

No. 2883. 18 size S. B. & B. three-ounce nickel case, plain polished or half engraved, fitted with the celebrated New Era nickel damaskeened movement, with assorted fancy or white dials. Price, each...**$1.85**
No. 2884. Same as above, in hunting case. Price. each.........**$2.15**

$40.00

12s Imitation Gold Filled Watches
VERY THIN MODEL, STEM-WIND, LEVER SET HUNTING WATCHES

A GENTLEMAN'S WATCH
The 12 Size

THE BEST SELLER IN YOUR STOCK

No. 40.

$35.00

These watches are made especially for us, extra care being taken in the finish of both case and movement, which makes them as good as some filled watches.

No. 42.

$35.00

If you do not want ^at you want let ^want yo. ee to fill and save you money

CASES AND MOVEMENTS ARE PRICED SEPARATELY AND MUST BE IN MINT CONDITION AND RUNNING.

No. 41.

$30.00

Our low prices a d our up-to-date m hod combined with reliable goods and prompt service make us the leading house of the west

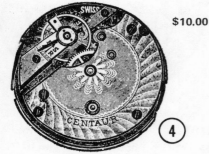

$10.00

No. B212. B. W. Special, 12 size, red raised jewel, exposed winding, patent regulator, finely damaskeened three-quarter plates, white enamel dial and gilt hands. Price, complete $2.50

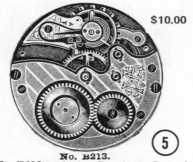

$10.00

No. B213. 12 size Senator. One of our best selling and most popular movements set with raised jewels, very showy and of rich finish, extra jeweled cylinder escapement, damaskeened plates, white enamel dial and gilt hand. Price, complete......$2.40

$10.00

No. B214. Seven jewel, nickel movement, damaskeened in nickel, cylinder, very finely adjusted and finished, highly tempered bearings, flat model, a very satisfactory low price movement, stem wind and setting, hunting. White, enameled dial. Complete, price $2.25

THESE CHEAPLY MADE WATCHES AND MOVEMENTS ARE TRADERS AND ARE NOT AT THE PRESENT BEING PUT IN COLLECTIONS. THESE WATCHES ARE STILL BEING MISREPRESENTED WHEN OFFERED FOR SALE IF THEY ARE IN MINT CONDITION.

18 Size Gold Plated Cases and Complete Watches
Raised Imitation Gold Ornamented. Looks Like a $50 Watch.

① CASE MINT $75.00

Case $1.25 ②

CASE ONLY MINT $75.00 FINE $35.00

GOOD $5.00

③ CASE MINT $75.00

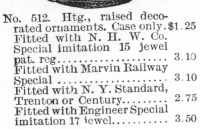

No. 512. Htg., raised deco-rated ornaments. Case only.$1.25
Fitted with N. H. W. Co.
Special imitation 15 jewel
pat. reg..................... 3.10
Fitted with Marvin Railway
Special 3.10
Fitted with N. Y. Standard,
Trenton or Century......... 2.75
Fitted with Engineer Special
imitation 17 jewel.......... 3.50

No. 513. Htg., raised deco-rated ornaments. Case only.$1.25
Fitted with N. H. W. Co.
Special imitation 15 jewel
pat. reg..................... 3.10
Fitted with Marvin Railway
Special..................... 3.10
Fitted with N. Y. Standard,
Trenton or Century......... 2.75
Fitted with Engineer Special
imitation 17 jewel.......... 3.50

No. 514. Htg., raised deco-rated ornaments. Case only.$1.25
Fitted with N. H. W. Co.
Special imitation 15 jewel
pat. reg..................... 3.10
Fitted with Marvin Railway
Special..................... 3.10
Fitted with N. Y. Standard,
Trenton or Century......... 2.75
Fitted with Engineer Special
imitation 17 jewel.......... 3.50

CASE ONLY $75.00

MOVEMENTS ARE PRICED ON ANOTHER PAGE
Case $1.25 ④

CASE MINT $75.00
Case $1.25 ⑤

⑥ CASE MINT $75.00

No. 515. Htg., raised deco-rated ornaments...........$1.25
Fitted with N. H. W. Co.
Special imitation 15 jewel
pat. reg..................... 3.10
Fitted with Marvin Railway
Special.....................
Fitted with N. Y.
Trenton or Ce
Fitted with Lo
cial imitation 1

No. 516. Htg., raised deco-rated ornaments...........$1.25
Fitted with N. H. W. Co.
Special imitation 15 jewel
pat. reg.....................
................3.10
.....tandard,
....Century........ 2.75
Fitted with Locomotive Special imitation 17 jewel...... 3.50

No. 517. Htg., raised deco-rated ornaments...........$1.25
with N. H. W. Co.
imitation 15 jewel
.... 3.10
Fitted with Marvin Railway
Special 3.10
Fitted with N. Y. Standard,
Trenton or Century......... 2.75
Fitted with Locomotive Spe-
cial imitation 17 jewel...... 3.50

THESE CASES IN MINT TO FACTORY NEW CONDITION ARE VERY HARD TO IDENTIFY AS BEING IMITATION GOLD CASES, WITHOUT A CLOSE LOOK.

6, 16 and 18 Size Imitation Gold Flexible and Ornamented Cases and Watches

LOOKS LIKE GOLD AND BENDS LIKE GOLD

FINEST IMITATION OF A GOLD CASE MADE

① MINT CASE $55.00

② CASE MINT $60.00 FINE $25.00 GOOD $5.00

③ CASE MINT $80.00

No. 151. 16 size flexible imitation solid gold hunting case. Looks like solid gold; handsomely engraved, E. T. or plain polish. Price, each.. **$0.90**
Fitted with 15-jewel imitation Algiers. **2.50**
Fitted with Vallon embossed dial, each **2.30**
Fitted with 11-jewel SH. Elgin movement, each. **4.00**

No. 152. 6 size flexible imitation gold hunting case, asst. engraving or E. T. Price, each. **$0.90**
Fitted with imit. 15-jewel Algiers.. **2.50**
Fitted with Vallon embossed dial, each **2.50**
Fitted with Victor or Vallon movement, each. **2.15**

No. 153. 18 size flexible imitation gold hunting case, asst. engraving or E. T. Price, each. **$0.90**
Fitted with 21-jewel No. Western Spec. **2.75**
Fitted with 23-jewel Marvin fancy dial, each. **3.00**
Fitted with 7-jewel Vallon movement, each. **2.15**

④ CASE MINT $75.00 FINE $35.00 GOOD $5.00

⑤ CASE MINT $75.00

⑥ CASE MINT $80.00

No. 154. 18 size flexible imitation gold raised hunting case. A great seller. Each. **$1.50**
Fitted with 23-jewel Marvin Spec... **3.50**
Fitted with 21-jewel Algiers. **3.35**
Fitted with Vallon embossed dial. **2.75**

No. 155. 6 size flexible imitation gold raised hunting case, assorted designs, each. **$1.50**
Fitted with 15-jewel Algiers. **2.75**
Fitted with 15-jewel Malton, metallic dial, each. **2.80**
Fitted with Vallon, white dial. **2.65**

No. 156. 18 size, white metal raised decorated cases, asst. designs, each. **$1.25**
Fitted with 21-jewel Algiers. **3.30**
Fitted with 17 or 21-jewel U. P. Flyer **3.00**
Fitted with 7-jewel Century American movement. **2.65**

Low Price American Watches
Nickle, Gun Metal and Gilt

**ME
NEAR MINT
CONDITION
AND RUNNING**

58c   62c   62c

Madison Special

Every box marked price $2.00

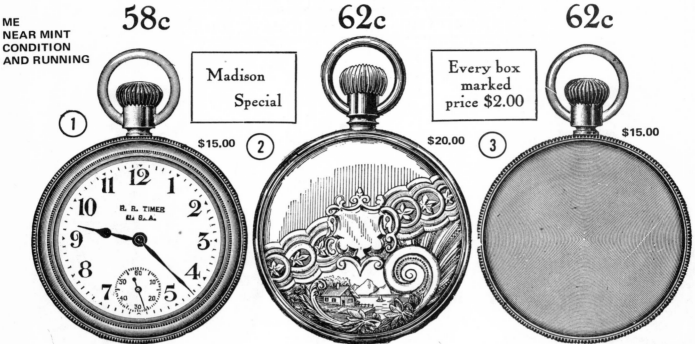

No. 141. Madison special, nickel, stem wind and stem set, American watch. Best of its kind on the market. A good timepiece. Each..**$0.58**

No. 142. Madison Special, gold plated, stem wind and stem set, American watch, very showy, guaranteed for one year. Price, each.**$0.62**

No. 143. Madison Special Gun Metal, stem wind and stem set American, watch. A great watch for the boys. Everyone guaranteed for one year. Price, each ....**$0.£2**

½ Size

½ Size

The American

$10.00

49 cents

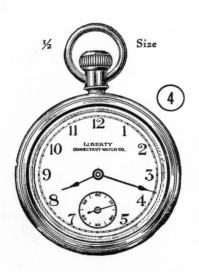

No. 144. Liberty Nickel, 16 size, highly polished nickel case- (hinged back), fitted with our American lever escapement movement, winds and sets in the back without the use of key and is timed and tested, regulated and fully guaranteed for one year.
Each **$0.52**
In lots of 50, each............. .50

No. 145. Defiance Nickel, 16 size, highly polished nickel case, fitted with our American lever escapement, stem wind and pendant set movement, which is timed, tested, regulated and fully guaranteed for one year.
Each **$0.63**
In lots of 50, each............. .60
No. 146. Defiance Oxidized. Same as above, in black gun metal case.
Each **$0.65**
In lots of 50. Each............. .62
No. 147. Defiance Gilt. Same as above in 14k gold plated case.
Each **$0.65**
In lots of 50. Each............. .62

No. 148. The American stem wind nickel watch. The greatest clock watch on the market.
Price, each **$0.49**

WRITE FOR PRICES IN LOTS OF 100 OR MORE

18 Size S. B. & B.
Nickel Cases

MINT CONDITION CASE PRICED ONLY ON THIS PAGE

43c

CASE MINT $25.00
FINE $15.00
GOOD $3.00

No. 157, 18 size, open face, screw bezel and back.
OUR PRICE (case only)........... $0 43

FITTED COMPLETE WITH

7-jewel Century movement.........	$1 95
7-jewel Standard movement........	2 00
7-jewel Hampden or Rockford.......	2 60
11-jewel Hampden..........	3 00
11-jewel gilt Springfield movement....	2 85
11-jewel Keystone or Seth Thomas mvt.	2 00
15-jewel Springfield movement........	2 50

CASE MINT $25.00

NO. 160. SILVERINE.

No. 160, 18 size, solid metal, solid back, swing ring and screw bezel.
OUR PRICE (case only)........... $0 75

FITTED COMPLETE WITH

7-jewel Century or Trenton movement.	2 15
7-jewel Elgin or Waltham movement.	3 25
11-jewel Elgin or Waltham..........	3 75
15-jewel Elgin, Waltham or Hampden movement..................	4 75
17-jewel special imitation Amer. mvt.	2 50
11-jewel old model American movement.	2 90

No. B.2005. SILVERINE.
Same as above. Dust proof........ $0 95

SILVEROID

CASE MINT $25.00

NO. 159. SILVEROID.
No. 159, 18 size, open face watch case, jointed back and front.
OUR PRICE (case only)........... $0 35

FITTED COMPLETE WITH

7-jewel Century movement.........	1 80
7-jewel Standard movement........	1 80
7-jewel Illinois movement..........	2 65
11-jewel Hampden, Rockford or Springfield movement.	3 00
15-jewel imitation Swiss S. H. mvt....	2 15

16 Size
S. B. & B.
Nickel
Cases
45 Cents

CASE MINT $50.00
FINE $25.00
GOOD $10.00

ASSORTED DECORATIONS SILVERINE INLAID.
No. 158, 18 size, S. B. & B., silverine, gold inlaid.
OUR PRICE (case only)....... $0 73

FITTED COMPLETE WITH

7-jewel Trenton or Century movement.	2 30
15-jewel imitation American lever set movement....................	3 00
7-jewel American Waltham movement.	3 35
15-jewel American Waltham movement.	4 85

CASE MINT $40.00
FINE $35.00
GOOD $15.00

ANY KIND OF KEYWIND CASE IS IN DEMAND AT THIS TIME

KEY WIND.
No. 161, 18 size, silverine, open face, key wind.
OUR PRICE (case only)........... $0 35

FITTED COMPLETE WITH

11-jewel imitation American movement.	1 30
7-jewel steel balance movement......	1 40
11-jewel steel balance movement....	1 65
7-jewel Elg. or Walt. comp. bal. mvt.	1 75
11-jewel Elg. or Walt. comp. bal. mvt.	2 00
15-jewel Elg. or Walt. comp. bal. mvt.	2 25

Nickel or Silverine Cases

All Sizes

Hunting
and
Open Face

MINT
$25.00
FINE $10.00
GOOD $3.00

No. B800. 18 size, Hunting, Nickel or Silverine Case. Plain Polish, Engine Turned or Engraved. Price, each 75c

MINT
$30.00
FINE
$10.00
GOOD $3.00

No. B801. 16 size, Hunting, Nickel or Silverine Case. Plain Polish, Engine or Engraved. Price each....75c

MINT $60.00

No. B802. 18 size, 3-oz. Nickel Swing Ring, Dustproof Nut. Gilt Reflection Cup Case. Screw Bezel and Solid Back. Solid Gold Inlaid, assorted subjects—stag, engine, etc. Price each $1.75

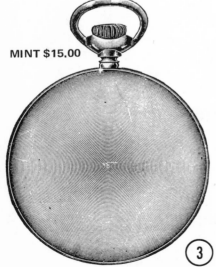

MINT $15.00

No. B803. 16 size, Nickel or Silverine, Screw Back and Bezel Round Bow. Price each...............45c
No. B804. Same as above, Antique Bow. Price each.............50c

HC
MINT
$30.00

OF
MINT
$15.00

No. B805. 6 size, Hunting, Nickel or Silverine Case, Engraved, Engine Turned or Plain Polish. Price, each 80c

No. B806. Same as above in Open Face. Price each.............60c

18 Size Grand Central Chronometer Complete Watches

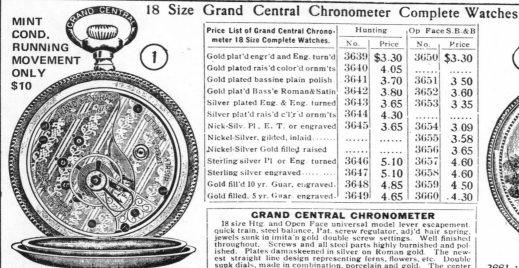

MINT
COND.
RUNNING
MOVEMENT
ONLY
$10

No. 1695 18 size Grand Central Chronometer Htg. & O. F., Universal model, lever esc'm't, quick train, steel Bal. Pat. screw regula'r Jwls sunk in imita'n gold double screw settings.

Price List of Grand Central Chronometer 18 Size Complete Watches.	Hunting		Op Face S.B.&B	
	No.	Price	No.	Price
Gold plat'd engr'd and Eng. turn'd	3639	$3.30	3650	$3.30
Gold plated rais'd color'd ornm'ts	3640	4.05	......	......
Gold plated bassine plain polish	3641	3.70	3651	3 50
Gold plat'd Bass'e Roman&Satin	3642	3.80	3652	3.60
Silver plated Eng. & Eng. turned	3643	3.65	3653	3 35
Silver plat'd rais'd c'l'r'd ornm'ts	3644	4.30	......	......
Nick-Silv. Pl., E. T. or engraved	3645	3.65	3654	3.09
Nickel-Silver, gilded, inlaid.......	......	......	3655	3.58
Nickel-Silver Gold filled raised	......	......	3656	3 65
Sterling silver Pl or Eng. turned	3646	5.10	3657	4.60
Sterling silver engraved.....	3647	5.10	3658	4.60
Gold fill'd 10 yr. Guar, engraved.	3648	4.85	3659	4.50
Gold filled, 5 yr. Guar. engraved.	3649	4.65	3660	.4.30

GRAND CENTRAL CHRONOMETER

18 size Htg. and Open Face universal model lever escapement. quick train, steel balance. Pat. screw regulator, adj'd hair spring. jewels sunk in imita'n gold double screw settings. Well finished throughout. Screws and all steel parts highly burnished and polished. Plates damaskeened in silver on Roman gold. The newest straight line design representing ferns, flowers, etc. Double sunk dials, made in combination, porcelain and gold. The center and second circles are gold plated on an Engine Turned metal surface. Outer circle is made of porcelain, tinted in ivory, rose and other colors. Black Arabic figures, red marginals. Extra heavy spade black hands.

CASE
$75.00

3661 18 size Htg. flexible, extra gold plated colored ornaments,. Grand Central Chronometer. $4.55

MINT
$45.00

3662 18 size S. B. & B. 3oz. nickel gilded inlaid ornaments, Loco. stag., horse, trolley, etc., Grand Central Chronometer.................$3.58

MINT — $75.00
FINE — $30.00
GOOD — $10.00

3663 18 size Htg. gold plated, extra quality raised colored ornaments, raised stone center, Grand Central Chronometer. $4.30

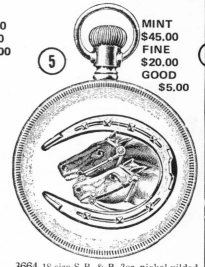

MINT
$45.00
FINE
$20.00
GOOD
$5.00

3664 18 size S B. & B. 3oz. nickel gilded inlaid ornaments, Loco., Stag, horse, trolley, etc., Grand Central Chronometer................. $3 58

MINT
$75.00
FINE
$35.00
GOOD
$10.00

3665 18 size Htg. 14 k. gold filled col'r'd engraved, guaranteed for 10 years, Grand Central Chronometer. $5.65

MINT
$85.00

3666 18 size Htg. gold filled, engraved and engine turned, guaran'd for 10 yrs., Grand Central Chronometer.........$4.85

MINT
$65.00

3667 18 size Htg gold filled engr'v'd and engine turned, guaranteed for 5 years, Grand Central Chronometer.....$4.65

18 size Woldorf Anchor Complete Watches

MINT
CONDITION
RUNNING
MOVEMENT
ONLY
$10.00

1434 18 size Woldorf, nickel silvered ¾ plate mvt, impr'd lever escapem't, quick train

WOLDORF 18 SIZE MOVEMENTS

Nickel silvered ¾ plate Hunting and Open Face, improved lever escapement, quick train, gilt balance in recess, patent screw regulator, concave visible winding wheels, hardened and finely tempered hair spring, bright flat screws,, all steel parts highly polished. Decorated with artistic damaskeened new art ray designs on nickel silvered plates, gold inlaid lettering and ornamental scrolls. Highly colored jewels in imitation gold settings, extra large red stone over center pinion, imitation double sunk, white enameled French dial, Roman or Arabic figures, red and blue marginals, blue steel pear shaped hands.

The general construction of the Woldorf movement is mechanically correct. Every piece of material is thoroughly well finished.

$35.00

3687 18 size O. F. screw bezel, solid back, swinging Mvt. ring, 3oz. nickel cup Pl. Pol., Woldorf $3.58

M—$30.00
F—$15.00
G—$5.00

3688 18 size open face screw bezel, solid back, swinging movement ring, 4 oz. nickel cup plain polish, Woldorf..........$4.25

Price List of Woldorf 18 size Complete Watches.	Hunting		Op. Face S. B. & B.	
	No.	Price	No.	Price
Gold Plated Engrav'd and engine turned ..	3668	$3.30	3679	$3.30
Gold plated, raised colored ornaments..	3669	4.05	......	....
G. plat., bass'e, pl. pol.	3670	3.70	3680	3.50
G. plat. bass, Rom & Sa.	3671	3.80	3681	3.60
Silver plat. eng. & E. T.	3672	3.65	......	....
Silver plated, raised colored ornaments..	3673	4.30	......	....
Nick'l Silv. Pl. or E. T.	3674	3.65	3682	3.09
Sterling Silver plain or engine turned....	3675	5.10	3683	4.60
Sterling silver eng. assorted designs ..	3676	5.10	3684	4.60
Gold Filled 10 year guarantee, eng......	3677	4.85	3685	4.50
Gold Filled, 5 year guarnteed eng......	3678	4.65	3686	4.30

M—$75.00
F—$30.00
G—$5.00

3690 18 size open face screw bezel, solid back, swinging movement ring, 4oz. nickel cup solid gold inlaid, Loco., stag, trolley, horse, etc., Woldorf......$5.18

M—$65.00
F—$30.00
G—$5.00

3692 18 size O. F. S. B. & B. 3 oz. nickel gilded inlaid, Woldorf......$3.58

M—$40.00

3689 18 size open face S. B. & B. 6 oz. plain polish Woldorf............$3.60

3691 18 size O. F. S. B. & B. 2 oz. nickel, plain pol., Woldorf....$3.30

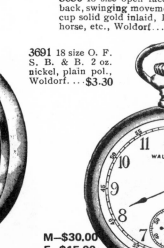

M—$30.00
F—$15.00
G—$5.00

GENUINE STERLING SILVER WATCH CASES
GUARANTEED $\frac{925}{1000}$ FINE
Can Furnish in all Sizes and a Large Variety of Designs

MINT
CASE $55
7J—$65.00
15J—$70.00

2116

No. 2116 16 size hunting sterling silver case, good heavy weight, assorted fancy engravings....................$2.50
Fitted with 7-jewel Trenton Bridge Model......................................5.00
Fitted with 15-jewel Trenton Bridge Model......................................6.50
Fitted with 7-jewel Elgin or Waltham S. H. M'vt...............................6.75
Open face screw case 60 cents less.

MINT
7J – $45.00
15J –$50.00

2117

No. 2117 6 size hunting sterling silver case, good weight, fancy engraved....$2.00
Fitted with 7-jewel Bridge Model Trenton...4.00
Fitted with 7-jewel Elgin or Waltham S. H. Mv't...................................5.80
Fitted with 15-jewel Elgin or Waltham S. H. Mv't...................................6.65

MINT
7J $40.00
15J $45.00

2118

No. 2118 12x6 size hunting sterling silver case, heavy weight fancy engraved....................$2.25
Fitted with 7-jewel Bridge Model Trenton...4.25
Fitted with 7-jewel Elgin or Waltham S. H. M'vt...................................6.05
Fitted with 15-jewel Elgin or Waltham S. H. Mv't...................................6.90

MINT
CASE
$55.00
7J $60.00
11J $65.00

2119

No. 2119 18 size hunting sterling silver case, heavy weight, assorted fancy engravings....................$2.60
Fitted with 7-jewel Century or Standard Mv't......................................4.10
Fitted with 7-jewel Elgin or Waltham S. H. Mv't...................................5.10
Fitted with 11-jewel Hampden or Illinois S. H. Mv't...............................5.25
Open face screw cases 60 cents less.

MINT CASE
$30.00
7J $40.00
15J $45.00

2120

No. 2120 0 size hunting sterling silver case, good weight, fancy engraved....$1.90
Fitted with 7-jewel nickel Trenton..5.85
Fitted with 7-jewel nickel U. S..6.40
Fitted with 11-jewel Wellington..4.15
Fitted with 15-jewel U. S. nickel..7.65

MINT
CASE
$40.00
7J $45.00
11J $50.00

2121

No. 2121 18 size open face screw bezel and back sterling silver case, heavy weight, plain polished.....................$2.00
Fitted with 7-jewel Century or Standard Mv't......................................3.50
Fitted with 7-jewel Elgin or Waltham S. H. Mv't...................................4.50
Fitted with 11-jewel Hampden or Illinois...4.65

The "CYMA"

The Perfect Watch

Adjusted to Heat and Cold

FULLY GUARANTEED   **A WORLD - BEATER**

MINT $20.00
FINE $10.00
GOOD $3.00

No. 426.

MINT $45.00
FINE $20.00
GOOD $5.00

No. 429.

Finished Material

Thin Model

Accurate Timepiece

Best Watch ever made for the Money

MUST BE MINT & RUNNING

MINT $20.00

No. 428.

"Cyma," 16 size, O. F., thin model watch, with finely finished jeweled movement, polished steel exposed winding wheels, lever escapement, compensation balance, quick train. Adjusted to heat and cold and thoroughly non-magnetic. It is manufactured, like the American watches, by automatic American machinery, and all parts are interchangeable and can be had in finished form, thereby making it a very easy matter to have one of these watches repaired if they should become broken. It is positively the best watch made for the money, and fully guaranteed.

G. M. case, with white enamel dial $3.15

Nickel case, with white enamel dial $3.15

"Cyma," 16 size, O. F., thin model, in French grey case (white metal with raised figures). Will always hold its color and never wear out. A most attractive watch. White enamel dial. Price............$4.05

This watch comes in various designs; some with flowers and some with figures and landscape scenery.

"Cyma," 16 size, O. F., thin model watch, in gun metal case, with black enamel dial and gold hands and figures.........$3.47

Same, with gold dial and black steel hands $3.47

Same, with silver dial and black steel hands $3.47

MINT $75.00
FINE $25.00
GOOD $5.00

No. 427.

"Cyma," 16 size, O. F., thin model, in sterling silver jointed case, beautifully decorated in the Niello finish, black background with silver ornamentation. Assorted patterns. White enamel dial $6.98

These Watches are Electric Proof. No Danger of Getting Magnetized when near Dynamos, Etc.

MINT $45.00

No. 430.

"Cyma," 16 size, O. F., thin model, in a gold-filled screw back and bezel plain polished case, guaranteed to wear 20 years. Makes a very neat and attractive watch.

With white enamel dial. Price..$6.17

With gold dial. Price........ 6.48

FULLY ADJUSTED = NO BETTER TIMEPIECE MADE

Prices on this Page subject to 6 per cent discount.

MINT $45.00 FINE $20.00 GOOD $5.00

The Enigma Watches are all Pendant Set

MINT – $50.00 FINE – $25.00 GOOD – $5.00

Most Beautiful Models Now Before the Public

MINT $25.00

① No. 194.
French gray white metal, fancy embossed raised effects, variety of patterns, fitted with the Enigma movement, cream inlaid dial and gold hands. Price..........$2.50

② No. 193.
The new French gray, etched patterns, a variety of beautiful designs, cream inlaid dial and gold hands. Fitted with the Enigma movement. Price..........$2.40

③ No. 192.
16 size, gun metal case, hinged back, inside cap, thin model, fitted with the Enigma movement, fancy raised sash dial, as shown in cut. A great seller. Price........$2.10

MINT $20.00

MINT $35.00

MINT $20.00

④ No. 182.
16 size, gun metal case, hinged back, inside cap, thin model, fitted with the Enigma movement, with gold or silver plated shaded dial. A showy watch. Price......$1.95

⑤ No. 190.
16 size, gun metal, hinge back, inside cap, thin model, fitted with the Enigma movement, raised embossed glass enameled dial, assorted colors, gilt fancy hands. Price..........$1.90
No. 200. Same as the above, in nickel case. Price..........$2.00

⑥ No. 187.
16 size, gun metal case, hinge back, inside cap, thin model, fitted with the Enigma movement, plain white dial and black hands. Price....................$1.70
No. 202. Same as above, in nickel case. Price..............$1.75

Gun Metal Fancy Steel and French Gray Complete Watches

All up-to-date jewelers sell these watches. Your stock is not complete without them. Great Sellers. Order Today.

MINT $45.00
FINE $20.00
GOOD $5.00

No. 406. The new French gray watch, assorted designs in raised embossed work, very handsome, fitted with fine quality Swiss movement, cream dial and gold hands. Best seller in the world. Our price, each. **$2.10**

MINT $95.00
FINE $50.00
GOOD $5.00

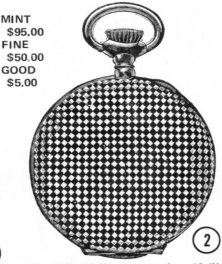

No. 407. 18 ligne, open face Neillo, highly polished, checkered back and bezel case, filled pendant and crown, hinge back and inside cap, fitted with fine Swiss movement, cream dials and gold hands. Good timekeeper. Each **$2.70**

MINT $85.00
FINE $40.00
GOOD $5.00

No. 408. 18 ligne, Neillo, highly polished, blue steel case in assorted patterns, filled pendant and crown, hinge back and inside cap, fitted with fine Swiss movement, cream dials and gold hands. A great seller. Each **$2.70**

MINT $75.00
$100.00
$160.00

PRICES ARE FOR COMPLETE WATCH MINT & RUNNING

MINT $45.00

MINT $150.00

"8-Day Watch."
No. 409. Open face, 16 size, 11 jewel, visible lever escapement, stem wind and set, Breguet hairspring, decorated dial, fancy hands. Runs a week with one winding. In gun metal case.
In gun metal case............ **$ 4.40**
In solid silver case........... **5.35**
In 14k solid gold case........ **28.00**

No. 410. 18 ligne, gun metal, open face panorama watch, showing pictures of scenes, presidents, actresses; full bassine case, fitted with fine jeweled nickel movement, with fancy dial **$3.00**

No. 411. Gun metal perpetual calendar watch, denoting the month, day of month, day of week, also phases of the moon; rich porcelain dial and fancy gilt hands; Swiss cylinder escapement. Each **$3.20**

THE LARGEST LINE IN AMERICA

Blue Steel and Gun Metal Complete Watches
OPEN FACE PENDANT SET
Good lookers.   Watches that make your store look bright.   Up-to-date goods.

COMPLETE
WATCH MUST BE
MINT & RUNNING

MINT
$40.00

MINT
$20.00

MINT
$40.00

No. 418. 12 size, full Bascine case, antique pendant bow. Fancy sash dial, nickel damaskeened movement. Price complete watch, each....$2.20

No. 419. 16 ligne, gun metal, highly polished, hinged back case with inside back cap, fitted with a pendant set, Swiss cylinder movement, fancy irridescent dial in blue, red, etc., with fancy gold hands, gilt crown and bow, a very showy watch.
Price, complete, each $2.35

No. 420. 16 ligne, gun metal, highly polished case, hinged back, inside back cap, jeweled cylinder nickel movement, raised embossed glass enameled dial in colors, gilt hands, pendant set, gilt crown and bow.$2.20

MINT — $40.00
FINE — $20.00
GOOD — $3.00

$120.00

MINT $40.00

No. 421. 18 ligne, blue steel, hinge back and inside cap, case fitted with good quality nickel, Swiss movement, with embossed metallic dial, assorted colors. Each $2.20

No. 422. 18 ligne O. F. gun metal, thin model, visible escapement, stem wind, pendant set. Best seller on the market. Each $2.25
Same as above, metallic dial.... 2.50
Same as above, blue steel...... 2.40

No. 423.. 12 size, gun metal, very thin model, with good cylinder movement, pendant set, antique gold and metal bows and crowns. Dials are metal, in gold and silver colors, with raised numerals on panels of crystal in various rich tints of blue, green, red and turquoise. A beautiful watch for a little price. Each........$2.50

Complete Fancy Watches

Thin model open face, pendant set, up-to-date in every respect. Very showy.

Watches that attract attention. Money makers for the live jeweler.

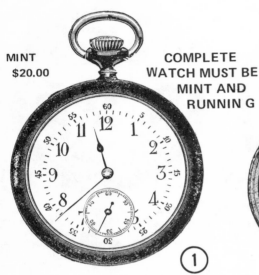

MINT $20.00

COMPLETE WATCH MUST BE MINT AND RUNNING

No. B412. Gold plated, plain polish, 16 size case, hinge back, antique bow fitted with a good, reliable three-quarter plate, highly polished damaskeen movement, white enameled dial and gilt hands. This watch is pendant set and a very thin basseen model. Price, each **$1.90**

MINT $17.50

No. B413. 16 size, gold plated, plain polish, full basseen case with antique pendant bow, fitted with good split plate movement, fine damaskeen nickel plates. Gilt metallic dial with black steel hands. This watch is pendant set and a very thin model. A great seller. Price, each **$2.20**

MINT $55.00
FINE $25.00
GOOD $5.00

No. 414. 16 size, gold plated, thin model, joint back, assorted beautifully engraved designs, antique bow case, fitted with a good bridge model, jeweled movement, fancy gold metallic dial, black steel hands pendant set. A beauty in every respect. Price, each **$2.65**

MINT $40.00
FINE $20.00
GOOD $3.00

No. 415. 16 size, fancy raised gun metal inlaid case, assorted designs. fitted with three-quarter plate nickel damaskeen movement, white enameled dial gilt hands. A very showy watch. Price, each **$2.25**

MINT $15.00

No. 416. 16 or 18 ligne, gun metal, snap back, gilt bow and crown case, fitted with pendant set, cylinder nickel movement. Each ...... **$1.60** Same as above, joint back, inside cap **$1.75**

MINT $15.00

No. 417. Nickel open face Swiss, thin model. Each .... **$1.70** **No. 116.** Gun metal open face, thin model, Swiss movement, pendant set; a nice watch for a young man. Each **1.75**

THE LARGEST ASSORTMENT IN AMERICA

Complete Swiss Watch

Get out of the old fogy way. You have to be on the jump now days if you want business. Get in line today and order these novelty watches. The best trade winners and money maker in the watch line.

Prices lower than the lowest. We lead them all.

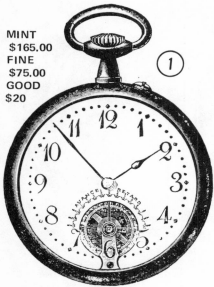

MINT
$165.00
FINE
$75.00
GOOD
$20

①

No. B401. Open-face, 16 size, thin model, visible escapement, stem wind, pendant set, lever escapement, b r e g u e t hair-spring, fancy hands, lever, jeweled rich colored enamel embossed dial, as shown in illustration. Price, each $3.95

MUST BE MINT AND RUNNING

②

MINT
$75.00

No. B402. The Alarm watch, 16 size gun metal case, fitted with a good reliable Alarm, watch movement guaranteed to give perfect satisfaction, hinge back cap gilt crown and bow white enameled dial, blue steel hands. A most reliable alarm watch on the market at an exceptionally low price. Good seller. Price each.... $4.35

You will never know the great bargains our stock contains unless you send us that trial order.

The Latest

MINT
$250.00
FINE
$150.00
GOOD
$50.00

④

No. B400. The Gun Metal Roskoff Pendulum Watch, assorted fancy subject dial and gilt hands. The Roskoff lever escapement movement, which has given service for the past twenty years, guaranteed to keep good time. This is the latest novelty watch on the market. A money maker and a fine looker. A watch that will attract everybody's attention. Has joint back with glass inside cap. Price, each..........$2.75

MINT
$250.00
FINE
$125.00
GOOD
$75.00

③

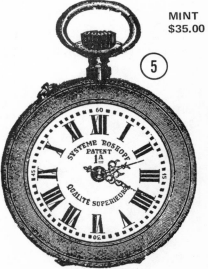

MINT
$35.00

⑤

No. B403. The GooGoo Roskoff Watch. A sister to the Pendulum watch. This is the celebrated Roskoff movement which has given satisfaction for many years. Lever escapement, assorted subject dials, with movable eyes, incased in a gunmetal steel case, joint back with glass inside cap. One of the latest novelties on the market. A great seller, as well as a fine time keeper. Price, each........$2.70

No. B404. The GooGoo Roskoff Watch. A sister to the Pendulum watch. This is the celebrated Roskoff movement which has given satisfaction for many years. Lever escapement, assorted subject dials, with movable eyes, incased in a solid nickel joint back glass inside cap. Price, each.$2.70

No.. B405. Roskoff System Watch. 18 size gunmetal case, joint back with glass inside cap, fitted with the celebrated Roskoff lever movement which has stood the test for many years, proven a fine timekeeper, mounted with white enameled dial, roman or arabic figures, fancy gilt hands. A reliable watch in every respect. Price, each $1.50

Same as the above in nickel case, price, each...........$1.50

The largest stock of Swiss watches in America.

Black Niello on Silver Engraved Background

MINT
$125.00

①

12 — SIZE

②

MINT
$125.00
FINE
$60.00

GOOD
$10.00

Niello is a solid pliable substance, very similar to black enamel, embedded in a white background. The decorations are cut through the black surface, forming a most beautiful contrast, silver on black. The interior of the back back and cap is heavily silver plated, large variety of designs. Nickel pendant set cylinder movements.

2583 Open Face Niello......$2.90

2584 Open Face Niello......$2.90

Gold & Silver Decorated Gun Metal Open Face Watches

MINT
$100.00

④

12 — SIZE

⑤

MINT
$100.00

Solid gold and silver raised lillies, fir. de lis, and other fancy designs. Inlaid on a solid black back ground, bassine shape case, nickel pendant set. ¾ plate nickel silver movement well finished throughout. Tinted dial, Arabic figures red marginals, black steel hands. Most attractive watches of this class on the market,

2585 Open Face gold and silver decorated gun metal......$3.20

2586 Open Face decorated gold and silver gun metal.........$3.20

Gray Embossed Metal Artistic Open Face Watches

MINT
$50.00

⑦

12 — SIZE

⑧

MINT
$50.00

Gray silver metal artistic art reproductions of raised gold styles, usually placed on very high priced cases only; assorted subjects stags, horses, hunting and boating scenes, floral designs, etc. ¾ plate nickel cylinder movement, pendant set. Cream colored dial, Arabic figures. These watches are without question the most attractive of their kind.

2587 Open Face gray metal artistic.................$2.50

2588 Open Face gray metal artistic.........: 2.50

Open Face Gun Metal Empire Cylinder Watches

③

MINT
$25.00

2589 Gun Metal Empire open face gold and silver engraved dial. $3.25

2590 Gun Metal Empire open face solid colored dial, red blue, green, turquoise, etc.................. 3.25

Flat Empire shape open face black gun metal, extra heavy, gold plated oval back and bezel border. Flat, straight knurl center. Gold engraved and fancy colored dial, red, blue, green and turquoise. French antique shaped bow. ¾ nickel cylinder, pendant set movement.

Open Face Winslow Complete Cylinder Watches

⑥

MINT
$25.00
to
$50.00

2591 O. F., S. B. & B. nickel plain polish......................$2.60

2592 O.F., S.B. & B. extra gold plated bassine shape plain polish......2.65

2593 O F., S.B.& B. black gun metal bassine shape, oval pend't & bow 2.90

2594 O. F., S. B. & B. Sterling silver, plain polish, E. T. or engraved 3.80

2595 O. F., S. B. & B. gold filled 10 yr. guarantee, engr. or E.T. 3.70

All movements used in the completion of the watches illustrated on this page are ¾ nickel silver. Plates elaborately damaskeened, straight line and circle designs. Imitation Anchor balance gilded center wheels, well finished throughout. Flat blue steel screws. White enameled dials, Roman and Arabic figures. Red marginals, gold or blue steel hands.

These cylinder movements are the best of their class, nevertheless their system of construction does not warrant a positive guarantee for accuracy. We deliver them in good running order, but assume no further responsibility.

The watches illustrated Nos. 2591-5 are composed of 16 size O F., S. B. & B. thin model cases, fitted with ¾ plate nickel cylinder pendant set movements. Equipped with fancy dials, raised colored enameled figures, red, blue, green, etc.

Utmost One-Quarter Hour Repeating Full Jeweled Open Face Watches.

MINT

2340 Gun metal black open face ¼ hour repeater....$17.50 $350.00
2341 Silver engine turned bassine ¼ hour repeater.. 19.50 $375.00
2342 Gold filled bassine plain ¼ hour repeater....... 27.50 $400.00

The UTMOST repeaters are very simply constructed on the plan of regular high-grade movements. Free from all the complications usually associated with watches of this sort. Repairing can easily be accomplished by any competent watchmaker. Every part that enters into the construction of the UTMOST repeaters is finished in the best manner possible. The exposed winding wheels and all bright steel parts are burnished and highly polished. TOP PLATES ARE SILVERED. Striking hammers and sound coil act perfectly, producing a silver bell sound. Free from buzzing mechanical noise.

WE GUARANTEE THE TIMEKEEPING ACCURACY OF EVERY UTMOST TO BE EXACTLY THE SAME AS MAY BE EXPECED FROM ANY HIGH GRADE WATCHES.

No. 2340 Utmost repeater gun metal, front view............ $17.50

No. 2342 Utmost repeater gold filled, movement view....... $27.50

30 Minute Register Chronograph, Start, Stop and Fly Back. Extra Fine Quality.

2343 Chronograph in black gun metal cases........$12 50 50.00
2344 Chronograph in silver engine turned cases.... 15.00 60.00
2345 Chronograph in gold filled or engine turned cases 18.50 75.00
2346 Chronograph in 14 K. solid gold E.-T. cases ... 55.00 200.00

Minute Register Split Second Chronograph, Start, Stop and Fly Back. High Quality.

2347 Split second chronograph in 18 size black gun 200.00
metal cases.....................$35.00
2348 Split second chrongraph in 18 size silver engine 225.00
turned cases...... .... .36 00
2349 Split second chronograph in 18 size gold filled 250.00
bassine plain or engine turned cases....... .. 42.00

All chronographs illustrated and quoted on this page are guaranteed in every sense. They are absolutely reliable timekeepers. Chronographs and split seconds attachments are exceptionally strong and will always act correctly consistent with ordinary care. Repairing can be done by any first-class watch-maker. In fact, these watches are practical in every respect. Selections for immediate inspection forwarded to RESPONSIBLE JEWELERS ONLY.

No. 2343 Gun Metal Chronograph, front view $12.50

No 2345 Gold filled chronograph, movement view $27.50

30 Minute Register Chronograph, Start, Stop and Fly Back. High Grade.

MINT $75.00

2350 Chronograph in black gun metal cases........$12.00
2351 Chronograph in silver engine turned cases..... 15 00

MINT $100.00

The Chronographs illustrated herewith are the nearest to mechanical perfection. Constructed to perform accurately the functions of high-grade time recorders and sporting watches. Our Chronograph attachment is simple and extremely strong in construction, resting entirely on the solid top plate. When in operation it does not in the slightest manner interfere with the timekeeping mechanism. The 30 minute register is a splendid acquisition and especially desired by doctors, autoists, etc.

WE GUARANTEE THE TIMEKEEPING ACCURACY OF THESE CHRONOGRAPHS TO EXACTLY THE SAME AS MAY BE EXPECTED FROM ANY HIGH GRADE WATCHES.

No. 2350 Gun Metal Chronograph, front view $12.00

No. 2351 Silver Chronograph movement view.... .... $15.00

One-quarter and Minute Repeating Chronograph Watches
14 Karat Solid Gold Hunting, 12 to 18 size

2250--$95.00

Minute Repeating chronograph, 14 K. solid gold Hunting, plain and engine turned.

No. 2250 illustrates one of the best 19 ligne solid gold 14 Karat Minute Repeating Chronographs.

The general construction is first-class in every particular; full jewelled movement, finely finished throughout. Every part is highly burnished and polished. Exposed concave display winding wheels. The entire chronograph attachment is clearly exposed on the movement surface. There are no hidden or delicate parts to become dislocated. The Minute Repeating striker falls onto a coil spring, producing a clear silver bell sound. Free from all buzzing noise. Mechanically these Minute Repeating chronographs are very simple, and the most accurate service may be expected. They can be repaired by any competent watchmaker.

No. 2250 Illustration of 14 K. solid gold Minute repeating Chronograph, showing movement view $95.00

No. 2250 Illustration of 14 K. solid gold Minute Repeating Chronograph, showing case view $95.00

COMPLETE WATCH MINT

No.	Price
2250	$1,800.00
2251	1,500.00
2252	1,750.00
2253	600.00
2254	750.00
2255	1,800.00
2256	1,800.00
2257	800.00
2258	1,600.00
2259	1,500.00
2260	1,500.00
2261	1,400.00
2262	1,600.00
2263	3,000.00
2264	800.00
2265	1,000.00
2266	2,500.00

PUSH BUTTON TYPE NOT AS FINE AS SLIDES

Price List of 12 size Solid Gold 14 and 18 K. Plain and Engine Turned Repeating Watches

2251 Minute Repeater, fully jeweled extra heavy case, plain or E. T., ... $115.00
2252 Minute Repeater, with Chronograph attachment, fully jeweled, extra heavy case, plain or E. T.... 125.00
2253 One-quarter Repeater, fully jeweled, extra heavy case, plain or E. T 87.50
2254 One-quarter Repeater, with Chronograph attachment, fully jeweled, extra heavy case, plain or E. T. 97.50
2255 Minute Repeater, extra thin model 18 K. Htg. bassine, extra heavy, plain polished case, Geneva movement jeweled in every part. The very finest watch that can possibly be constructed $295.00
2256 Minute Repeater, extra thin model 18 K., O. F., bassine, extra heavy, plain polished case, Geneva movment jewelled in every part. The very finest watch that can possibly be constructed 275.00

Special attention is directed to Nos. 2255 and 2256 These are the thinnest model and the finest grade of Minute Repeaters that can possibly be produced. They represent the highest science of modern watch making.

2257 12 size One-quarter Repeater. $87.50
2258 12 size Minute Repeater, Htg. 115.00
Plain or engine turned heavy Hunting cases.

12 SIZE REPEATER, SOLID GOLD, 14 K

2257 One-quarter Repeater $87.50
2228 Minute Repeater 115.00
2259 Minute Repeater, with Chronograph, 125.00
Plain or Engine Turned Hunting cases.

Solid gold 14 Karat, plain or engine turned, and Minute Repeaters, made with and without chronograph attachment. Full jewelled, fine finished throughout. Nickel silvered plates and bridges. Steel exposed concave display winding wheels. Finest tempered hair and main spring. Every piece of material that enters into the construction of these Repeaters is the nearest mechanical perfection. White glaze enamel French porcelain dial. Marginals divided indicate 1-5 seconds stops.

2261 Minute Repeater, with Chronograph attachment, 17 jewels, extra heavy case, plain or E. T $130.00

Price List of 14 K. Solid Gold Plain and Engine Turned Hunting Repeating Watches

2260 Minute Repeater, 17 jewels, extra heavy case, plain or E. T $120.00
2261 Minute Repeater, with Chronograph attachment, 17 jewels, extra heavy case, plain or E. T 130.00
2262 Minute Repeater, with Chronograph and 30 minute Register attachment, 17 jewels, extra heavy case, plain or E. T 135.00
2263 Minute Repeater, with Chronograph and Moon Calendar attachment, fully jeweled, medium weight case, plain or E. T 125.00
2264 One-quarter Repeater, 17 jewels, extra heavy case, plain or E. T 95.00
2265 One-quarter Repeater, with Chronograph attachment, 17 jewels, extra heavy case, plain or E. T 100.00
2266 One-quarter Repeater, with Chronograph and Automatic Striking Attachment, medium weight case, fully jeweled 95.00

Special attention is directed to No. 2266 Automatic One-quarter Repeater. The dial portrays, in raised colored enamel, two moving human figures, striking, with miniature hammers, a suspended bell. The figure representing the man strikes the hours; the woman strikes the quarters. The dials are executed in bright colors.—red, blue, green, etc. The entire watch represents a positively unique effect. Samples submitted to any responsible jeweler upon application.

2260 Minute Repeater, 17 jewels, extra heavy case plain or E. T 120.00

I MAY NOT BE VERY CLOSE ON THESE PRICES. REPEATERS HAVE ADVANCED RAPIDLY IN VALUE IN THE PAST 3 YEARS. CONDITION IS IMPORTANT. NOT ENOUGH INFORMATION ON THIS PAGE TO VALUE PROPERLY. THE MAIN MESSAGE HERE IS THEY ARE VERY EXPENSIVE AND VERY DESIREABLE.

Solid Silver Chatelaines and Boys' Watches

A Page of Money Makers That Can't Be Beat
Order From Us and SAVE MONEY

① $15.00

② MINT $15.00

③ $15.00

④ $45.00

No. 440. Solid silver, open face, chatelaine, stem wind and set, fine jeweled nickel movement, case engraved in a handsome selection of the latest designs.
Snap back............... $2.00
Hinge back............... 2.05

No. 441. Solid silver, open face, stem wind and set, fitted with an 8-jewel nickel movement, fancy sash, handsome assortment of patterns.
Snap back............... $1.95
Hinge back............... 2.10

No. 442. 13 ligne, open face, solid silver, engraved or E. T., case fitted with cylinder movement, stem wind and set.
Each............... $1.75
Hinge back............ 1.95

No. 443. Solid silver, hunting case, chatelaine, fitted with fine jeweled nickel movement, stem wind and set, handsome engraved case or E. T.
Each............... $2.45

⑤ $15.00

WE SAVE YOU MONEY

⑥ $20.00

MUST BE MINT AND RUNNING

⑦ $15.00

No. 444. 16 ligne, O. F. nickel boy's watch, fitted with cylinder, nickel movement, stem wind and stem set, snap back. Each. $1 65
Hinge back............ 1 80

No. 445. Boys' solid silver watch, fitted with a fine Swiss movement. Each..... $2.50
No. B-1011. Same as above, in hunting.
Each............... 3.00

No. 446. Boys' open face, gun metal, plain polished case, with fine grade nickel jeweled cylinder movement, stem wind and set. Each............... $1.60

⑧ $25.00

⑨ $35.00

⑩ $25.00

"The Congress Watch."
No. 447. 12 size, solid silver, open face with antique pendant and bows with gold crown, handsomely engraved or engine-turned, with good cylinder movement.
Snap B. and B............... $2 35
Jointed............... 2 65

No. 448. 16 or 18 ligne, solid silver hunting case, assorted hand engraved beautiful designs, engine-turned, fitted with fine nickel movement, stem wind and stem set. Good time keeper. Each............... $3.25

No. 449. Nickel horse-timer, start, stop and fly-back from crown, minute register; most reliable watch on the market.
Each............... $3 95
Solid silver............... 5 70
Solid silver horse-timer and timer... 7 70

Transparent Enamel Silver O. F. Pendant Set Chatelaine Watches.

Painted Miniatures Solid Gold and Pearl Inlaid Decorations.

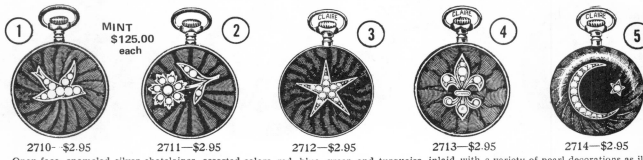

MINT $125.00 each

2710—$2.95   2711—$2.95   2712—$2.95   2713—$2.95   2714—$2.95

Open face, enameled silver chatelaines, assorted colors, red, blue, green and turquoise, inlaid with a variety of pearl decorations as illustrated above, crescent, flr. de lis, star, sunflower and bird. Cylinder bridge model movements with tinted Arabic dials, gold hands, gold plated centers, bows and crowns.

MINT $150.00 each

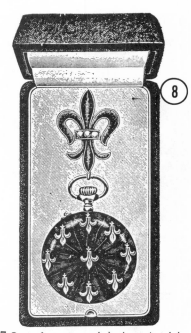

2715 Open face enameled silver chatelaine, red, blue, green and turquoise, extra quality, gold filled centers, bows and crowns, gold inlaid decorations assorted designs, enameled chatelaine pin, plush, satin lined box....$4.25

This quotations includes watch, enameled pin and plush box.

2716 Open face, enameled silver chatelaine, red, blue, green and turquoise, heavily gold filled centers, pendants, bows and crowns, decorated with painted miniature, assorted subjects, enamel chatelaine, pin, silk plush, satin lined box............ ....$4.50

This quotation includes watch, enameled pin, and plush box.

27,17 Open face, enameled silver chatelaine, red, blue, green and turquoise, gold plated centers, bows and crowns, decorated with gold inlaid assorted designs, enamel chatelaine pin, plush, satin lined box..................$3.40

This quotation includes watch, enameled pin and plush box.

MINT $125.00 each

2718—$2.65   2719—$2.65   2720—$2.65   2721—$2.40   2722—$2 65

Open face, enamel silver chatelaines, assorted colors, red, blue, green and turquoise, solid gold inlaid decorations in large variety, stars, floral designs, leaves, flr. de lis, etc. Gold plated centers pendant, bows and crowns.

2721 Open face, enameled silver chatelaine, transparent fancy engine turned back ground, finished entirely plain in red, blue, green and turquoise. Time keeping accuracy not guaranteed.

Highest Grade Enameled Gold Filled O. F. Pendant Set Chatelaine Watches.

Decorated with Painted Miniatures and Pearl Inlaid.

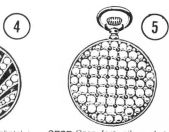

MINT $125.00 each

FINE $50.00 each

GOOD $10.00 each

2723 Open face chatelaine, transparent colored enamel on silver, solid gold inlaid massive designs in large variety, exceptionally brilliant. The light shading on the illustration show the gold decoration. Gold filled center, pendant, bow and crown. Jeweled cylinder movement $5.50

2724 Open face chatelaine, transparent colored enamel on silver, hand painted top designed inlaid with solid gold Transparent Sandaw enamel in colors, red, blue, green, etc. Gold filled center, pendant, bow and crown. Jeweled cylinder movement $6.00

2725 Open face chatelaine, enameled on silver, pearl border and pearl bezel surrounding hand painted transparent miniature, assorted designs on opal light colored back ground. Gold filled center, pendant, bow and crown. Jeweled cylinder movement $6.50

2726 Open face chatelaine, enamel on silver, pearl, shell and other pearl inlaid designs in red, blue, turquoise and green Sandaw enamel back ground A most attractive contrast. Gold filled center, pendant, bow and crown. Jeweled cylinder movement $5.75

2727 Open face silver chatelaine, full pearl inlaid back, pearl border and bezel, ruby turquoise, or green stones. set alternately between each set of four pearls. Jeweled cylinder nickel pendant set, bridge model movement. Gold filled center pendant bow and crown $6.00

MINT $110.00 each

FINE $40.00 each

GOOD $10.00 each

2728 Open face chatelaine, transparent colored enameled on silver, pearl border and bezel, solid gold inlaid decorations brilliant designs, red, blue and turquoise. Jeweled cylinder movement, pendant set. Gold filled center, pendant, bow and crown. $4.75

2729 Open face chatelaine, transparent colored enamel on silver, pearl border and bezel, solid gold inlaid decorations, brilliant designs, red blue and turquoise. Jeweled cylinder movement, pendant set. Gold filled center, pendant, bow and crown. $4.75

2730 Open face chatelaine, transparent colored enamel on silver, hand painted, brilliantly tinted miniatures in red, blue, green and turquoise. Jeweled cylinder movement, pendant set. Gold filled center, pendant, bow and crown $4.50

2731 Open face chatelaine, transparent colored enamel on silver, pearl border and bezel, hand painted, brilliantly tinted miniatures in red, blue, green and turquoise. Jeweled cylinder movement, pendant set. Gold filled center, pendant, bow and crown $5.35

2732 Open face chatelaine, transparent colored enamel on silver, pearl border and bezel, hand painted brilliantly tinted miniatures in red, blue, green and turquoise. Jeweled cylinder movement, pendant set. Gold filled center, pendant, bow and crown $5.35

MINT $100.00 each

FINE $40.00 each

GOOD $10.00 each

2733 Open face silver chatelaine, transparent colored enamel on silver, single pearl center in white center, pearl border and bezel, red, blue, green and turquoise Cylinder pendant set movement Gold filled center pendant bow and crown $3.50

2734 Open face chatelaine, transparent colored enamel on silver, pearl border and bezel, assorted pearl designs set in white back ground, red, blue, green and turquoise Cylinder pendant set movement Gold filled center, pendant, bow and crown $4.00

2735 Open face chatelaine, transparent colored enamel on silver, pearl border and bezel, hand painted brilliantly tinted miniature heads in red, blue, green and turquoise. Cylinder movement, pendant set. Gold filled center, pendant, bow and crown $4.75

2736 Open face chatelaine, transparent colored enamel on silver, pearl border and bezel, hand painted, brilliantly tinted miniatures in red, blue, green and turquoise. Cylinder movement, pendant set. Gold filled center, pendant, bow and crown $4.75

2737 Open face silver chatelaine, full pearl inlaid back, pearl border and bezel, ruby, turquoise, or green stone, set alternately between each set of four pearls. Jeweled cylinder pendant set movement. Gold filled center, pendant, bow and crown $6.00

MINT $100.00 each

2738 Open face chatelaine, transparent colored enamel on silver, solid gold inlaid designs, red, blue, green and turquoise. Nickel cylinder movement. Gold filled center, pendant, bow and crown. **Reversible pendant** $3.75

2739 Open face chatelaine, transparent colored enamel on silver, solid gold inlaid designs, red, blue, green and turquoise Nickel cylinder movement. Gold filled center, pendant, bow and crown $3.50

2740 Open face chatelaine, transparent colored enamel on silver, hand painted, brilliantly tinted miniatures in red, blue, green and turquoise Cylinder movement, pendant set. Gold filled center, pendant, bow and crown $3.75

2741 Open face chatelaine, transparent enamel on silver, inlaid with fancy engine turned designs, a large variety in red, blue, green and turquoise. Nickel cylinder movement. Gold filled center, pendant, bow and crown. **Reversible pendant** $3.50

2742 Open face chatelaine, transparent colored enamel on silver, inlaid with fancy engine turned designs, a large variety in red, blue, green and turquoise. Nickel cylinder movement. Gold filled center, pendant, bow and crown $3.25

Oxydized Black Gun Metal Pendant Set O. F. Chatelain Watches.
Painted Decorations, Gold and Silver Dials.

① $50.00 ② $50.00 $40.00 $40.00 ⑤ $40.00

2743 Black Gun metal O.F. square shaped, half bassine gold and silver decorations on back and bezel. Pendant set cylinder movem't **$4.00**

2744 Black gun metal O.F. heart shape, gold and silver inlaid decorations on back and bezel. Pendant set cylinder movement.....**$4.00**

2745 Black gun metal O.F. heart shaped, bassine case, snap back and bezel medium size, pendant set, nickel cylinder movement..**$2.65**

2746 Black gun metal O F. heart shaped, bassine case, snap back and bezel, small size, pendant set, nickel cylinder movement..**$3.50**

2747 Black gun metal O.F. square shaped, half bassine gold and silver decorations on back and bezel, pendant set cylinder movem't **$4.00**

⑥ MINT $30.00 each   ⑦ FINE $15.00 each   ⑧ GOOD $3.00 each   ⑨   ⑩

2748 Black gun metal open face, bassine, pendant set, nickel cylinder movement, assorted colored decorations **$3.25**

2749 Black gun metal open face, bassine, pendant set, nickel cylinder movement, assorted colored decorations **$3.25**

2750 Black gun metal open face, bassine, pendant set, nickel cylinder movement, gold and silver inlaid decorations..............**$3.00**

2751 Black gun metal open face, tinted white dial, nickel cylinder movement, snap back and bezel, pendant set steel hands.........**$2.10**

2752 Black gun metal open face, nickel cylinder movement, transparent colored dial, Arabic figures in contrast. **$2.75**

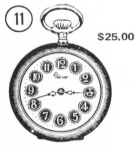    

⑪ $25.00   ⑫ $20.00   ⑬ $20.00   ⑭ $30.00   ⑮ $20.00

2753 Black gun metal open face, white dial with raised red colored enamel figures, nickel cylinder pendant set movement **$2.25**

2754 Black gun metal open face, nickel cylinder movement, white dial Roman and Arabic figures, pendant set gold hands.........**$1.85**

2755 Black gun metal open face, extra thin, knife edge assorted floral designs, decorated in gold and silver, Pendant set, cylinder movement **$2 50**

2756 Black gun metal open face, extra thin, knife edge assorted floral designs, decorated in gold and silver, pendant set, cylinder movement.. ... .**$2.50**

2757 Black gun metal open face, extra thin, knife edge plain black, white dial, Arabic figures, pendant set cylinder movement..**$1.95**

⑯ $30.00   ⑰ $30.00   ⑱ $35.00   ⑲ $30.00   ⑳ $20.00

2758 Black gun metal open face, bassine shape, silver and gold, Arabesque designs, white dial, Arabic figures, nickel cylinder movement.........**$3.00**

2759 Black gun metal open face, extra thin, knife edge raised crescent set with pearls, Pendant set cylinder movement **$3.25**

2760 Black gun metal open face, enameled gold inlaid, and decorated in several colors, with painted miniatures, pendant set, cylinder movement.........**$3.50**

2761 Black gun metal open face, extra thin, knife edge raised fleur de lis set with pearls, pendant set cylinder movement...... ....**$3.25**

2762 Black gun metal open face, nickel cylinder movement, white dials, Roman and Arabic figures, gold hands, Second hands **$2 00**

DO NOT COMPARE US with other jobbers. We can always sell you goods at much lower prices than any house in the U. S. because we are constantly buying stocks for spot cash.

Exceptional Bargains on Chatelaine Watches

NOTE LOW PRICES.

MINT EACH

① $40.00   ② $50.00   ③ $40.00   ④ $50.00   ⑤ $40.00

Enameled Gold Inlaid, with row of Pearls on Brezel and Back. Full jeweled Swiss movement, fine seller; special reduced price $4.00

Solid gold, Open Face, 10½ ligne, jeweled movement, plain polished. No. 946. White dial. $4.85

No. 606. Gold filled center, enameled back, 11½ ligne, Open Face, chatelaine watch; plain, red, sapphire blue, green or turquoise $2.65

Solid gold, Open Face, 10½ ligne, jeweled movement. No. 956. Colored enamel dial .... $5.00 Turquoise, Red, Blue or Green.

ASSORTED DESIGNS

No. 913. Gold filled center, enameled back, 11½ ligne, Open Face chatelaine watch, gold etched, assorted subjects in red, sapphire blue, green or turquoise. $2.90

We have all colors.   State colors desired.

ALL WATCHES MUST BE MINT AND RUNNING CYLINDER MOVEMENTS ARE HARD TO FIX.

$65.00

$70.00

$60.00

⑥ ⑦ ⑧

A PAIR OF BARGAINS.

Open Face sterling chatelaine or oxidized gun metal chatelaine watch, very neat, staple, standard goods, with jeweled movement, all complete in box.
Oxidized, each ....$2.40 Complete outfit.
Sterling silver, each........... 2.40 Complete outfit.

Plush or leatherette box. Each..**$0.45**
Gold plated sterling chatelaine brooch. Each .... .45
No. 810. Beautiful chatelaine watch, size 13 ligne, any color. This makes a very handsome outfit, all complete, watch, box and pin. Each net **$4.00**

Plush box. Each..............**$0.45**
Gold plated sterling pin. Each.. .45
No. 811. Inlaid, enameled watch, any color, gold filled crown and antique bow, finely made jeweled movement, complete, box, pin and watch. Each **$4.25**

Pins and Boxes at all prices.   Boxes $2.50 doz. up, and Pins from $1.00 doz. up.

ABOVE GOODS GUARANTEED, and are the best quality on the market for the price.

GUARANTEED 10 YEAR GOLD FILLED WATCHES

These cases are too well known to need any special commendation on our part. They have been made for years, and have given satisfaction. There is no doubt but that they will continue to give satisfaction, and that every dealer is safe in depending on them. Our prices are a little lower than you can get elsewhere, and if you send us your orders they will be filled correctly, and shipped same day as received.

TOP 3 MINT	TOP 3 FINE	TOP 3 GOOD
$ 80.00	$40.00	$20.00
$100.00	$50.00	$25.00
$100.00	$50.00	$25.00
$100.00	$50.00	$25.00
$105.00	$50.00	$25.00

2855

2865

2606

No. 2855 18 size, 10 year gold filled, **Victory**, hunting case; made by the **Philadelphia Watch Case Co.** of Riverside, N. J. Each case is stamped with the makers' guarantee. Case only $1.98
Fitted with 7-jewel Century or Standard... 3.50
Fitted with SH. 7-jewel gilt Elgin or Waltham 4.50
Fitted with SH. 11-jewel gilt Hampden or Springfield..................... 4.45
Fitted with SH. 15-jewel Elgin, Waltham or Hampden................. 6.00

No. 2865 18 size, 10 year, gold filled, **Victory**, open face, S. B. & B. case, made by the **Philadelphia Watch Case Co.** of Riverside, N. J. Each case is stamped with the maker's guarantee and is fully warranted. Case only $1.65
Fitted with 7-jewel Century or Standard... 3.15
Fitted with SH. 7-jewel gilt Elgin or Waltham 4.15
Fitted with SH. 11-jewel gilt Hampden or Springfield................... 4.10
Fitted with SH. 15-jewel Elgin, Waltham or Hampden 5.65

No. 2606 16 size, 10 year, **Victory** hunting case, made by the **Philadelphia Watch Case Co.** of Riverside, N. J. Each case is stamped with the maker's guarantee and is fully warranted for 10 years.
Case only $1.87
Fitted with 7-jewel Bridge Model Trenton 4.35
Fitted with 15-jewel Bridge Model Trenton..................... 5.85
Fitted with SH. 7-jewel Elgin or Waltham................... 6.10
Open face, screw B. & B. 33 cents less.

12S MINT	6S MINT	OS MINT
$50.00	$60.00	$70.00
$60.00	$70.00	$90.00
$65.00	$70.00	$75.00
$70.00	$70.00	$95.00

1250

C155

88

No. 1250 12x6 size, 10 year, **Victory**, hunting case; made by the **Philadelphia Watch Case Co.** of Riverside, N. J. whose guarantee is stamped in every case.
Case only $1.76
Fitted with Bridge Model nickel Fortuna 3.75
Fitted with SH. 7-jewel Elgin or Waltham 5.80
Fitted with SH. 15-jewel Elgin or Waltham.................... 6.70
Open face, screw B. & B. 28 cents less.

No. C155 6 size, 10 year gold filled **Victory** hunting case. This case is made by the **Philadelphia Watch Case Co.** of Riverside, N. J. and is fully warranted by this company for 10 years' wear.
Case only $1.48
Fitted with Fortuna or Standard.... 3.45
Fitted with SH. 7-jewel Elgin or Waltham 3.55
Fitted with 15 imitation jewel Algiers 3.00

No. 88 0 size, 10 year gold filled **Victory** hunting case. This case is made by the **Philadelphia Watch Case Co.** of Riverside, N. J. and is fully warranted by this company for 10 years' wear.
Case only $1.43
Fitted with 7-jewel nickel U. S........ 5.65
Fitted with 11-jewel Wellington...... 3.75
Fitted with 15-jewel U. S. nickel..... 6.85

A PAGE OF COMPLETE WATCHES
That No Live Jeweler Will Pass
Good Lookers and Good Sellers

=== 10-YEAR CASES STAMPED 20 YEARS ===

TOP 2 MINT
$60.00
$70.00
$75.00
$80.00
$70.00

TOP 2 FINE
$25.00
$30.00
$30.00
$35.00
$30.00

BIG
PROFITS
MADE
ON
THESE
WATCHES

TOP 2 GOOD
$10.00
$10.00
$10.00
$10.00
$10.00

No. 168. 18 size, gold filled 10 year case, stamped 20 years. Case only......$2 00
Fitted with 7-jewel gilt Elgin or Waltham........................... 4 50
Fitted with 11-jewel gilt Hampden or Springfield.................. 4 45
Fitted with 15-jewel Elgin, Waltham or Hampden.................... 6 00
Fitted with 21-jewel Northwestern Special........................ 3 90

No. 169. 16 size, gold filled 10 year case, stamped 20 years. Case only......$2 00
Fitted with 7-jewel Bridge Model Trenton.......................... 4 50
Fitted with 15-jewel Bridge Model Trenton.......................... 6 00
Fitted with 7-jewel Elgin or Waltham 6 25

MINT
$60.00
$70.00
$70.00
$75.00

MINT
$60.00
$80.00
$65.00
$85.00

MINT
$50.00
$60.00
$65.00
$55.00

No. 170. 12-6 size, gold filled 10 year case, stamped 20 years. Case only...$1 90
Fitted with Bridge Model nickel Fortuna........................... 3 90
Fitted with 7-jewel Elgin or Waltham 5 65
Fitted with 15-jewel Elgin or Waltham........................... 6 50

No. 171. 0 size, gold filled 10 year case, stamped 20 years................$1 50
Fitted with 7-jewel nickel U S...... 5 75
Fitted with 11-jewel Wellington..... 3 75
Fitted with 15-jewel U. S. nickel.... 6 75

No. 172. 6 size, gold filled 10 year case, stamped 20 years................$1 70
Fitted with Fortuna or Standard.... 3 65
Fitted with 7-jewel Elgin or Waltham 5 50
Fitted with 15 imitation jewel Algiers 3 25

THE ABOVE CASES COME IN PLAIN POLISH, E. T. AND ENGRAVED

More Watch Bargains.

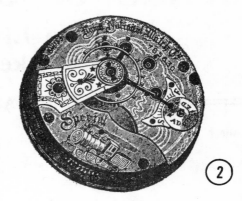

UNION NATIONAL WATCH

A Complete Watch for less than the usual price of the case alone.

MINT
HC
$85.00
OF
$45.00

No. 775 20 year filled case, assorted designs.

No. 775 Men's Union National gold filled watch, 18 size, gold filled, 20 year guaranteed case, engraved in a variety of late designs, fitted with the well known Union National movement, extra quality highly jeweled, specially adjusted, stem wind, lever set, patent regulator, polished screws, jewels in settings.

Price, complete. Hunting...$4.75
Open Face Screw B. & B...$4.00

Illustration shows 20 year filled case.

MINT
OF
$45.00
HC
$85.00

Southern Express Watch

Looks like a High Grade Railroad Watch.

No. 850 Case, assorted designs.

No. 850 Men's gold filled Southern Express watch, 18 size, gold filled, 20 year guaranteed case, engraved in a variety of the very latest designs, fitted with a Southern Express movement, fancy gold damaskeened plates, ruby jewels in cup settings, stamped "extra quality, highly 23 jeweled, specially adjusted," fancy gold decorated dial and gold hands. Very similar to a high grade railroad movement.

Price complete. Hunting...$5.25
Open Face Screw B. & B...$4.50

Illustration shows 20 year filled case.

Algier Special Watch

This is a special offer of a special Watch very much below its usual price.

OF
MINT
$45.00
FINE
$20.00
GOOD
$3.00

HC
MINT
$85.00
FINE
$40.00
GOOD
$10.00

No. 925 Case, assorted designs.

No. 925 Men's gold filled Algier watch, 18 size. 20 year gold filled case, fitted with the well-known and reliable Algier, nickel finish movement, ruby jewels in cup settings, fancy engraved plates, patent regular, double sunk dial, heavy hands, stamped 21 jewel, very similar to a high grade railroad movement.

Price complete. Hunting..$5.20
Open Face Screw B. & B..$4.45

Do You Want to Make Money?

By these 20 Year Cases at a Never-before-heard-of Price

They are from a special purchase, and because of the low prices we can't use the name of the manufacturer, but it is one of the best known and most reputable makes in the world. These cases come in plain polish, engine turned, and a variety of beautifully engraved designs. Every one will give perfect satisfaction.

OF MINT $40.00
FINE $15.00
GOOD $5.00

HC MINT $80.00
FINE $35.00
GOOD $10.00

No. 1005.
18 size hunting, engraved.
Price $3.00
Same in open face..........2.25

MINT OF $40.00
HC $80.00

No. 1008.
18 size hunting, ray line engraved. Price $3.00
Same in open face 2.25

OF $35.00
HC $70.00

No. 1007
18 size hunting, plain polish.
Price $3.00
Same in open face..........2.25

MINT OF $40.00
HC $80.00

No. 1006.
18 size hunting, engine turn.
Price $3.00
Same in open face..........2.25

MINT OF $40.00
HC $80.00

No. 1009.
18 size hunting, top and bottom engraved. Price $3.00
Same in open face..........$2.25

Orders Filled same day as received

Order today, and if you do not like them send them back

Write for prices complete with Elgin and Waltham Movements

STOP! Do Not Pass This Page
THE BEST VALUES EVER OFFERED

Place your order today. It means big money for you.
16 size 20-year hunting and open face complete watches.

These cases are made by one of the largest watch case manufacturers of the country and are reliable goods, very fine finished in beautiful designs fitted with good time-keepers at prices which speak for themselves.

Every watch we guarantee to give perfect satisfaction.

MINT
$95.00
$100.00
$80.00

RUNNING
$15.00

No. 130.

Bridge model, 16 size, 7 jewels, nickel damaskeened, quick train, straight line lever escapement, exposed pallets, cut expansion balance, hardened and tempered Breguet hair spring, safety pinion, screw bankings, exposed polished steel winding wheels, dust band, Roman or Arabic depressed center and second white enamel dial and red marginal figures. Each, net $2.50

No. 1010.

16 size, basket, engraved in beautiful designs. Complete, with No. 130, 7 jewels............$5.50
Complete, with No. 140, 15 jewels $6.90
Price of case...............3.00

MINT
$80.00
$85.00
$70.00

No. 1012.

16 size, Sunray, engraved hunting. A great seller. Complete, with No. 130, 7 jewels.....$5.50
Complete, with No. 140, 15 jewels $6.90
Price of case...............3.00

MINT
$80.00
$85.00
$70.00

RUNNING
$20.00

No. 140.

Bridge model, 16 size, 15 jewels, 4 pairs in settings, micrometer regulator, nickel damaskeened, quick train, straight line lever escapement, exposed pallets, cut expansion balance, hardened and tempered Breguet hair spring, safety pinion, screw bankings, exposed polished steel winding wheels, dust band, Roman or Arabic depressed center and second white enamel dial and red marginal figures. Each, net, $3.90

No. 1011.

16 size, engine-turned hunting, the old reliable pattern. Complete, with No. 130, 7 jewels.$5.50
Complete, with No. 140, 15 jewels $6.90
Price of case...............3.00

MINT
$105.00
$110.00
$90.00

No. 1013.

16 size, plain polish, beaded and vermicellia border. Complete, with No. 130, 7 jewels............$5.50
Complete with No. 140, 15 jewels $6.90
Price of case...............3.00

These watches furnished in open face at 75c less.

Watches That Sell at Sight

6 and 0 Sizes

Beautiful 20-year cases set with fine white stones, in an assortment of designs fitted with good American movements. Every watch is guaranteed to give perfect satisfaction at very low prices.

Every case is guaranteed for 20 years.

MINT $70.00
$90.00

FINE $25.00
$30.00

No. 1014.
6 size hunting star and crescent, decorated with fine white stones. Price, each $3.15
Fitted with No. 310 Trenton. Price, complete $5.40

MINT $70.00
$90.00

FINE $25.00
$30.00

No. 1015.
6 size, hunting, fleur de lis decorated with fine white stones $3.15
Fitted with No. 310 Trenton. Price, complete $5.40

MINT $60.00
$80.00

No. 1016.
6 size, hunting, single star decorated with fine white stones..$3.15
Fitted with No. 310 Trenton. Price, complete $5.40

MINT $10.00

No. 310.
Bridge model, 6 size, 7 jewels, nickel damaskeened, cut expansion balance, safety pinion, screw bankings, straight line lever escapement, hardened and tempered Breguet hairspring, quick train, exposed winding wheels, Roman or Arabic white enamel dial and red marginal figures. Each, net $2.25

MINT $15.00

No. 176.
0 size, nickel, 7-jewel, quick train, straight line escap.; exp. pall., cut expans. bal., breg. h. spr., sunk sec. dial, dam. pl., gilded cent. wheel.........$4.25

MINT $15.00

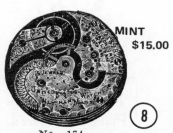

No. 174.
0 size, nickel, 11-jewel, top pl. jew. in settings, quick tr., straight line escap., exp. pall., cut expans. bal., breg. h. spr., sunk sec. dial, dam. pl., gilded center wheel.$4.50

MINT $100.00
$120.00
$120.00

No. 1017.
0 size, hunting, star and crescent design, decorated with fine white stones $3.15
Fitted with No. 176 U. S. Price, complete $7.25
Fitted with No. 174 U. S. Price, complete $7.50

MINT $100.00
$120.00
$120.00

No. 1018.
0 size, hunting, fleur de lis, decorated with fine white stones. Price, each $3.15
Fitted with No. 176 U. S. Complete $7.25
Fitted with No. 174 U. S. Complete $7.50

MINT $80.00
$100.00
$100.00

No. 1019.
0 size, hunting, single star decorated with fine white stone. Price $3.15
Fitted with No. 176 U. S. Complete $7.25
Fitted with No. 174 U. S. Complete $7.50

Notice to
Wide Awake Jewelers

We have just closed a deal with one of the largest case manufacturers of this country for several thousand of their 20-year cases; by doing so we received a special price, much lower than they were ever sold at before. We are going to give you the benefit of that low price,

Twenty Years

MINT
$80.00
EX FINE
$70.00
GOOD
$10.00

① No. B 700. 18 Size.

② MINT
$80.00
No. B 702. 18 Size.

18 and 16 size
Hunting

$4.⁴⁰
NET

Every case is guaranteed by the manufacturer.

MINT
$80.00
③ No. B 704. 16 Size.

④ MINT
$75.00
FINE
$35.00
GOOD
$10.00
No. B 705. 16 Size.

18 and 16 size
Open Face

$3.⁰⁰
NET

The cases come in Plain Polished, Engine Turned and Engraved.

MINT
$100.00
⑤ No. B 703. 16 Size.

⑥ MINT
$75.00
No. B 701. 18 Size.

12, 12-6, 6 and 0 Size 20-Year Cases

THESE ARE FROM OUR GIGANTIC PURCHASE IN WHICH WE SECURED THE LOW PRICES

Remember, every one of these cases are guaranteed by the manufacturer to give perfect satisfaction and to wear for 20 years. Beautiful designs in plain polish, engine turn and engraved.

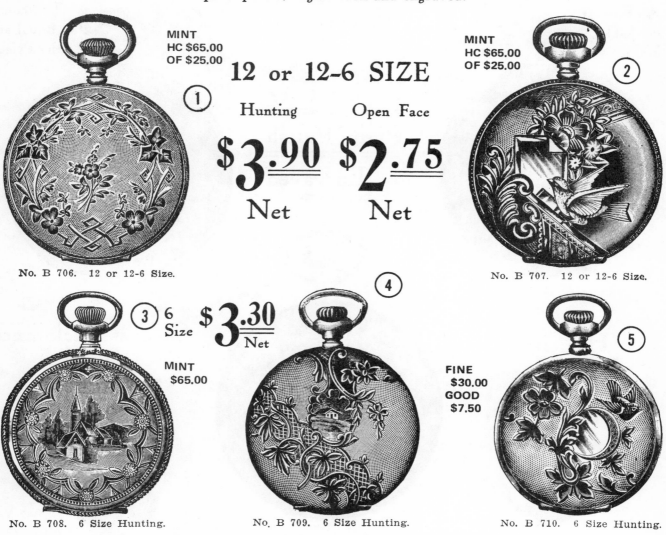

MINT
HC $65.00
OF $25.00

12 or 12-6 SIZE

Hunting — Open Face

$3.90 Net — **$2.75** Net

No. B 706. 12 or 12-6 Size.

MINT
HC $65.00
OF $25.00

No. B 707. 12 or 12-6 Size.

6 Size **$3.30** Net

MINT
$65.00

No. B 708. 6 Size Hunting.

No. B 709. 6 Size Hunting.

FINE
$30.00
GOOD
$7.50

No. B 710. 6 Size Hunting.

—— BARGAINS AT ALL TIMES ——

0 Size

$3.00 Net

MINT
$80.00
FINE
$30.00
GOOD
$10.00

No. B 711. 0 Size Hunting.

No. B712. 0 Size Hunting.

No. B 713. 0 Size Hunting.

We Do Not Want ALL the Profit

THIS PAGE IS WHERE WE PROVE IT

18 size Hunting and Open Face Double Stock 20-Year Cases.   Made by one of the largest and most reliable watch case manufacturing companies in this country.   They are all hand engraved in a large assortment of beautiful designs. Every case guaranteed to give perfect satisfaction.   Order today and if they are not just as we say, return at our expense.

A Remarkable Value

① MINT $90.00
FINE $40.00
GOOD $10.00

No. 1000.
18 size, hunting, hand engraved.
Price, each $5.15

These Cases may be had in

Engine Turn
Plain Polish
and Engraved

② MINT $90.00

Without an Equal at the Price

No. 1003.
18 size, hunting, hand engraved.
Price, each $5.15

Hunting
EACH

$5.15 NET

③ MINT $90.00

No. 1001.
18 size, hunting, hand engraved.
Price, each $5.15

Screw Back and Bezel
EACH

$3.40 NET

④ MINT $50.00

No. 1002.
18 size, S., B. & B., hand engraved. Price, each........$3.40

⑤ MINT $30.00

No. 1004.
18 size, S., B & B., plain polish.
Price, each $3.40

SOME MORE PROOF

16 size Hunting and Open Face 20-Year Double Stock Case, made by the same manufacturer as cases on page 21. Everyone guaranteed to give perfect satisfaction. A large assortment of beautiful up to date cases.

HONEST GOODS AT VERY LOW PRICES

MINT
$90.00
FINE
$45.00
GOOD
$10.00

No. 714.
16 size hunting, hand engraved.
Price, each $4.60

CASES PRICED AS SHOWN
FACTORY NEW, MINT, EX. FINE
AND GOOD

These Cases may be had
in

Engine Turn Plain Polish and Engraved

MINT
$90.00

No. 716.
16 size hunting, hand engraved.
Price, each $4.60

MINT
$90.00

No. 717.
16 size hunting, hand engraved.
Price, each $4.60

Hunting, Each,
$4.60 NET

Open Face, Each,
$2.90 NET

MINT
$40.00
FINE
$20.00
GOOD
$5.00

No. 715.
16 size S. B. & B., hand engraved. Price, each.......$2.90

Write for Prices

Complete with

Elgin and Waltham Movements

MINT
$40.00

No. 718.
16 size S. B. & B., hand engraved. Price, each........$2.90

12, 6 AND 0 SIZE 20-YEAR CASE

GOLD FILLED CASES AT EXCEPTIONALLY LOW PRICES

SEND US YOUR ORDERS AND WE WILL SAVE YOU FROM 15 TO 20 %

6 SIZE 20-YEAR, $3.57 NET

FIRST 4 — 6S
MINT $70.00
GOOD $7.50
FINE $35.00

No. 1500. 6 Size 20-Year
Hunting.

No. 1501. 6 Size 20-Year
Hunting.

No. 1502. 6 Size 20-Year
Hunting.

12 AND 12-6 SIZE 20-YEAR, $4.15 NET

A BEZEL FOR
A HUNTING CASE
IS WORTH $25.00
IF YOU NEED IT
FOR A MINT
CASE.

12—S
MINT $70.00
FINE $35.00
GOOD $7.50

No. 1503. 6 Size 20-Year
Hunting.

No. 1504. 12 or 12-6 size
20-Year Hunting.

No. 1505. 12 or 12-6 size
20-Year Hunting.

0 SIZE 20-YEAR, $3.30 NET

OS CASES
MINT $85.00
FINE $40.00
GOOD $10.

No. 1506. 0 Size 20-Year
Hunting.

No. 1507. 0 Size 20-Year
Hunting.

No. 1508. 0 Size 20-Year
Hunting.

No. 1509. 0 Size 20-Year
Hunting.

WE CARRY A COMPLETE LINE OF ELGIN AND WALTHAM MOVEMENTS

25 Year Watch Cases

Manufactured by the Wadsworth Watch Case Co.

THE NAME WADSWORTH IS ENOUGH GUARANTEE

The Most Beautiful Designs that can be Produced.   Every One a Beauty.

18 Size Hunting and Open Face

Lack of space prevents us from showing more designs. We carry a complete line, all sizes.

No. 3024. 18 Size Hunting, fancy color, engraved. Price, each..**$6.98**

No. 3027. 18 Size Screw Back and Bezel, fancy color, engraved. Price, each **$4.50**

18 size Hunting in plain polish and Engine turned.
Price each,   -   - $6.53

18 size S. B. & B., Plain polish and engine turned.
Price each,   -   - $4.28

No. 3026. 18 Size Hunting, fancy color, engraved. Price, each...**$6.98**

	H. C.	O. F.
MINT	$110.00	$ 60.00
EX FINE	80.00	45.00
FINE	50.00	25.00
GOOD	15.00	10.00
PARTS	7.50	5.00

No. 3025. 18 Size Hunting, fancy color, engraved. Price, each...**$6.98**

No. 3028. 18 Size Screw Back and Bezel, fancy color, engraved. Price, each **$4.50**

25 Year Watch Cases The Wadsworth Line of 16 Size in Hunting and Open Face

No. 3029. 16 Size Hunting, fancy color; engraved. Price, each..**$6.75**

No. 3032. 16 Size Screw Back and Bezel, fancy color; engraved. Price, each **$4.28**

All these Cases are hand Engraved and finished in that Cately colored effect in the most beautiful designs that skilled workmanship can produce.

No. 3030. 16 Size Hunting, fancy color; engraved. Price, each...**$6.75**

No. 3033. 16 Size Screw Back and Bezel, fancy color, engraved. Price, each **$4.28**

FANCY—COLOR

	H.C.	O.F.
MINT	$200.00	$125.00
EX FINE	125.00	75.00
FINE	50.00	25.00
GOOD	20.00	10.00
PARTS	10.00	5.00

No. 3031. 16 Size Hunting, fancy color, engraved. Price, each...**$6.75**

16 Size Swing Ring Cases can be furnished in Engraved for $5.63 in plain polish or Engine Turned for $5.40.

Prices on this page subject to 6 per cent for cash.

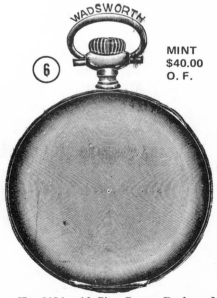

MINT
$40.00
O. F.

No. 3034. 16 Size Screw Back and Bezel, plain polish or engine turned. Price, each **$4.05**

25 Year Watch Cases—Hunting and Open Face
12 and 12-6 Sizes
The Finest American Watch Case Made
KNIFE EDGE

Multi-Color Mint
$150.00

No. 3035. 12 or 12-6 Size Hunting, fancy color, engraved.
Price, each **$6.50**

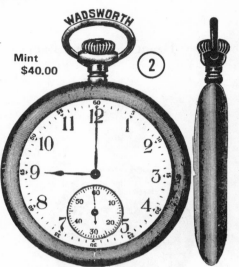

Mint $40.00

No. 3038. 12 or 12-6 Screw Back and Bezel, knife edge; plain polish.
Price, each **$4.00**

The Gentleman's Watch

Any of these cases fitted with an Elgin or Waltham Movement make the swellest watch of the age.

MINT $70.00

No. 3036. 12 or 12-6 Size Hunting, engine turned on plain polish.
Price, each **$6.00**

Do not destroy this book—it is valuable.

MINT Multi-Color $125.00

No. 3039. 12 or 12-6 Screw Back and Bezel; fancy color; engraved.
Price, each **$4.30**

MINT Multi-Color $150.00

No. 3037. 12 or 12-6 size Hunting, fancy color, engraved.
Price, each **$6.50**

Send Us Your Orders

and they will not be delayed. We carry a complete stock.

MINT $80.00

No. 3040. 12 or 12-6 Screw Back and Bezel; fancy engraved.
Price, each **$4.30**

Prices on this page subject to 6 per cent for cash

25 Year Watch Cases
6 and 0 Sizes

Beautiful Hand-Engraved Color Effects   Plain Polish and Engine Turned

"THE WADSWORTH"

0 - S
MULTI
COLOR
MINT
$200.00

O - S
FANCY
MINT
$125.00

No. 3041. 0 Size Hunting, fancy color; engraved. Price, each...**$5.15**

No. 3042. 0 Size Hunting, fancy engraved. Price, each.........**$5.15**

No. 3043. 0 Size Hunting, fancy color; engraved. Price, each...**$5.15**

No. 3044. 0 Size Hunting, fancy color; engraved. Price, each...**$5.15**

No. 3045. 0 Size Hunting, fancy engraved. Price, each.........**$5.15**

No. 3046. 0 Size Hunting, fancy color; engraved. Price, each...**$5.15**

6 - S
MULTI
COLOR
MINT
$175.00

6 - S
FANCY
MINT
$110.00

No. 3047. 6 size Hunting, fancy color; engraved. Price, each...**$5.60**

No. 3048. 6 Size Hunting, fancy color; engraved. Price, each...**$5.60**

No. 3049. 6 Size Hunting, fancy color; engraved. Price, each...**$5.60**

Prices on this Page Subject to 6 per cent for Cash

18s. IMITATION AMERICAN RAILROAD MOVEMENTS.

Stem wind and lever set.   The line of movements that sell on sight.   At prices that make other jobbers take notice.   Every one we guarantee to be in perfect running order when received.

No. 150. 18 Size Htg. and open face, improved lever escapement, quick train, steel balance, patent screw regulator, adjusted hair spring, bright red jewels set in imitation gold triple screw settings.
Price $2.25

MVT'S ONLY – NO CASE

MUST BE RUNNING DIAL EXTRA FINE

No. 107. The Rock Island Special. Imit. railroad movement, fancy cream and assorted color dials, gilt hands, very fancy gilt and nickel damaskeen plates stamped, specially adjusted, extra quality, highly jeweled, patent regulator. The best imitation railroad movement on the market. Price................$2.20

No. 125. The Helmet. The latest imitation railroad movement on the market. 18 size, full plate, beautifully nickel damaskeened, six pairs in settings, imitation ruby jewels, patent regulator, standard non-magnetic, adjusted six positions, double sunk white enameled dial and black steel hands, a good movement. Price, each....................$2.30

No. 100. 18 Size, full plate, fancy engraved highly, 23 jewels, patent regulator, metallic frame and assorted colored dials. A great seller. Our price, only....................$2.20

No. 108. 18 Size Nickel Hunting, highly polished plates, self-exposed winding wheels, sunk balance, patent regulator, double sunk glass enameled dial, one of the showiest watches on the market today for the money, an accurate time keeper. Price for movement only .$2.40

No. 106. Railway regulator, 18 size, lever escapement, ¾ fine flowered damaskeened plates stamped, highly jeweled, exposed winding wheels, imitation red ruby jewels and double sunk white enameled dial. Our price................$2.00

DIAL PERFECT
$15.00

ADD $10.00 TO $20.00 FOR FANCY DECORATED DIAL

Dial view of the Train Despatcher. Fancy raised sash, assorted color dials.

The movements on this and the next three pages are excellent examples of the low grade European import watches sold in this country. By far the larger share were Swiss made. Literally hundreds of styles were sold and this book only shows selected examples.

No. 109. 18 Size Empire Special movement, imitation 21 jewel American made Vanguard, highly polished damaskeened nickel and gilt plates, sunk balance, patent bridge regulator, four pair jewels in settings, stamped 17 or 21 jewels and adjusted, glass enameled, double sunk dial. Price $2.10

18 Size Swiss Imitation American Movements

MOVEMENTS ONLY – NO CASE MUST BE RUNNING DIAL AT LEAST FINE

STEM-WIND AND LEVER SET

FANCY DIAL $10.00 TO $20.00 EXTRA

Fit any 18 size American case made. All good sellers.

$10.00

No. 110. 18 size imitation American Railroad movement, highly polished nickel and gilt damaskeened plates, lever escapement, four pair jewels in settings, non-magnetic hairspring, patent bridge regulator, stamped 17 or 21 jewels and adjusted, double sunk, white glass enameled dial. Price each **$1.85**

$10.00

No. 112. A good Special, Union National, hunting or open face, full plate, imitation 15 jewels in setting, patent regulator, white sunk second dial, fancy nickel and gilt damaskeened. Price each **$1.80**

$10.00

No. 130. 18 size, W. P. Flyer, full plate, lever escapement, stem wind, lever set, imitation 17 jewels in settings, patent regulator, white dial and heavy railroad hands. Price each **$1.85**

NOT RUNNING $2.00

$10.00

Locomotive Special.

No. 135. 18 size, hunting and open face, imitation 17 ruby jewels, patent regulator, damaskeened, nickel or gilded plates, in composition settings, stamped adjusted, white enamel dial, spade hands. Engineer's Special stamped on dial. Price........ **$2.25**

$10.00

No. 114. 18 size, nickel, lever escapement, two exposed steel winding wheels, highly polished, patent regulator, double sung glass enameled dial **$1.75**

$10.00

No. 115. The Vallon. 18 size, three-fourths plate, cylinder escapemnet, lever set, white enamel dial, in hunting only. Price................ **$1.20**

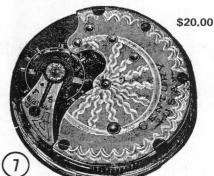

$20.00

No. 116. Seth Thomas Century. 18 size, nickel, finely damaskeened, 7 jewels, expansion balance, composition time screws, depressed second hand. Each **$1.48**

$15.00

No. 117. 18 size, New York Standard, 7-jewel, ¾ plate, nickel damaskeened, quick train, cut expansion balance, Breguet hairspring, fine white enamel dial. Hunting, lever set, open face arc, pendant set. Price **$1.48**

$10.00

No. 118. 18 size, nickel, cylinder movement, damaskeened plates, fancy raised embossed spot dial in colors, red, green, blue, etc. Price, for movement only, each.......... **$1.30**

16 Size Swiss Movements

Hunting Lever and Cylinder Escapement. All good lookers and fine sellers. Compare these prices and see for yourself that we save you money.

ALGIERS   MADISON   U. N. SPECIAL

MOVEMENT MUST BE RUNNING NO CASE DIAL AT LEAST FINE

① $10.00

② $10.00

③ $10.00

NOT RUNNING $2.00

B102

B103

B104

B104. 16 size U. N. Special, hunting cylinder, lever set, imitation raised ruby jeweled, exposed winding wheels, patent regulator, finely damaskeen plates. Name in full, Union National Watch Company, on dial and plate. White enameled dial, gilt hands. A very showy movement. Price each $1.50
B105. Same as above in fancy dial, gilt hands. Price $1.60

B102. The Algier, 16 size, ¾ plate cylinder imitation red ruby jeweled, exposed winding wheels, patent regulator, finely damaskeen plates, fancy assorted colored dials, gilt hands. The best jeweled cylinder movement on the market. Sells at sight. A fine looker. Price each.............$1.60

B103. 16 size Madison, ¾ plate cylinder imitation raised jeweled exposed winding wheels, patent regulator, finely damaskeen plates, white enameled dial, gilt hands, a good seller. Price each.............$1.50

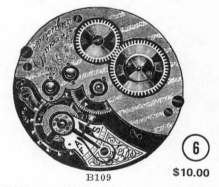

④ $10.00

⑤ $10.00

⑥ $10.00

B106

B108

B109

B106. 16 size Malton, three-quarter plate, nickel cylinder escapement, damaskeen plates, white enameled dial, gilt hands. Price, each...$1.25
B107. Same as above in assorted fancy tinted dial, gilt hands. Price each $1.30

B108. 16 size Malton, three-quarter plate, cylinder, hunting, nickel cylinder movement, fancy damaskeen plates, raised embossed dial, assorted colored gilt hands. A good seller, and a showy movement. Price, each.$1.35

B109. 16 size Washington, three-quarter plate, cylinder lever set, imitation raised ruby jewels, exposed winding wheels, patent regulator, nickel damaskeened plates, white enameled dial and gilt hands. Price, each $1.60

⑦ $10.00

⑧ $7.50

B898

B899

THE SWISS MOVEMENTS SHOWN ON THESE 5 PAGES ARE HARD TO REPAIR ESPECIALLY THE CYLINDER ESCAPEMENT. ALL OF THESE ARE STANDARD SIZE AND IT IS USUALLY BETTER TO TAKE THEM OUT OF THE CASE AND PUT IN ANOTHER MOVEMENT.

B898. 16 size, Bridge model, 7-jewel, lever escapement, nickel damaskeened pendant set, swiss movement, with exposed winding wheels and white double sunk dial and black hands. A good timepiece. Price, each $2.85

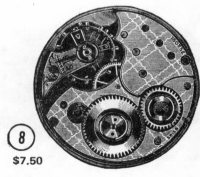

B899. 12 size split plate lever escapement, 7-jewel, nickel damaskeened pendant set, swiss movement, with exposed winding wheels and white double sunk dial and black hands. Thin model. Price, each $2.85

0 and 6 Size Swiss Movements
Hunting, Lever and Cylinder Escapements
Note Low Prices

6-Size
MOVEMENTS
ONLY MUST
BE RUNNING
DIAL MINT
$10.00
NOT MINT
$2.00

(1)

No. B85. The Algier, 6 size, ¾ plate, cylinder imitation raised, red ruby jeweled; exposed winding wheels, patent regulator, fancy damaskeen plates. Assorted colored fancy dial and gilt hands. A great seller. This movement is finished better than any other movement of this class, being made specially for us. Price, each..............$1.60

(2)

No. B86. 6 size Madison, ¾ plate, cylinder imitation, raised red ruby jeweled, exposed winding wheels, patent regulator, fancy damaskeen plates, white enamel dial, gilt hands. Price, each $1.50

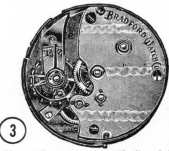

(3)

No. B87. 6 size B. W. Special, cylinder escapement, ¾ plate movement, imitation jeweled and setting, exposed winding wheels, patent regulator, white enameled dial, gilt hands. Price, each $1.50
B88. Same as above with fancy dial and gilt hands. Price, each...$1.60

O-SIZE
MOVEMENTS
ONLY MUST
BE RUNNING
DIAL MINT
$12.50
NOT RUNNING
$2.00

(4)

No. B89. 6 size Malton, ¾ plate cylinder imitation screw setting, jeweled, fancy damaskeen plates, raised embossed dials in assorted colors, gilt hands. A very showy movement. Price, each $1.35

(5)

No. B90. 6 size Malton, ¾ plate cylinder imitation screw setting, jeweled, fancy damaskeen plates, raised, with fancy assorted colored dials, gilt hands. Price, each........$1.30
B91. Same as above, with raised white dial, gilt hands. Price, each.$1.25

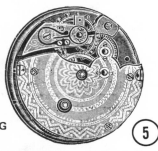

(6)

No. B92. The Victor, 6 size, ¾ plate, stem wind, lever set, nickel imitation jeweled movement, raised setting, white enamel dial, gilt hands, complete. Price, each. **$1.25**

(7)

No. B93. The Malton Special, 0 size, ¾ plate, exposed winding wheels, patent regulator, 11 j. movement, with fancy damaskeen plates. A very showy and good seller. Has the appearance of a 15 j. movement. Double sunk white enameled dial, blue steel hands. Complete. Price, each $2.25

(8)

B94. The Wellington, 0 size, ¾ plate, exposed winding wheels, jeweled cylinder, white double sunk dial, blue steel hands, full damaskeen plates, complete. Price, each...$2.25

(9)

No. B95. 0 size, Bijou, solid nickel lever movement, exposed pallet and winding wheels, compensation balance, pendant set, fine white enameled dial, black steel hands, 7 j. Very good timekeeper. A movement that can be relied upon. Price, each $3.00

(10)   B 96   **(11)**   B 98

No. B96. 0 size, Lady Suffolk, lever Swiss movement, ¾ plate exposed winding wheels, 7 j. damaskeen plate, white enameled dial. A very good seller. Price, each......$2.90
No. B97. Same as above, with fancy embossed dial. Price, each.$3.20
No. B98. The Alpine, 0 size, Bridge model, jeweled, exposed winding wheels, patent regulator, fancy colored dial, gilt hands. A very good movement, fine seller. Price each.$2.00

(12)   B 99

No. B99. The Mignon, 0 size, Bridge model, cylinder escapement, imitation jeweled movement, exposed winding wheels, nickel damaskeen plates, white enameled dial, blue steel hands. Price, each.......$1.90

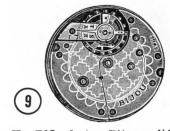

(13)   B 100   **(14)**   B101

No. B100. Malton, 0 size, ¾ plate, cylinder imitation screw setting, jeweled, white enameled, gilt hands. Best little movement on the market for the price. Price, each..$1.50
No. B101. 0 size Diana, ¾ plate, cylinder escapement, nickel damaskeen plates, exposed winding wheels, assorted fancy dial. A very showy little movement. Price, each..$1.60

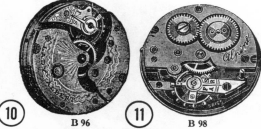

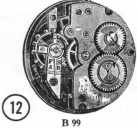

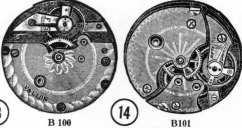

18 Size Elgin National Watch Co. Movements.

Prices Subject to Change Without Notice.

$160.00 (1)

Veritas No. 214.
¾ plate, nickel, 23 extra fine ruby jewels (raised gold settings); adjusted to temperature, isochronism and positions, double roller escapement with steel escape wheel, poised pallet and fork, pallet arbor and escape pinion cone-pivoted and cap-jeweled, exposed pallets, compensating balance, Breguet hairspring, micrometric regulator, patent safety barrel with spring box rigidly mounted on bridge, barrel arbor pivots running in jewels, display winding work, patent recoiling click, patent self-locking setting device, double sunk glass enamel dial, dust ring, plates beautifully damaskeened, carefully timed and finely finished throughout.
No. 214. Open Face only, lever set **$60.00**

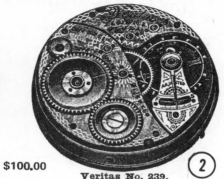

$50.00 (4)

B. W. Raymond.
Nickel, 17 ruby jewels (gold settings), adjusted to temperature, isochronism and positions, steel escape wheel, exposed pallets, compensating balance, Breguet hairspring, micrometric regulator, patent recoiling click, double sunk dial, dust ring, damaskeened plates, carefully timed and finely finished throughout.
No. 183. Hunting, lever set... **$37.00**
No. 180. Open Face, lever set.. **37.00**

$20.00 (7)

No. 335. Hunting. No. 336. O. F.
Nickel, 17 jewels (settings), exposed pallets, cut expansion balance, Breguet hairspring, micrometric regulator, sunk second dial, dust ring, damaskeened plates **$12.00**

$100.00 (2)

Veritas No. 239.
¾ plate, nickel, 21 fine ruby jewels (raised gold settings), adjusted to temperature, isochronism and positions, steel escape wheel, pallet arbor and escape pinion cone-pivoted and cap-jeweled, exposed pallets, compensating balance, Breguet hairspring, micrometric regulator, patent safety barrel with spring box rigidly mounted on bridge, display winding work, patent recoiling click, patent self-locking setting device, double sunk glass enamel dial, dust ring, damaskeened plates, carefully timed and finely finished throughout.
No. 239. Open Face only, lever set **$55.00**

$25.00 (5)

G. M. Wheeler.
Nickel, 17 jewels (gilded settings), adjusted to temperature, exposed pallets, compensating balance, Breguet hairspring, micrometric regulator, sunk second dial, dust ring, damaskeened plates.
Hunting, lever set............ **$16.00**
Open Face, pendant set........ **16.00**
Nameless movement, description as above:
No. 144. Hunting, lever set... **$16.00**
No. 148. Open Face, pendant set **16.00**

$15.00 (8)

Nickel, 15 jewels (settings), exposed pallets, cut expansion balance, Breguet hairspring, polished oval regulator, nickel index, dust ring, damaskeened plates.
No. 316. Hunting, lever set... **$10.00**
No. 317. Open Face, pendant set **10.00**

$65.00 (3)

B. W. Raymond No. 240.
¾ plate, nickel, 19 fine ruby jewels (raised gold settings), adjusted to temperature, isochronism and positions, steel escape wheel, exposed pallets, compensating balance, Breguet hairspring, micrometric regulator, patent safety barrel with spring box rigidly mounted on bridge, barrel arbor pivots running in jewels, display winding work; patent recoiling click, patent self-locking setting device, double sunk glass enamel dial, dust ring, damaskeened plates, carefully timed, and finely finished throughout.
No. 240. Open Face only, lever set **$40.00**

$100.00 (6)

Father Time.
Full plate nickel, 21 fine ruby jewels (gold settings), adjusted to temperature, isochronism and positions, steel escape wheel, pallet arbor and escape pinion cone-pivoted and cap-jeweled, exposed pallets, compensating balance, Breguet hairspring, micrometric regulator, patent recoiling click, double sunk dial, dust ring, damaskeened plates, carefully timed, and finely finished throughout.
No. 252. Open Face, lever set. **$45.00**
No. 149. Hunting, lever set... **45.00**

$15.00 (9)

Nickel, 7 jewels, exposed pallets, cut expansion balance, Breguet hairspring, polished steel regulator, nickel index, dust spring, damaskeened plates.
No. 287. Hunting, lever set.... **$8.00**
No. 288. Open Face, pendant set **8.00**

We Carry a Complete Line of Elgin Movements.

16 and 12 Size
Elgin National Watch Company's Movements

RR GRADE
$110.00

Nickel, 21 fine ruby jewels, gold settings, adjusted to temperature, isochronism and positions, steel escape wheel, pallet arbor and escape pinion cone-pivoted and cap-jeweled, exposed pallets, compensating balance, Breguet hairspring, micrometric regulator, display winding work, patent recoiling click, patent self-locking setting device, double sunk glass enamel dial, dust ring, engraving inlaid with gold, damaskeened plates, closely timed and finely finished throughout.
No. 270. Bridge. Open Face only, lever set $50.00

① $40.00

Nickel, 17 jewels, gilded settings, adjusted to temperature, exposed pallets, compensation balance, Breguet hairspring, micrometric regulator, display winding work, patent recoiling click, patent self-locking setting device, sunk second glass enamel dial, dust ring, damaskeened plates, thoroughly well finished.
No. 242. Hunting, bridge $35.00

② $30.00

Nickel, 17 jewels, gilded settings, adjusted to temperature, exposed pallets, compensating balance, Breguet hairspring, micrometric regulator, display winding work, patent recoiling click, patent self-locking setting device, sunk second glass enamel dial, dust ring, damaskeened plates.
No. 241. Hunting, bridge $23.00
No. 244. Open Face, bridge... 23.00

$25.00 ④

Nickel, 17 jewels, settings, exposed pallets, cut expansion balance, Breguet hairspring, micrometric regulator, display winding work, patent recoiling click, patent self-locking setting device, sunk second dial, dust ring, damaskeened plates.
No. 339. Hunting, bridge.....$18.00
No. 340. Open Face, bridge.... 18.00

$15.00 ⑤

Nickel, 15 jewels, settings, exposed pallets, cut expansion balance, Breguet hairspring, polished regulator, display winding work, patent self-locking setting device, sunk second dial, dust ring, damaskeened plates.
No. 312. Hunting, ¾ plates...$14.00
No. 313. Open Face, ¾ plate.. 14.00

$10.00 ⑥

Nickel, 7 jewels, exposed pallets, cut expansion balance, Breguet hairspring, polished regulator, display winding work, patent self-locking setting device, sunk second dial, dust ring, damaskeened plates.
No. 290. Hunting, ¾ plate....$10.00
No. 291. Open Face, ¾ plate.. 10.00

12 Size

$25.00 ⑦

No. 344. Hunting. $18.00.
No. 345. Open Face. $18.00
Hunting and Open Face, Pendant Set.

Nickel, 17 jewels (settings), exposed pallets, cut expansion balance, Breguet hairspring, micrometric regulator, exposed winding wheels, patent recoiling click, patent self-locking setting device, sunk second dial, dust ring, damaskeened plates......$18.00

$20.00 ⑧

No. 314. Hunting. $14.00.
No. 315. Open Face. $14.00.
Hunting and Open Face, Pendant Set.

Nickel, 15 jewels, settings, exposed pallets, cut expansion balance, Breguet hairspring, micrometric regulator, patent recoiling click, patent self-locking setting device, sunk second glass enamel dial, damaskeened plates.

$15.00 ⑨

Nickel, 7 jewels, exposed pallets, cut expansion balance, Breguet hairspring, polished steel regulator, display winding work, patent recoiling click, patent self-locking setting device, sunk second glass enamel dial, dust ring, damaskeened plates.
No. 301. Hunting $10.00
No. 303. Open Face 10.00

6 and 0 Size
Elgin National Watch Co. Movements.

$20.00 ①

No. 295. Nickel, $11.00.
Hunting and Open Face, Pendant Set.
15 jewels, settings, exposed pallets, cut expansion balance, Breguet hairspring, polished regulator, sunk second dial, damaskeened plates.

$15.00 ②

No. 286. Nickel, $9.00.
Hunting and Open Face, Pendant Set.
7 jewels, exposed pallets, cut expansion balance, Breguet hairspring, polished regulator, sunk second dial, damaskeened plates.

$15.00 ③

No. 289. Gilded. $8.00.
Hunting and Open Face, Pendant Set.
7 jewels, exposed pallets, cut expansion balance, Breguet hairspring, polished regulator, sunk second dial, damaskeened plates.

$25.00
$15.00
$15.00

No. 318. Hunting. $16.00.
No. 319. Open Face. $16.00.
No. 319s. Skylight. $16.00.
Hunting and Open Face have second hand.
Nickel, 15 jewels, settings, exposed pallets, cut expansion balance, Breguet hairspring, polished regulator, patent recoiling click, patent self-locking setting device, sunk second dial, damaskeened plates.

$75.00

No. 263. Hunting.
No. 264. O. F., with Seconds.
Nickel, 17 ruby jewels (raised gilded settings), adjusted to temperature, quick train with gold wheels, straight line escapement with gold escape wheel, exposed pallets, compensating balance, Breguet hairspring, micrometric regulator, display winding work, patent recoiling click, patent self-locking setting device, sunk second glass enamel dial, dust ring, engraving inlaid with gold frosted and damaskeened plates, pendant set $26.00

$25.00
$15.00
$15.00

No. 320. Hunting. $13.00.
No. 324. Open Face. $13.00.
No. 324s. Skylight. $13.00.
Hunting and Open Face, with second Hand Skylight have no second hand.

Nickel, 7 jewels, exposed pallets, cut expansion balance, Breguet hairspring, patent recoiling click, patent self-locking setting device, sunk second dial, damaskeened plates.

AMERICAN WALTHAM CO. MOVEMENTS.

$25.00 ④

"V." Nickel. $11.00.
15 jewels, settings, exposed pallets, cut expansion balance, patent Breguet hairspring, hardened and tempered in form, tempered steel safety barrel.

$15.00 ⑤

"Y." Nickel. $9.00.
7 jewels, exposed pallets, cut expansion balance, patent Breguet hairspring, hardened and tempered in form tempered steel safety barrel.

$15.00 ⑥

"J." Gilded. $8.00.
7 jewels, exposed pallets, cut expansion balance, patent Breguet hairspring, hardened and tempered in form, tempered steel safety barrel.

$25.00 ⑦

Lady Waltham. Nickel. $25.00.
Hunting or Open Face.
16 ruby jewels, raised gold settings, exposed pallets, compensation balance, adjusted, patent Breguet hairspring, hardened and tempered in form, patent micrometric regulator, tempered steel safety barrel, red gold center wheel.

$25.00 ⑧

No. 115. Nickel. $16.00.
Hunting or Open Face.
15 jewels settings, exposed pallets, cut expansion balance, patent Breguet hairspring, hardened and tempered in form, tempered steel safety barrel, red gilded center wheel, and jewel settings.

$15.00 ⑨

No. 61. Nickel. $13.00.
Hunting and Open Face.
7 jewels, exposed pallets, cut expansion balance, patent Breguet hairspring, hardened and tempered in form, tempered steel safety barrel.

18 Size American Waltham Watch Co. Movements

Prices Subject to Change Without Notice.

$125.00

(1)

Vanguard, 23 Jewels.

Nickel, 23 diamond and ruby jewels, both balance pivots running on diamonds (raised gold settings), jewel pin set without shellac, double roller escapement, steel escape wheel, exposed pallets, compensating balance in recess, adjusted to temperature, isochronism and five positions, patent Breguet hairspring hardened and tempered in form, embossed gold patent micrometric regulator, tempered steel safety barrel, exposed winding wheels, elaborately finished nickel plates with gold lettering, plate and jewel screws gilded, steel parts chamfered, double sunk dial. The Vanguard is the finest 18 size movement in the world.

Vanguard, 23 jewels, Hunting or Open Face, lever set...**$60 00**

$75.00

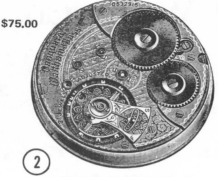

(2)

Vanguard, 21 Jewels.

21 diamond and ruby jewels, both balance pivots running on diamonds (raised gold settings), jewel pin set without shellac, double roller escapement, steel escape wheel, exposed pallets, compensating balance in recess, adjusted to temperature, isochronism and five positions, patent Breguet hairspring hardened and tempered in form, embossed gold patent micrometric regulator, tempered steel safety barrel, exposed winding wheels, elaborately finished nickel plates with gold lettering, plate and jewel screws gilded, steel parts chamfered, double sunk dial. The Vanguard is the finest 18 size movement in the world.

Vanguard, nickel, Hunting or Open Face **$55 00**

$65.00

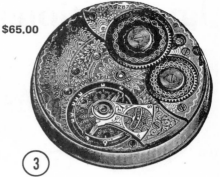

(3)

Crescent Street, 21 Jewels.

Nickel, 21 fine ruby jewels, gold settings, jewel pin set without shellac, double roller escapement, steel escape wheel, exposed pallets, patent micrometric regulator, compensation balance in recess, adjusted to temperature, isochronism and five positions, tempered steel safety barrel, exposed winding wheels, patent Breguet hairspring hardened and tempered in form, double sunk dial.

Crescent Street, 21 jewels, Hunting or Open Face....**$45 00**

$40.00

(4)

Appleton, Tracy & Co.

Nickel, 17 ruby jewels, gold settings, jewel pin set without shellac, double roller escapement, steel escape wheel, exposed pallets, patent micrometric regulator, compensation balance in recess, adjusted to temperature and three positions, tempered steel safety barrel, exposed winding wheels, patent Breguet hairspring hardened and tempered in form, double sunk dial.

Appleton, Tracy & Co., Hunting or Open Face.......**$30 00**

$25.00

(5)

P. S. Bartlett.

Nickel, 17 jewels, settings, exposed pallets, compensation balance, adjusted to temperature, patent micrometric regulator, patent Breguet hairspring hardened and tempered in form.

P. S. Bartlett, Hunting or Open Face **$16 00**

$20.00

(6)

No. 825. Nickel, 17 jewels, settings, exposed pallets, compensation balance, patent micrometric regulator, patent Breguet hairspring hardened and tempered in form.

No. 825 Hunting or open face.**$12 00**

$20.00

(7)

Nickel, 15 jewels, settings, exposed pallets, cut expansion balance, highly finished oval regulator, polished and gilded index plate, patent Breguet hairspring hardened and tempered in form.

No. 820 Hunting or Open Face.**$10 00**

$15.00

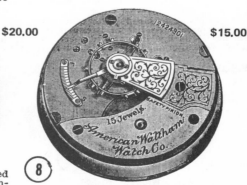

(8)

Gilded, 15 jewels, settings, exposed pallets, cut expansion balance, patent Breguet hairspring hardened and tempered in form.

No. 81 Hunting or Open Face.**$9 00**

(9)

Nickel, 7 jewels, settings, exposed pallets, cut expansion balance, highly finished oval regulator, polished and gilded index plate, patent Breguet hairspring hardened and tempered in form.

No. 18 Nickel, Hunting or Open Face **$8 00**

Same as above in Gilt........**$7 00**

We Carry a Complete Line of Boss & Crescent Cases.

16 & 12 Size American Waltham Watch Co.'s Movements

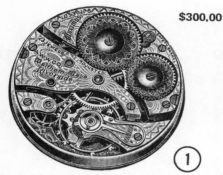

$300.00

$25.00

$20.00

Riverside Maximus. $100.00.
Hunting, pendant set. Open Face,
pendant or lever set.

Nickel, 23 diamond and ruby jewels, 2 pairs diamond caps, both balance pivots running on diamonds, raised gold settings, jeweled main wheel bearings, jewel pin set without shellac, double roller escapement, steel escape wheel, exposed sapphire pallets, compensating balance, accurately adjusted to temperature, isochronism and five positions, and carefully timed, patent Breguet hairspring, hardened and tempered in form, patent micrometric regulator, tempered steel safety barrel, exposed winding wheels, steel parts chamfered, gold train, fine glass hand-painted dial.

Royal. Nickel. $27.50.
Hunting and Open Face, Pendant Set.

17 jewels, red gold settings, exposed pallets, compensating balance, adjusted to temperature, patent Breguet hairspring, hardened and tempered in form, patent micrometric regulator, tempered steel safety barrel, exposed winding wheels, red gold center wheel.

P. S. Bartlett. Nickel. $23.00.
Hunting and Open Face, Pendant Set.

17 jewels, red gilded settings, exposed pallets, compensating balance, adjusted to temperature, patent Breguet hairspring, hardened and tempered in form, patent micrometric regulator, tempered steel safety barrel, red gilded center wheels.

$20.00

$20.00

$15.00

No. 620. 15 Jewels. $14.00.
Hunting and Open Face, Pendant Set.

15 jewels, red gilded settings, exposed pallets, cut expansion balance, patent Breguet hairspring, hardened and tempered in form, patent micrometric regulator, tempered steel safety barrel, exposed winding wheels, red gilded center wheel.

No. 610. Nickel. $10.00.
Hunting and Open Face, Pendant Set.

7 jewels, exposed pallets, cut expansion balance, patent Breguet hairspring, hardened and tempered in form, tempered steel safety barrel, exposed winding wheels.

No. 625. Nickel. $18.00.
Hunting and Open Face, Pendant Set.

17 jewels, red gilded settings, exposed pallets, compensating balance, patent Breguet hairspring, hardened and tempered in form, patent micrometric regulator, tempered steel safety barrel, red gilded center wheels.

12 Size

$25.00

$20.00

$15.00

No. 225. Nickel.
Hunting or Open Face.

17 jewels (settings), exposed pallets, polished and red gilded center wheel and jewel settings, cut expansion balance, patent micrometric regulator, patent Breguet hairspring, hardened and tempered in form. $18.00

No. 220. Nickel. $14.00.
Hunting and Open Face, Pendant Set.

15 jewels, settings, exposed pallets, cut expansion balance, patent Breguet hairspring, hardened and tempered in form, patent micrometric regulator, tempered steel safety barrel.

No. 210. Nickel. $10.00.
Hunting and Open Face, Pendant Set.

7 jewels, exposed pallets, cut expansion balance, patent Breguet hairspring, hardened and tempered in form, tempered steel safety barrel.

1904   10 Line= 9/0 Size
12 Line = 4/0 Size

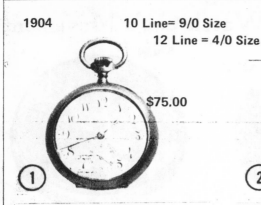

$75.00

$70.00

$65.00

151. O. F., 14K, 10 line anchor, 15 jewels, gold cap, plain bassine case, ... $87.50

152. O. F., 14K, 10 line anchor, 15 jewels, nickel movement, gold cap, plain bassine case; *"Omega"* $56.76

153. O. F., 14K, 10 line anchor, 15 jewels, nickel movement, 2d hand, fancy dial, gold cap; *Nameless,* $52.04

NOTE: This page through page 81 was taken from a 1904 Jos Brown wholesale catalog and represents the swiss import watches extremely well. There were thousands of these watches sold in the U.S. Most of them have little value now. (SEE BELOW)

$60.00
$55.00

$55.00
$50.00

$50.00
$45.00

154. O. F., 14K, 11 line anchor, 15 jewels, fancy dial, plain bass. case, gold cap; *"Lady Racine,"* . . . $43.75
155. Same in eng'd case, $44.94

156. O. F., 14K, 10 line cylinder, 10 jewels, plain case, gold cap; *"Lady Racine"* $31.92
157. Same in engraved case, $35.48

158. Hunting, 14K, 12 line cylinder, 7 jewels, engraved case p. c.; *"Guinand"* $23.05
159. Same in 9K case, $19.50

Page 65 to 75 represents low grade watches that have value only in the case metal and for trading watches. None of these at this point in time are being collected.

$45.00
$40.00

$40.00
$35.00

$40.00
$35.00

160. Hunting, 14K, 12 line cylinder, 7 jewels, plain case, p. c.; *"Guinand,"* $21.88
161. Same in 9K case, . $18.30

162. O. F., 14K, 12 line cylinder, 7 jewels, engraved case, p. c.; *"Guinand,"* $16.54
163. Same in 9K case, . $14.20

164. O. F., 14K, 12 line cylinder, 7 jewels, plain case. . . . $15.96
"Guinand,"
165. Same in 9K, . . $13.60

1904

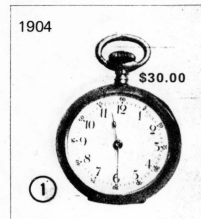

$30.00

$30.00
$25.00

$25.00
$20.00

166. O. F., silver 935 / 1000 fine, 11 line anchor, 15 jewels, plain bass case, silver cap; "Omega," $26.00
167. Same in E. T. or E. T. & E. case, . . $27.20

168. O. F., silver, 935 / 1000 fine, 11 line anchor, 10 jewels, E. T. & E. case, silver cap; "Lady Racine," . . $21.28
169. Same in plain case, $20.70

170. O. F., silver, 935 / 1000 fine, 10 line cylinder, 10 jewels, plain case, silver cap, fancy dial; "Lady Racine," . . . $14.20
171. Same, plain dial, . $13.60

NOTE: I apologize for the quality of these 20 pages, my original catalog was sorry, but I feel even with the bad quality they tell the story well.

$30.00
$20.00

$20.00

$20.00
$20.00

172. O. F., silver; 935 / 1000 fine, 10 line cylinder, 10 jewels, engraved or E. T. case, silver cap, fancy dial; "Lady Racine," $14.20
173. Same, plain dial, . $13.60

174. O. F., silver, 935 / 1000 fine, 10 line cylinder, 10 jewels, enamel niello case, silver cap; "Lady Racine," . . . $16.54

175. O. F., silver, 935 / 1000 fine, 10 line cylinder, 10 jewels, antique plain case, silver cap; "Lady Racine," . . . $17.72
176. Same, oxidized. . $23.65

$20.00

$20.00

$50.00

177. O. F., silver, 935 / 1000 fine, 12 line cylinder, 10 jewels, plain case, silver cap, 2d-hand; "Lady Racine," . . $11.24

178. O. F., silver, 935 / 1000 fine, 12 line cylinder, 10 jewels, engraved case, silver cap, 2d-hand; "Lady Racine," . . . $11.24

179. O. F., silver, 935 / 1000 fine, 12 line cylinder, 10 jewels, enamel niello case, silver cap; "Lady Racine," . . . $15.96

$20.00

180. Hunt'g, silver, 935/1000 fine, 12 line cylinder, 10 jewels, engraved case, silver cap, 2d-hand; *"Lady Racine,"* . . . $13.00

$20.00

181. Skylight, silver, 935/. fine, 12 line cylinder, 10 jewels, plain. case, silver cap; *"Lady Racine,"* . . . $13.00
182. Same, engraved case, $13.00

$20.00

183. O. F., silver, 12 line cylinder, 6 jewels, plain bassine case, silver cap; *"Lady Racine,"* $9.46

13 Line= O Size

$20.00

184. Hunting, silver, 12 line cylinder, 6 jewels, 2d-hand, engraved case, silver cap; *"Lady Racine,"* . . . $11.24

$20.00
$20.00

185. O. F., silver, 12 line cylinder, 6 jewels, engraved case, silver cap; *"Lady Racine,"* $9.16
186. Same, plated cap, $8.58

$20.00

187. O. F., silver, 935/1000 fine, 13 line cylinder, 10 jewels, assorted cases, silver cap; *"Lady Racine,"* . . . $10.64

$35.00

188. O. F., silver, 935/1000 fine, 13 line cylinder, 10 jewels, oxidized ornamented case, silver cap, *"Lady Racine,"* . . . $11.24

$20.00

189. Hunt'g, silver, 935/1000 fine, 13 line cylinder, 10 jewels, assorted cases, silver cap; *"Lady Racine,"* . . . $12.40

$25.00
$20.00

190. Skylight, silver, 935/. fine, 13 line cylinder, 10 jewels, engraved case, silver cap; *"Lady Racine,"* $12.40
191. Same, plain case, $12.40

$15.00

$20.00
$20.00

$20.00

192. O. F., silver, 12 line cylinder, engraved case, no cap, snap back, ... $5.56

193. O. F. silver, 12 line cylinder, engraved case, plated cap; "Fairy," $5.90
194. Same, silver cap, $6.15 Fancy dials 24 cts. list extra.

195. O. F., silver, 12 line cylinder, 7 jewels, engraved case, silver cap; "Fairy," . . . $6.40

$20.00
$20.00

$20.00
$20.00
$20.00

$25.00

196. O. F., silver, 12 line cylinder, 5 jewels, engraved case, silver cap, fancy bezel; "Fairy," $6.28
197. Same, 7 jewels, . . $6.50

198. O. F., silver, 12 line cylinder, 5 jewels, engraved case, silver cap, 2d-hand; "Fairy," $6.50
199. Same, 7 jewels, . . $6.75
200. Same, better grade movement, pendant set, $8.04

201. O. F., silver, 12 line cylinder, 7 jewels, fluted case, silver cap; "Fairy," $8.28

$20.00
$20.00

$20.00
$20.00

$20.00
$20.00

202. Hunting, silver, 12 line cylinder, 5 jewels, engraved case, plated cap; "Fairy," . $7.16
203. Same, silver cap, . $7.34
204. Same, sil. cap, 7 jewels, $7.58

205. Hunting, silver, 12 line cylinder, 5 jewels, engraved case, silver cap, 2d-hand; "Fairy," $7.58
206. Same, 7 jewels, . . $7.80

207. Hunting, silver, 12 line cylinder, 7 jewels, engraved case, silver cap, 2d-hand, inside lever set; "Fairy," . . $8.16
208. Better quality, with cases 935/1000 fine, . . $9.46

$15.00 Mint
$ 2.00 Not Running

$15.00

$15.00

209. O. F., silver, 10 line cylinder, 7 jewels, engraved case, silver cap; *"Fairy,"* $7.10

210. O. F., nickel, 10 line cylinder, 6 jewels, plain case, glass cap; *"Fairy,"* $6.22

211. O. F., nickel, 10 line cylinder, 6 jewels, plain case, nickel cap; *"Lady Racine,"* . . $9.78

$15.00

$15.00

$15.00

212. O. F., nickel, 12 line cylinder, 6 jewels, plain case, nickel cap, 2d-hand; *"Lady Racine,"* $7.98

213. O. F., nickel, 15 line cylinder, 6 jewels, plain case, nickel cap; *"Lady Racine,"* . . $7.68

214. O. F., nickel, 13 line cylinder, 6 jewels, plain case, nickel cap; *"Lady Racine,"* . . $7.58

$15.00

$15.00

$15.00

215. O. F., nickel, 12 line cylinder, plain case, glass cap; *"Fairy,"* $5.20

216. O. F., nickel, 15 line cylinder, plain case, glass cap; *"Eureka,"* $4 42
217. Same, pendant set, $4.62

218. O. F., nickel, 14 line cylinder, stamped engraved case, no cap; *"Wonder,"* $4.74

Watch, case and dial MUST be mint and running

 $20.00 ①

 $20.00 ②

 $25.00 ③

219. O. F., oxidized steel, polished or satin finish, 10 line cylinder, 10 jewels, steel cap, fancy dial, rolled plated bow and crown; *"Lady Racine,"* . . . $12.40
220. Same, silver bow and black dial, ... $12.40

221. O. F., oxidized steel, polished or satin finish, 10 line cylinder, 10 jewels, steel cap, white dial, rolled plated bow and crown, *"Lady Racine,"* . . . $11.82
222. Same, silver bow, $11.82

223. O. F., oxidized steel, satin finish, 11½ line cylinder, 10 jewels, steel cap, fancy dial, silver bezel, rolled plated bow and crown; *"Lady Racine,"* . . . $9.18
224. Same in 13 line, . $8.56

 $25.00 ④

 $20.00 ⑤

 $20.00 ⑥

225. O. F., oxidized steel, polished or satin finish, 12 line cylinder, 6 jewels, steel cap, fancy dial, rolled plated bow and crown, *"Lady Racine,"* . . . $9.18

226. O. F., oxidized steel, polished or satin finish, 12 line cylinder, 6 jewels, steel cap, white dial, rolled plated bow and crown; *"Lady Racine,"* . . . $8.56

227. O. F,. oxidized steel, polished or satin finish, 12 line cylinder, 6 jewels, 2d-hand, steel cap, white dial, rolled plated bow and crown; *"Lady Racine."* . $8.56

 $20.00 ⑦

 $20.00 ⑧

 Eagle Case $40.00 ⑨

228. O. F., oxidized steel, satin finish, 12 line cylinder, 5 jewels, glass cap, *"Fairy,"* $5.32
229. Same, with fancy dial, $5.64

230. O. F., oxidized steel, satin finish, 10 line cylinder, 6 jewels, glass cap, fancy dial *"Fairy,"* $6.22

231. O. F., oxidized steel, satin finish, 12 line cylinder, 5 jewels, glass cap, fancy dial, ornamented back, ... $7.40

18 Line = 13 Size
16 Line = 8 Size

Note: These swiss style pin set cases will not fit American made standard size movements.

① $25.00
$25.00

② $25.00
$25.00

NIELLO
$100.00

246. Hunt'g, silver, 935 / 1000 fine, 16 line anchor, 15 jewels, E. T. or E. T. & E. case; *"Racine,"* $18.92
247. Same in plain bassine case, ... $18.92

243. O. F., silver, 935 / 1000 fine, 16 line anchor, 15 jewels, silver cap, plain polished bassine case; *"Racine,"* $16.54
244. Same in E. T. or E. T. & E. case, ... $17.14

245. O. F., silver, 935 / 1000 fine, 16 line anchor, 15 jewels, silver cap, enameled niello case; *"Racine,"* $22.48

④ $25.00
$25.00

⑤ $25.00
$25.00

⑥ $25.00

248. Hunt'g, silver, 18 line anchor, 7 jewels, E. T. & E. or engraved case; *"Success,"* $11.82
249. Same in silver case, 900 / 1000 fine $12.42

Note:
If not running figure $1.00 for movement and scrap value or less than $10.00 for case.

250. O. F., silver, 18 line anchor, 7 jewels, E. T. & E. or engraved case; *"Success,"* . . . $10.64
251. Same in silver case, 900 / 1000 fine, $11.24

252. O. F., silver, 900 / 1000 fine, 18 line anchor, 7 jewels, plain bass. case, *"Success,"* $11.45

These Cylinder watches are not worth fixing if the staff is broken and would have scrap value only.

$25.00

$25.00

$25.00

253. O. F., silver, 18 line cylinder, 6 jewels, plated cap, engraved case; Nameless, ... $6.80

254. Hunting, silver, 18 line, cylinder, 6 jewels, plated cap, engraved case, Nameless, $8.04

18 Line = 13 size
20 Line = 18½ size

255. Hunting, silver, 20 line cylinder, 6 jewels, plated cap, engraved case; Nameless, ... $9.22

$25.00

$25.00

Note: All Prices in this book are retail.

256. O. F., silver, 18 line cylinder, 6 jewels, plated cap, engraved case; "Select," $8.58

257. Hunting, silver, 18 line cylinder, 6 jewels, plated cap, engraved case; "Select," . $9.78

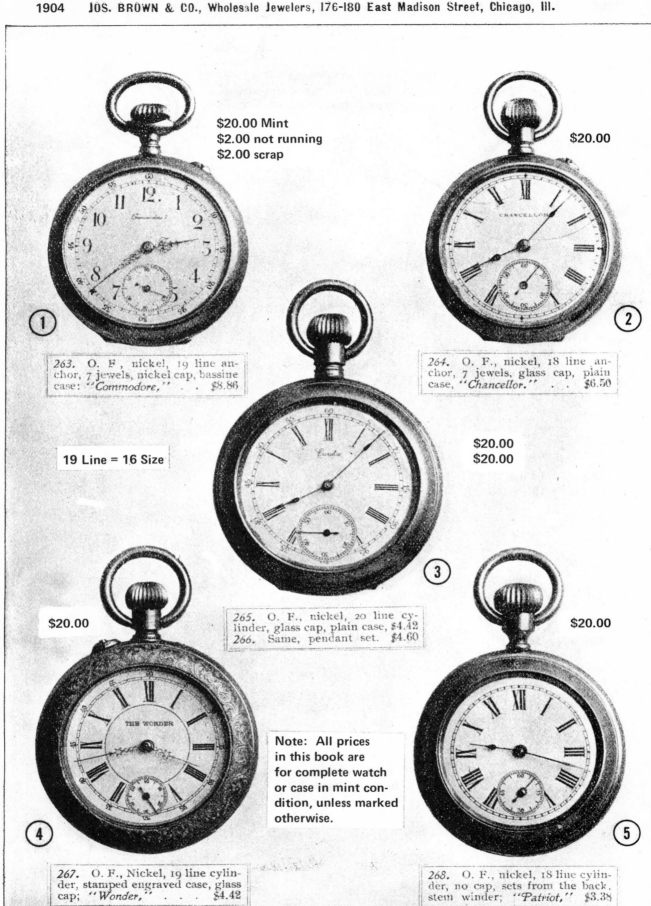

$20.00 Mint
$2.00 not running
$2.00 scrap

$20.00

263. O. F., nickel, 19 line anchor, 7 jewels, nickel cap, bassine case: *"Commodore,"* . . . $8.86

264. O. F., nickel, 18 line anchor, 7 jewels, glass cap, plain case, *"Chancellor."* . . . $6.50

19 Line = 16 Size

$20.00
$20.00

$20.00

265. O. F., nickel, 20 line cylinder, glass cap, plain case, $4.42
266. Same, pendant set. $4.60

$20.00

Note: All prices in this book are for complete watch or case in mint condition, unless marked otherwise.

267. O. F., Nickel, 19 line cylinder, stamped engraved case, glass cap; *"Wonder,"* . . . $4.42

268. O. F., nickel, 18 line cylinder, no cap, sets from the back, stem winder; *"Patriot,"* $3.38

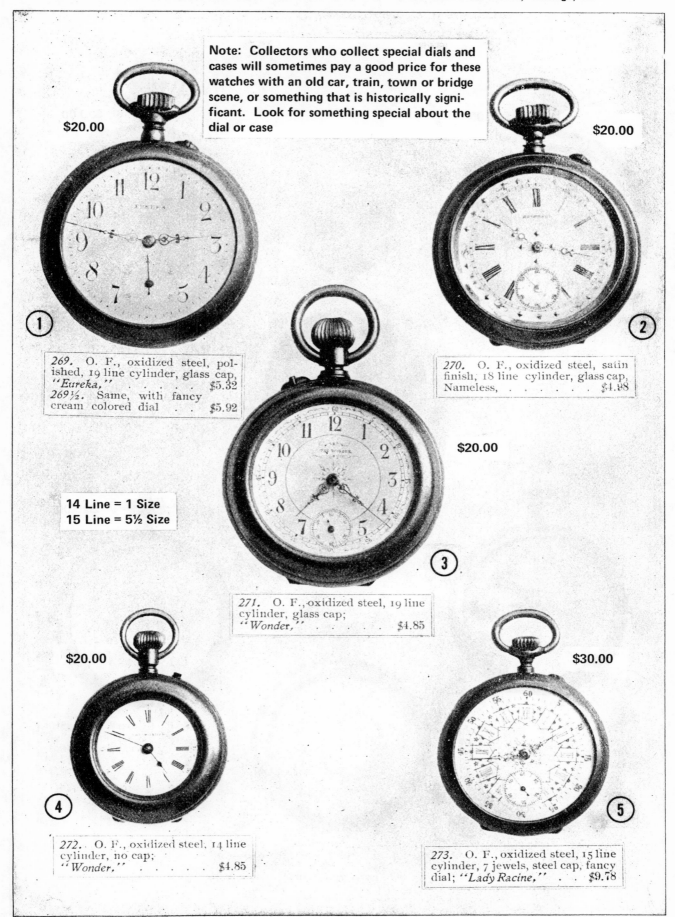

Note: Collectors who collect special dials and cases will sometimes pay a good price for these watches with an old car, train, town or bridge scene, or something that is historically significant. Look for something special about the dial or case

$20.00

$20.00

①

269. O. F., oxidized steel, polished, 19 line cylinder, glass cap, "Eureka," $5.32
269½. Same, with fancy cream colored dial . . $5.92

270. O. F., oxidized steel, satin finish, 18 line cylinder, glass cap, Nameless, ... $4.98

$20.00

14 Line = 1 Size
15 Line = 5½ Size

271. O. F., oxidized steel, 19 line cylinder, glass cap; "Wonder," $4.85

③

$20.00

$30.00

④

272. O. F., oxidized steel, 14 line cylinder, no cap; "Wonder," $4.85

⑤

273. O. F., oxidized steel, 15 line cylinder, 7 jewels, steel cap, fancy dial; "Lady Racine," . . . $9.78

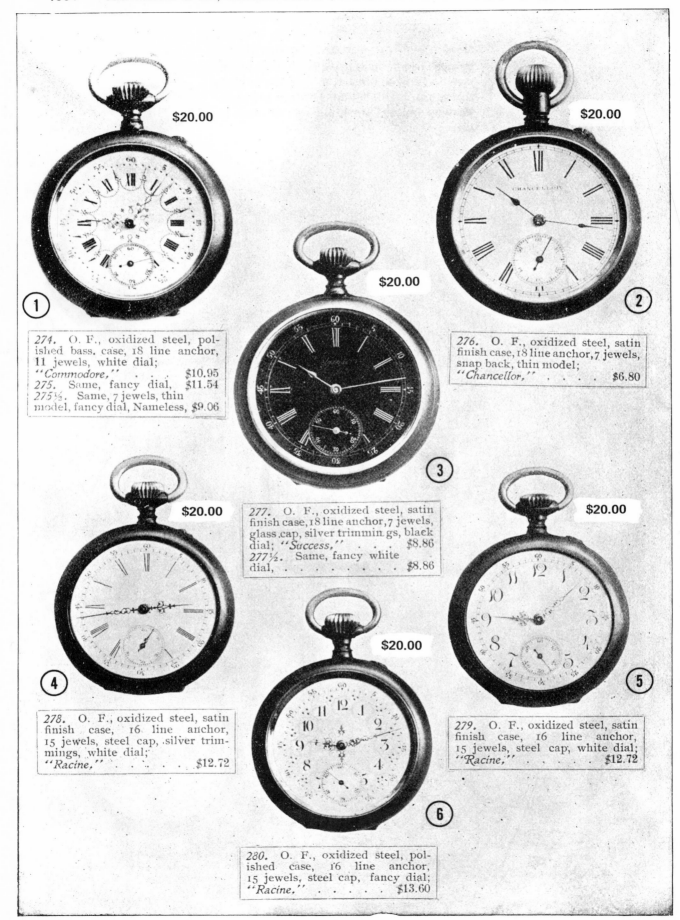

$20.00

$20.00

$20.00

1

274. O. F., oxidized steel, polished bass. case, 18 line anchor, 11 jewels, white dial; *"Commodore,"* . . . $10.95
275. Same, fancy dial, $11.54
275½. Same, 7 jewels, thin model, fancy dial, Nameless, $9.06

2

276. O. F., oxidized steel, satin finish case, 18 line anchor, 7 jewels, snap back, thin model; *"Chancellor,"* $6.80

3

277. O. F., oxidized steel, satin finish case, 18 line anchor, 7 jewels, glass cap, silver trimmings, black dial; *"Success,"* . . . $8.86
277½. Same, fancy white dial, ... $8.86

$20.00

$20.00

$20.00

4

278. O. F., oxidized steel, satin finish case, 16 line anchor, 15 jewels, steel cap, silver trimmings, white dial; *"Racine,"* $12.72

5

279. O. F., oxidized steel, satin finish case, 16 line anchor, 15 jewels, steel cap, white dial; *"Racine,"* $12.72

6

280. O. F., oxidized steel, polished case, 16 line anchor, 15 jewels, steel cap, fancy dial; *"Racine,"* $13.60

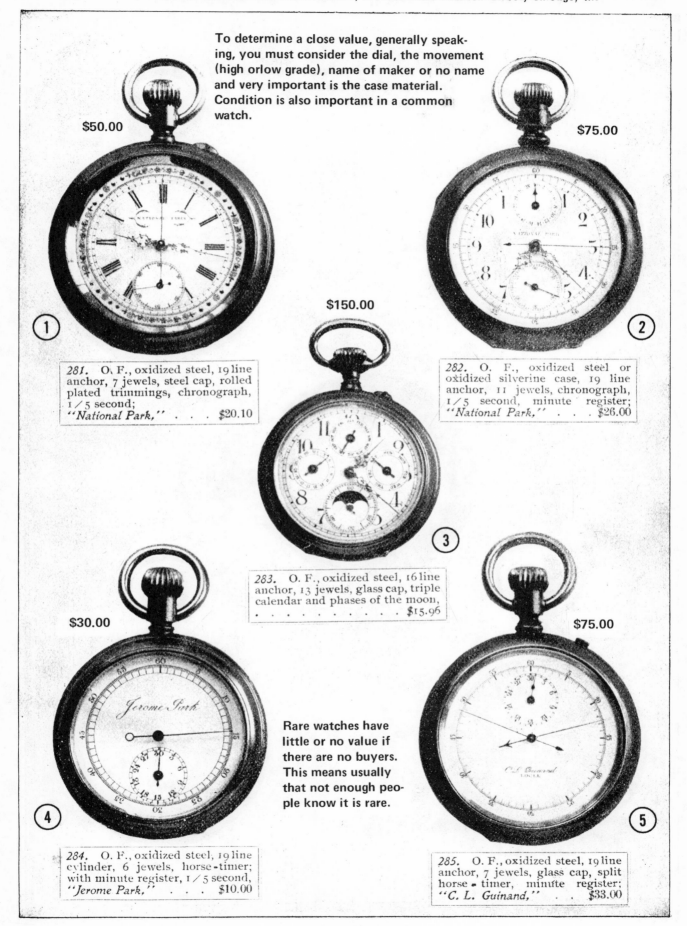

To determine a close value, generally speaking, you must consider the dial, the movement (high or low grade), name of maker or no name and very important is the case material. Condition is also important in a common watch.

$50.00

$75.00

$150.00

281. O. F., oxidized steel, 19 line anchor, 7 jewels, steel cap, rolled plated trimmings, chronograph, 1/5 second; *"National Park,"* . . . $20.10

282. O. F., oxidized steel or oxidized silverine case, 19 line anchor, 11 jewels, chronograph, 1/5 second, minute register; *"National Park,"* . . . $26.00

$30.00

$75.00

283. O. F., oxidized steel, 16 line anchor, 13 jewels, glass cap, triple calendar and phases of the moon, ... $15.96

Rare watches have little or no value if there are no buyers. This means usually that not enough people know it is rare.

284. O. F., oxidized steel, 19 line cylinder, 6 jewels, horse-timer; with minute register, 1/5 second, *"Jerome Park,"* . . . $10.00

285. O. F., oxidized steel, 19 line anchor, 7 jewels, glass cap, split horse-timer, minute register; *"C. L. Guinand,"* . . . $33.00

$60.00

Note: Rare or very scarce watches that a lot of collectors are looking for will bring high prices even in very poor condition.

Mint
$350.00

①

②

286. O. F., oxidized steel, 19 line anchor, 15 jewels, steel cap, 8 day watch, rolled plated trimmings, ... $20.10

287. O. F., oxidized steel, 19 line anchor, 15 jewels, glass cap, 15 minute repeater. Pull out the crown and press on it as long as it strikes, ... $34.20
287½. Same in silver case. $36.66

$200.00

③

$125.00

$200.00

288. O. F., oxidized steel, 19 line anchor, 15 jewels, automatic. A watch without hands, . $26.00
289. Same, in silver case, 935 / 1000 fine, ... $28.38

④

⑤

290. Hunting, nickel, 19 line anchor, 11 jewels. Blind-man's watch, ... $26.00

291. O. F., silver, 19 line anchor, 15 jewels, silver cap, 24 hour watch, shifting dial, . . 28.38

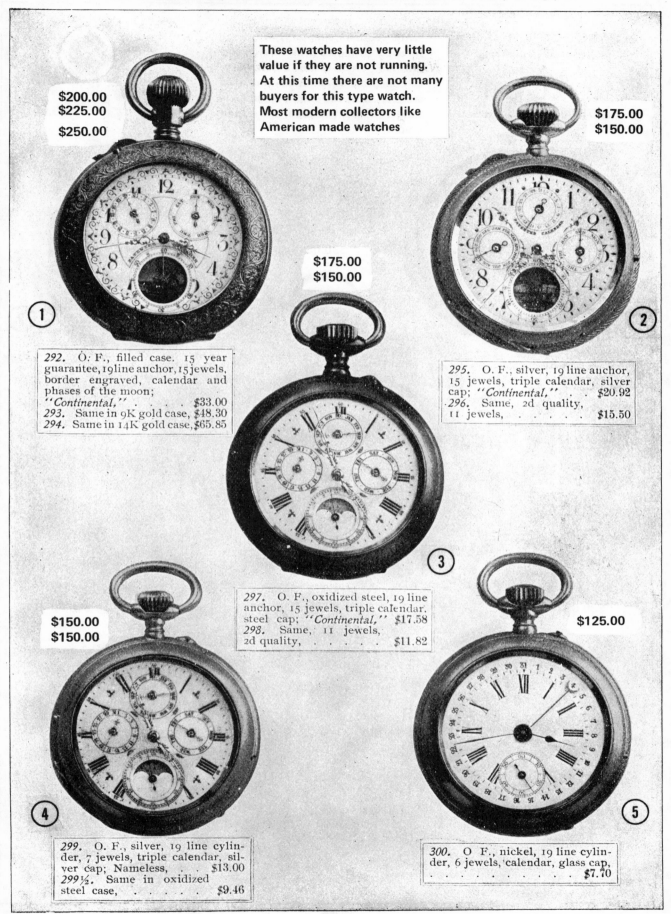

These watches have very little value if they are not running. At this time there are not many buyers for this type watch. Most modern collectors like American made watches

$200.00
$225.00
$250.00

$175.00
$150.00

$175.00
$150.00

$150.00
$150.00

$125.00

292. O. F., filled case. 15 year guarantee, 19 line anchor, 15 jewels, border engraved, calendar and phases of the moon; "Continental," $33.00
293. Same in 9K gold case, $48.30
294. Same in 14K gold case, $65.85

295. O. F., silver, 19 line anchor, 15 jewels, triple calendar, silver cap; "Continental," . . $20.92
296. Same, 2d quality, 11 jewels, ... $15.50

297. O. F., oxidized steel, 19 line anchor, 15 jewels, triple calendar. steel cap; "Continental," $17.58
298. Same, 11 jewels, 2d quality, ... $11.82

299. O. F., silver, 19 line cylinder, 7 jewels, triple calendar, silver cap; Nameless, . . $13.00
299½. Same in oxidized steel case, ... $9.46

300. O F., nickel, 19 line cylinder, 6 jewels, calendar, glass cap, ... $7.70

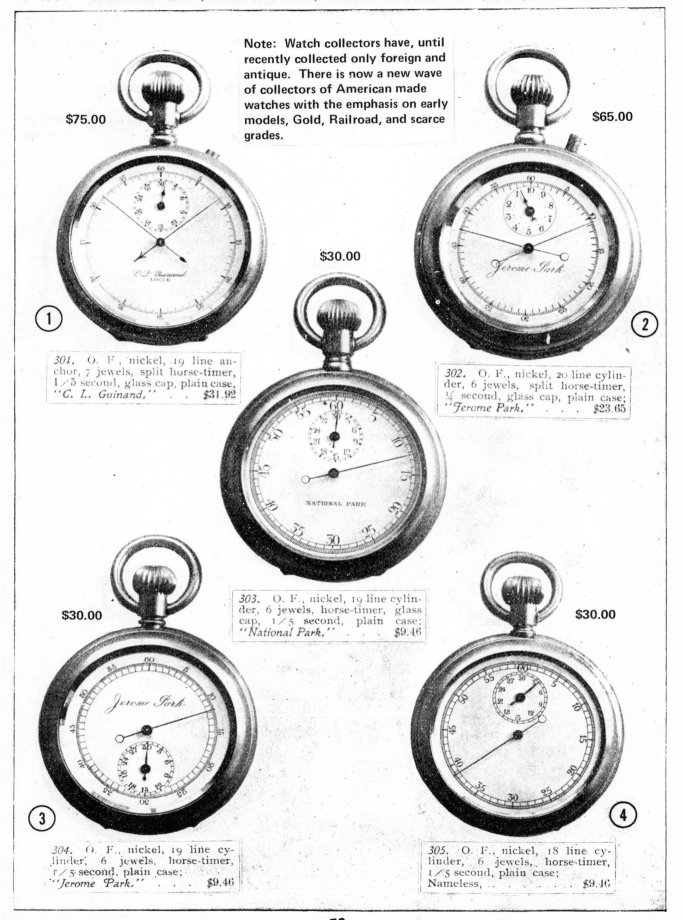

$75.00

Note: Watch collectors have, until recently collected only foreign and antique. There is now a new wave of collectors of American made watches with the emphasis on early models, Gold, Railroad, and scarce grades.

$65.00

$30.00

1

301. O. F., nickel, 19 line anchor, 7 jewels, split horse-timer, 1/5 second, glass cap, plain case, "C. L. Guinand," . . $31.92

2

302. O. F., nickel, 20 line cylinder, 6 jewels, split horse-timer, 1/4 second, glass cap, plain case; "Jerome Park," . . . $23.65

$30.00

3

303. O. F., nickel, 19 line cylinder, 6 jewels, horse-timer, glass cap, 1/5 second, plain case; "National Park," . . $9.46

$30.00

304. O. F., nickel, 19 line cylinder, 6 jewels, horse-timer, 1/5 second, plain case; "Jerome Park," . . . $9.46

4

305. O. F., nickel, 18 line cylinder, 6 jewels, horse-timer, 1/5 second, plain case; Nameless, ... $9.46

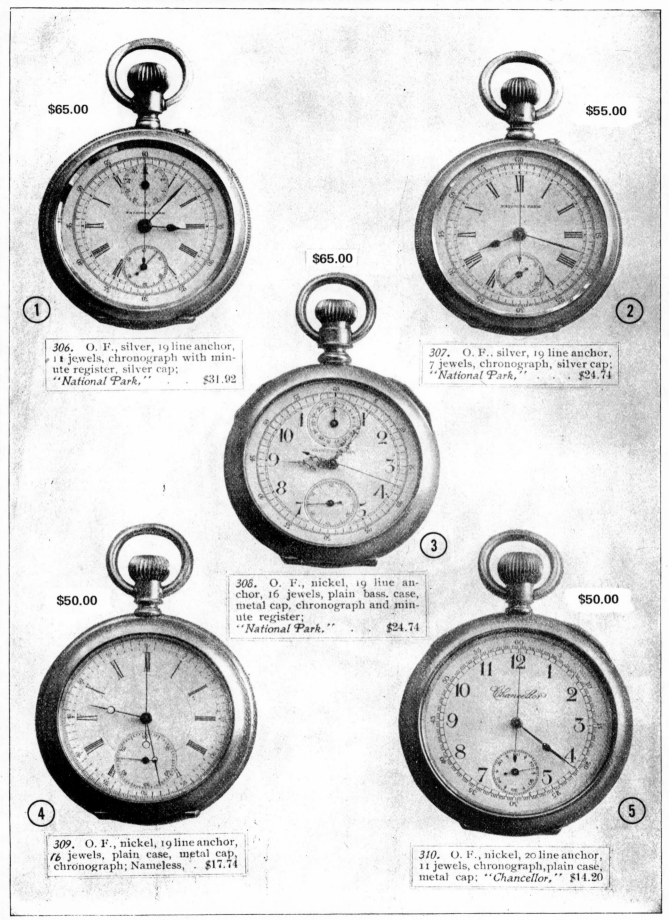

$65.00

$55.00

$65.00

1

306. O. F., silver, 19 line anchor, 11 jewels, chronograph with minute register, silver cap; "National Park," . $31.92

2

307. O. F., silver, 19 line anchor, 7 jewels, chronograph, silver cap; "National Park," . . . $24.74

3

308. O. F., nickel, 19 line anchor, 16 jewels, plain bass. case, metal cap, chronograph and minute register; "National Park." . . $24.74

$50.00

$50.00

4

309. O. F., nickel, 19 line anchor, 16 jewels, plain case, metal cap, chronograph; Nameless, . $17.74

5

310. O. F., nickel, 20 line anchor, 11 jewels, chronograph, plain case, metal cap; "Chancellor," $14.20

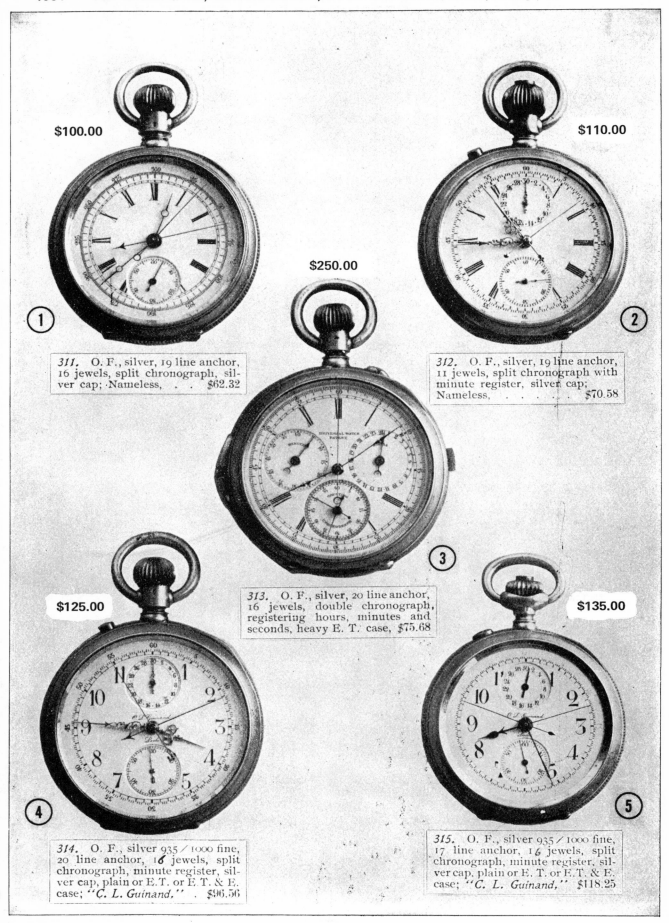

$100.00

$110.00

$250.00

$125.00

$135.00

1

2

3

4

5

311. O. F., silver, 19 line anchor, 16 jewels, split chronograph, silver cap; Nameless, . . . $62.32

312. O. F., silver, 19 line anchor, 11 jewels, split chronograph with minute register, silver cap; Nameless, ... $70.58

313. O. F., silver, 20 line anchor, 16 jewels, double chronograph, registering hours, minutes and seconds, heavy E. T. case, $75.68

314. O. F., silver 935 / 1000 fine, 20 line anchor, 16 jewels, split chronograph, minute register, silver cap, plain or E.T. or E.T. & E. case; *"C. L. Guinand,"* $96.56

315. O. F., silver 935 / 1000 fine, 17 line anchor, 16 jewels, split chronograph, minute register, silver cap, plain or E.T. or E.T. & E. case; *"C. L. Guinand,"* $118.25

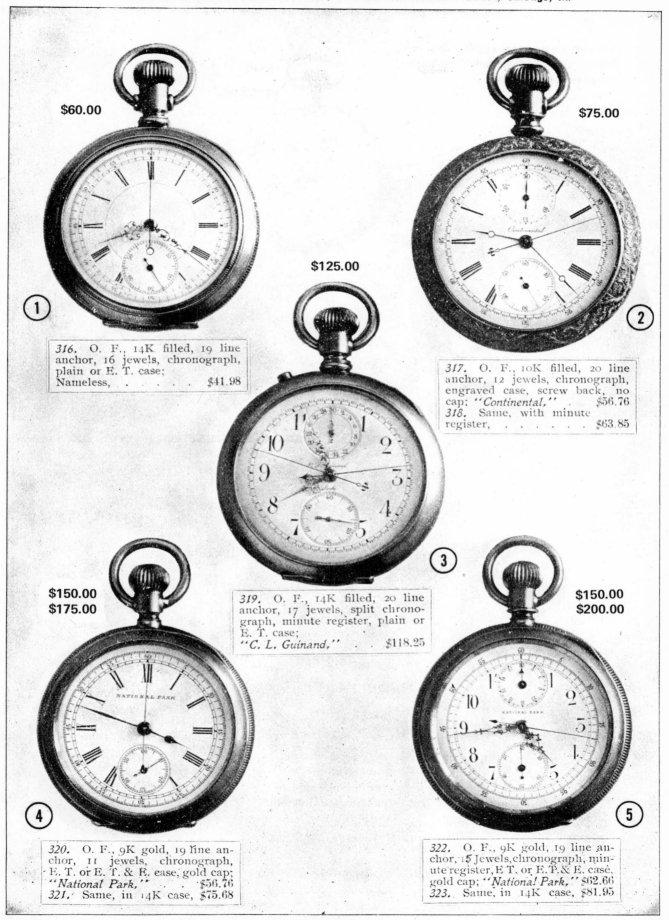

$60.00

$75.00

$125.00

316. O. F., 14K filled, 19 line anchor, 16 jewels, chronograph, plain or E. T. case; Nameless, ... $41.98

317. O. F., 10K filled, 20 line anchor, 12 jewels, chronograph, engraved case, screw back, no cap; "Continental," $56.76
318. Same, with minute register, ... $63.85

$150.00
$175.00

$150.00
$200.00

319. O. F., 14K filled, 20 line anchor, 17 jewels, split chronograph, minute register, plain or E. T. case; "C. L. Guinand," . $118.25

320. O. F., 9K gold, 19 line anchor, 11 jewels, chronograph, E. T. or E. T. & E. case, gold cap; "National Park," $56.76
321. Same, in 14K case, $75.68

322. O. F., 9K gold, 19 line anchor, 15 jewels, chronograph, minute register, E. T. or E. T. & E. case, gold cap; "National Park," $62.66
323. Same, in 14K case, $81.95

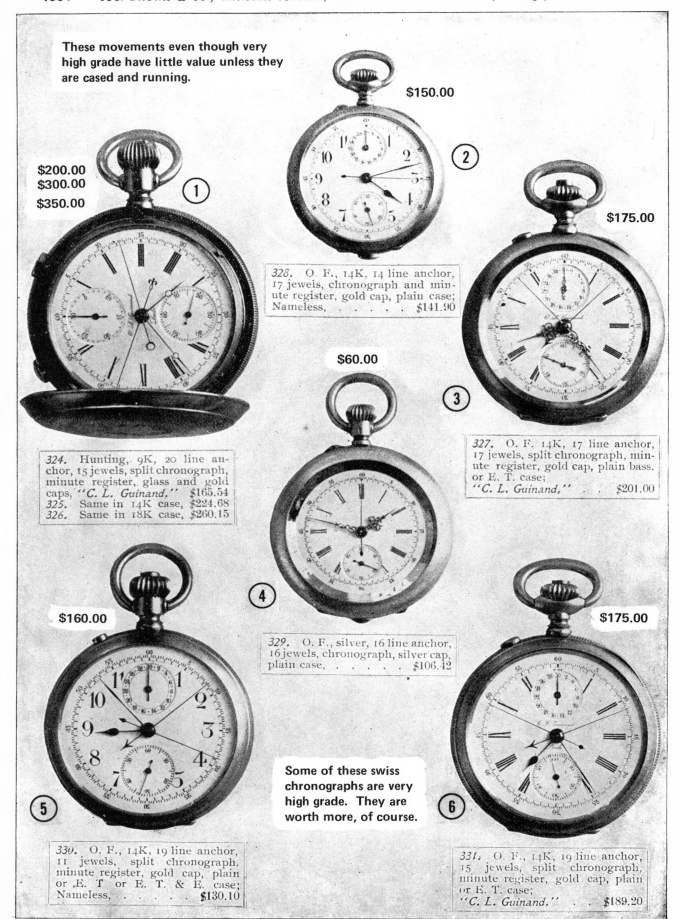

These movements even though very high grade have little value unless they are cased and running.

$150.00

②

$200.00
$300.00
$350.00

①

$175.00

③

328. O. F., 14K, 14 line anchor, 17 jewels, chronograph and minute register, gold cap, plain case; Nameless, ... $141.90

$60.00

324. Hunting, 9K, 20 line anchor, 15 jewels, split chronograph, minute register, glass and gold caps, "C. L. Guinand," $165.54
325. Same in 14K case, $224.68
326. Same in 18K case, $260.15

327. O. F. 14K, 17 line anchor, 17 jewels, split chronograph, minute register, gold cap, plain bass. or E. T. case; "C. L. Guinand," . . . $201.00

④

$160.00

329. O. F., silver, 16 line anchor, 16 jewels, chronograph, silver cap, plain case, ... $106.42

$175.00

⑤

Some of these swiss chronographs are very high grade. They are worth more, of course.

⑥

330. O. F., 14K, 19 line anchor, 11 jewels, split chronograph, minute register, gold cap, plain or E. T or E. T. & E. case; Nameless, ... $130.10

331. O. F., 14K, 19 line anchor, 15 jewels, split chronograph, minute register, gold cap, plain or E. T. case; "C. L. Guinand," . . $189.20

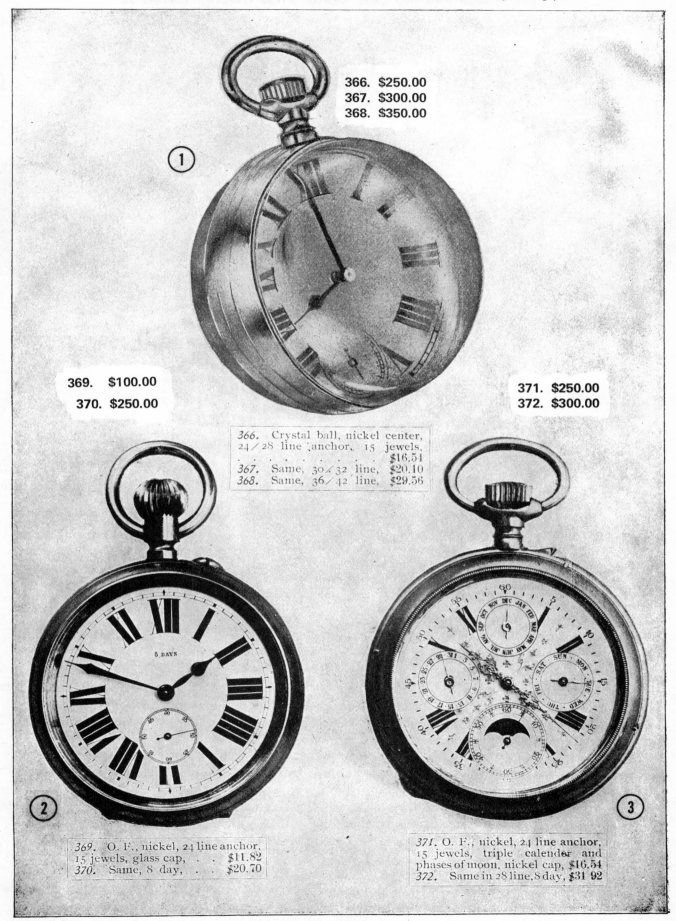

366. $250.00
367. $300.00
368. $350.00

369. $100.00
370. $250.00

371. $250.00
372. $300.00

366. Crystal ball, nickel center, 24/28 line anchor, 15 jewels, $16.54
367. Same, 30/32 line, $20.10
368. Same, 36/42 line, $29.56

369. O. F., nickel, 24 line anchor, 15 jewels, glass cap, . . $11.82
370. Same, 8 day, . . $20.70

371. O. F., nickel, 24 line anchor, 15 jewels, triple calender and phases of moon, nickel cap, $16.54
372. Same in 28 line, 8 day, $31.92

SOLID GOLD HUNTING CASE GENTS' STEM WINDING WATCHES.

1893 E. V. RODDIN

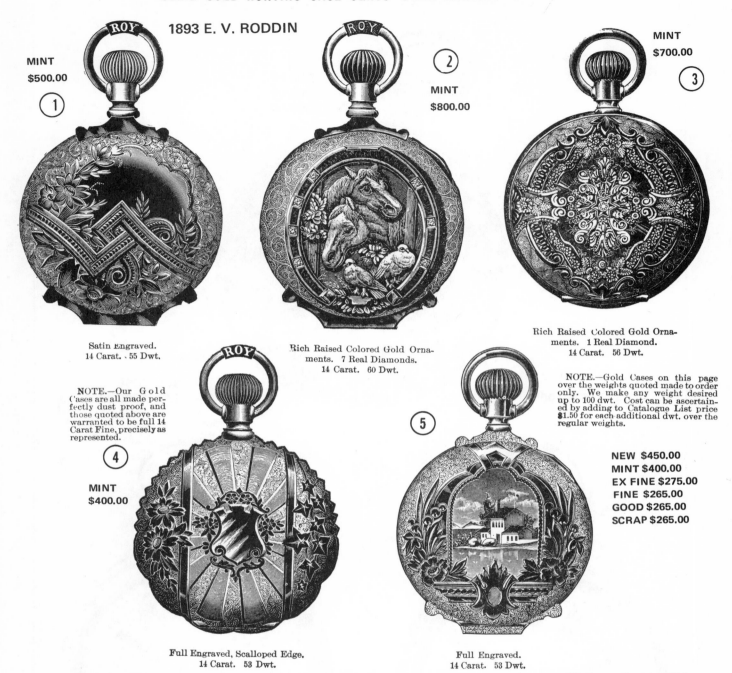

MINT $500.00 ①

Satin Engraved.
14 Carat. 55 Dwt.

NOTE.—Our Gold Cases are all made perfectly dust proof, and those quoted above are warranted to be full 14 Carat Fine, precisely as represented.

② **MINT $800.00**

Rich Raised Colored Gold Ornaments. 7 Real Diamonds.
14 Carat. 60 Dwt.

MINT $700.00 ③

Rich Raised Colored Gold Ornaments. 1 Real Diamond.
14 Carat. 56 Dwt.

NOTE.—Gold Cases on this page over the weights quoted made to order only. We make any weight desired up to 100 dwt. Cost can be ascertained by adding to Catalogue List price $1.50 for each additional dwt. over the regular weights.

④ **MINT $400.00**

Full Engraved, Scalloped Edge.
14 Carat. 53 Dwt.

⑤

Full Engraved.
14 Carat. 53 Dwt.

NEW $450.00
MINT $400.00
EX FINE $275.00
FINE $265.00
GOOD $265.00
SCRAP $265.00

The next few pages in this book were taken from an 1893 E. V. Roddin & Co., 151 State Street, Chicago Illinois, 37th Annual Catalog offering for sale fine watches — diamonds — jewelry and silverware.

These cases do not have the original cost shown because they were sold as cased watches only in this book. They did not come from the factory cased but were cased by E. V. Roddin.

These were to be considered the highest quality cases available to the general public at this time. This type of case had been produced for 15 to 20 years before and generally up until the crash or depression of the 1930's. These cases are most desireable and hunted for by collectors of today.

No. 16 Size watches were not offered for sale in this catalog although they were gaining in popularity. You can value 16 size similar cases by taking about 10% off the prices shown in 18 size.

The O size was the smallest U. S. made ladies watch available at this time. Waltham had introduced their 1 size earlier and the O size in 1890.

Condition is all important in the value of a watch case. Collectors and investors want them in new — mint — and some will accept them in extra fine. The value drops very rapidly and makes the watch or case hard to sell in any condition except mint or factory new.

All of the prices given in this book are retail. My definition of retail is "the price a man who has the money and wants the watch will pay to a dealer who knows the value".

SOLID GOLD HUNTING CASE GENTS' STEM WINDING WATCHES.

(Styles referred to on page 38.)

NOTE.—Gold Cases on this page over the weights quoted made to order only. We make any weight desired up to 100 dwt. Cost can be ascertained by adding to Catalogue List price $1.50 for each additional dwt. over the regular weights.

1 MINT $400.00

SIZE 18
MINT
$600.00

2

3 MINT $300.00

Scalloped and Full Engraved.
14 Carat. 52 Dwt.

Raised Colored Gold Ornaments.
Fancy Engraved.
14 Carat. 52 Dwt.

Full Engraved.
14 Carat. 48 Dwt.

1893 E. V. RODDIN

4
NEW $350.00
MINT $300.00
EX FINE $275.00
FINE $250.00
GOOD $250.00
SCRAP $250.00

5 MINT $450.00

Satin Engraved.
14 Carat. 50 Dwt.

Fancy Engraved
Border.
14 Carat. 50 Dwt.

6 MINT $300.00

7 MINT $325.00

8 MINT $300.00

Fancy Engraved.
14 Carat. 50 Dwt.

Fancy Engraved.
14 Carat. 48 Dwt.

NOTE.—Our Gold Cases are all made perfectly dust proof, and those quoted above are warranted to be full 14 Carat fine, precisely as represented

Fancy Engraved.
14 Carat. 50 Dwt.

GENTS' STEM WINDING WATCHES.

18—SIZE

IN "BOSS" PATENT GOLD FILLED HUNTING CASES.

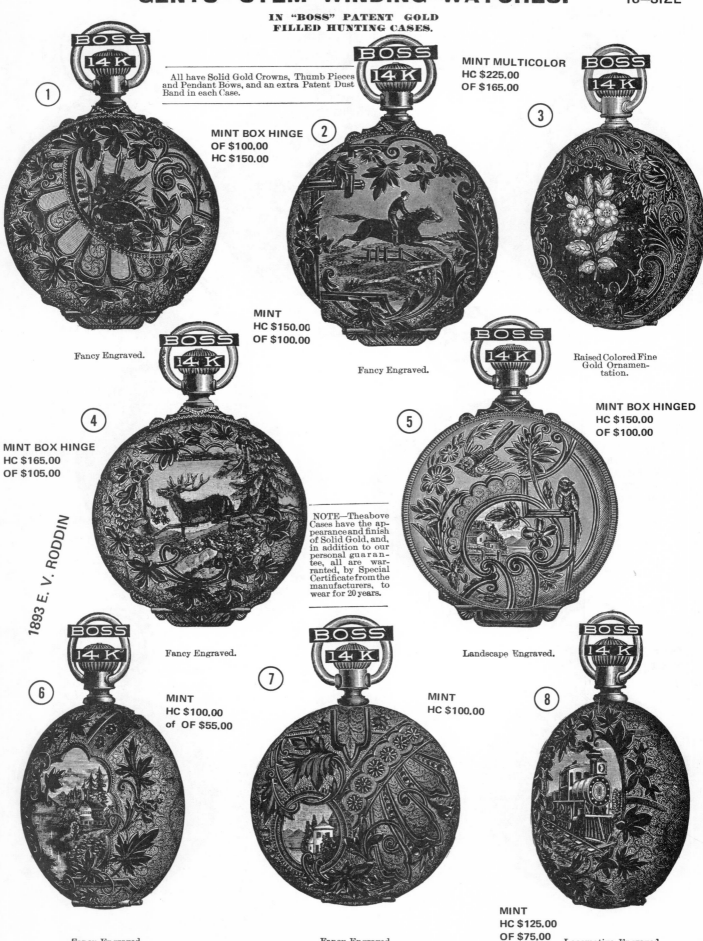

All have Solid Gold Crowns, Thumb Pieces and Pendant Bows, and an extra Patent Dust Band in each Case.

1 Fancy Engraved.

2 MINT BOX HINGE OF $100.00 HC $150.00

MINT HC $150.00 OF $100.00

Fancy Engraved.

3 MINT MULTICOLOR HC $225.00 OF $165.00

Raised Colored Fine Gold Ornamentation.

4 MINT BOX HINGE HC $165.00 OF $105.00

Fancy Engraved.

1893 E. V. RODDIN

NOTE—The above Cases have the appearance and finish of Solid Gold, and, in addition to our personal guarantee, all are warranted, by Special Certificate from the manufacturers, to wear for 20 years.

5 MINT BOX HINGED HC $150.00 OF $100.00

Landscape Engraved.

6 MINT HC $100.00 of OF $55.00

Fancy Engraved.

7 MINT HC $100.00

Fancy Engraved.

8 MINT HC $125.00 OF $75.00 Locomotive Engraved.

GENTS' STEM WINDING WATCHES.

18-SIZE

IN "BOSS" PATENT GOLD FILLED HUNTING CASES.

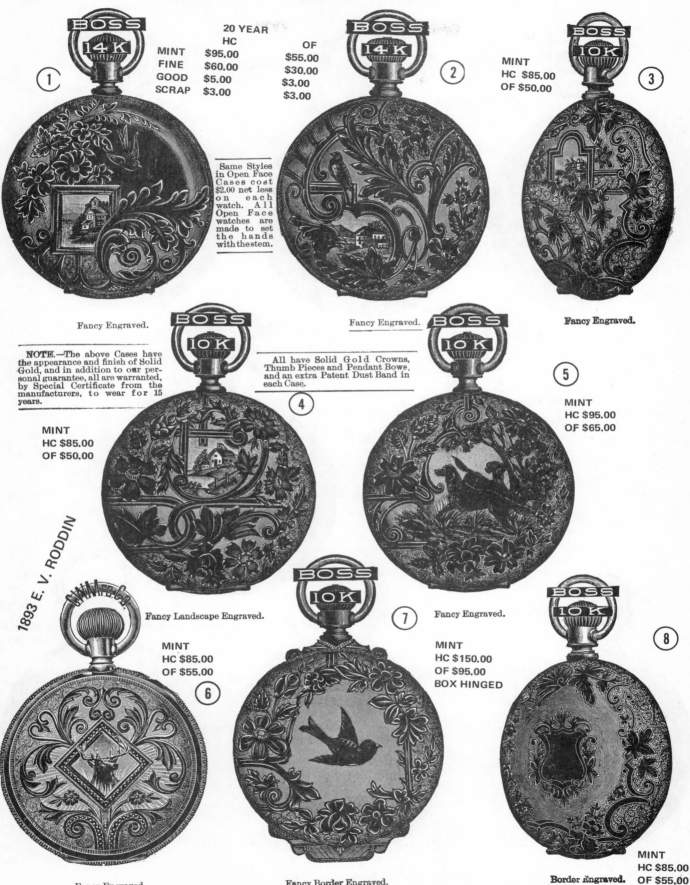

BOSS 14 K

① **20 YEAR**

	HC	OF
MINT	$95.00	$55.00
FINE	$60.00	$30.00
GOOD	$5.00	$3.00
SCRAP	$3.00	$3.00

Same Styles in Open Face Cases cost $2.00 net less on each watch. All Open Face watches are made to set the hands with the stem.

BOSS 14 K ②

BOSS 10 K ③

MINT
HC $85.00
OF $50.00

Fancy Engraved.

Fancy Engraved.

Fancy Engraved.

NOTE.—The above Cases have the appearance and finish of Solid Gold, and in addition to our personal guarantee, all are warranted, by Special Certificate from the manufacturers, to wear for 15 years.

All have Solid Gold Crowns, Thumb Pieces and Pendant Bows, and an extra Patent Dust Band in each Case.

BOSS 10 K ④

BOSS 10 K

⑤

MINT
HC $95.00
OF $65.00

MINT
HC $85.00
OF $50.00

1893 E. V. RODDIN

Fancy Landscape Engraved.

MINT
HC $85.00
OF $55.00

⑥

BOSS 10 K ⑦

Fancy Engraved.

MINT
HC $150.00
OF $95.00
BOX HINGED

BOSS 10 K ⑧

MINT
HC $85.00
OF $55.00

Fancy Engraved.

Fancy Border Engraved.

Border Engraved.

OPEN FACE STEM WINDING WATCHES.

IN " CRESCENT," "MONARCH" AND "MONTAUK" GOLD FILLED CASES, WITH SCREW BEZEL AND BACK.

All Open Face Watches are made to set the hands with the stem, and have heavy, thick Crystals.

1 — NEW $65.00 MINT $50.00 EX FINE $35.00 FINE $15.00 GOOD $3.00 SCRAP $3.00

18—SIZE

3 — MINT $85.00

1893 E. V. RODDIN

"Montauk" Gold Filled. Fancy Engraved.

'Crown" Gold Filled. Full Engraved.

"Montauk" Gold Filled. Fancy Engraved.

4 — MINT $65.00

5 — MINT $65.00

8 — MINT $65.00

"Crescent," Gold Filled, Screw Bezel and Back.

"Montauk," Gold Filled, Screw Bezel and Back.

6 — MINT $85.00

7 — MINT $85.00

"Monarch," Gold Filled, Screw Bezel and Back.

"Montauk," Gold Filled, Screw Bezel and Back.

"Crescent," Gold Filled, Screw Bezel and Back.

86

OPEN FACE STEM WINDING WATCHES.

IN "BOSS" PATENT GOLD FILLED CASES.

1 — **BOSS 14 K**
20 YEAR MINT
HC $85.00
OF $50.00

Open Face, Screw Back.

2 — **BOSS 14 K**
20 YEAR MINT
HC $85.00
OF $50.00

Full Engraved.
Open Face, Screw Back.

3 — **BOSS 14 K**
20 YEAR MINT
HC $115.00
OF $50.00

Locomotive, Engraved.
Open Face, Screw Back.

4 — **BOSS 10 K**
15 YEAR MINT
HC $100.00
OF $50.00

18—SIZE

Full Engraved.
Open Face, Screw Back.

5 — **BOSS 10 K**

15 YEAR	HC	OF
NEW	$125.00	$65.00
MINT	$100.00	$50.00
EX FINE	$70.00	$35.00
FINE	$30.00	$15.00
GOOD	$5.00	$3.00
SCRAP	$3.00	$3.00

Full Engraved.
Open Face, Screw Back.

6 — **MONARCH 14 K**
MINT
HC $85.00
OF $50.00

"Monarch" Gold Filled. Fancy
Half Engraved.

7 — **CROWN**
20 YEAR MINT
HC $100.00
OF $40.00

"Crown" Gold Filled. Fancy
Half Engraved.

All have Solid Gold
Crowns, Thumb
Pieces and Pendant
Bows, and an extra
Patent Dust Band
in each Case.

**THESE ARE ALL HIGH
QUALITY CASES**

NOTE. — The above
Cases have the appear-
ance and finish of *Solid
Gold*, and in addition
to our *personal guar-
antee*, all are *warrant-
ed* by *Special Certifi-
cate* from the manu-
facturers.

1893 E. V. RODDIN

HUNTING AND OPEN FACE
GENTS' STEM WINDING WATCHES.

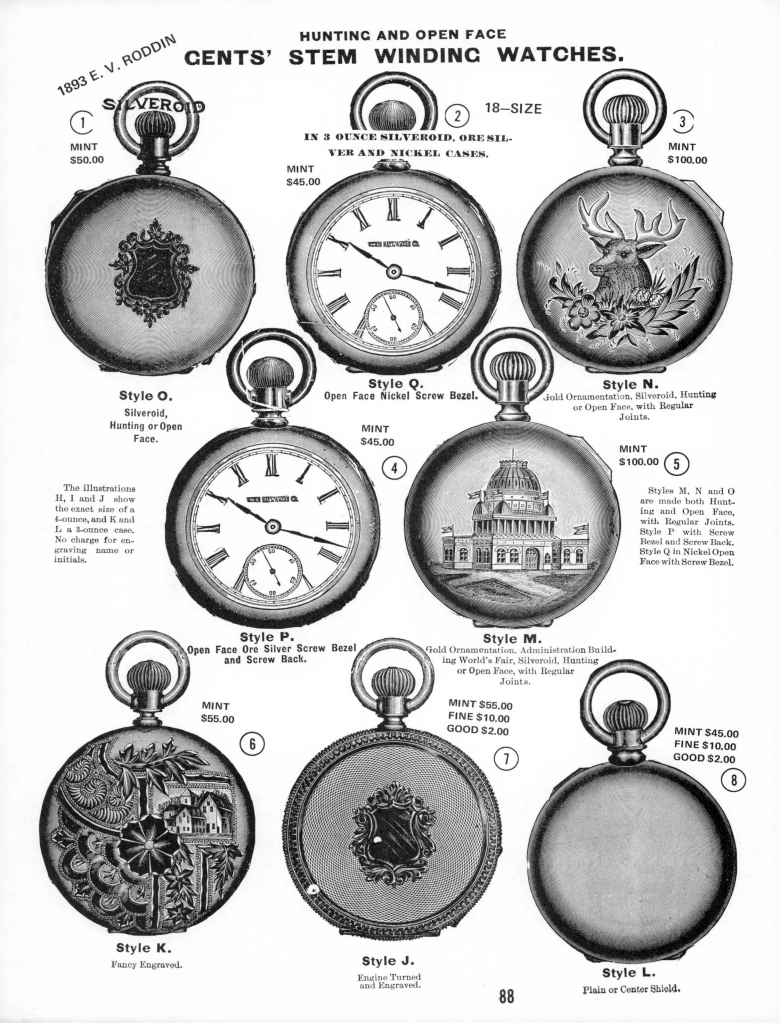

SILVEROID

① MINT $50.00

② 18—SIZE

IN 3 OUNCE SILVEROID, ORE SIL-VER AND NICKEL CASES.

MINT $45.00

③ MINT $100.00

Style O.

Silveroid, Hunting or Open Face.

Style Q.
Open Face Nickel Screw Bezel.

Style N.

Gold Ornamentation, Silveroid, Hunting or Open Face, with Regular Joints.

The illustrations H, I and J show the exact size of a 4-ounce, and K and L a 3-ounce case. No charge for engraving name or initials.

MINT $45.00

④

⑤ MINT $100.00

Styles M, N and O are made both Hunting and Open Face, with Regular Joints. Style P with Screw Bezel and Screw Back. Style Q in Nickel Open Face with Screw Bezel.

Style P.
Open Face Ore Silver Screw Bezel and Screw Back.

Style M.
Gold Ornamentation, Administration Building World's Fair, Silveroid, Hunting or Open Face, with Regular Joints.

MINT $55.00

⑥

MINT $55.00
FINE $10.00
GOOD $2.00

⑦

MINT $45.00
FINE $10.00
GOOD $2.00

⑧

Style K.

Fancy Engraved.

Style J.

Engine Turned and Engraved.

Style L.

Plain or Center Shield.

GENTS' SOLID SILVER
OPEN FACE STEM WINDING WATCHES.
WITH GOLD INLAID DECORATIONS.

18—SIZE

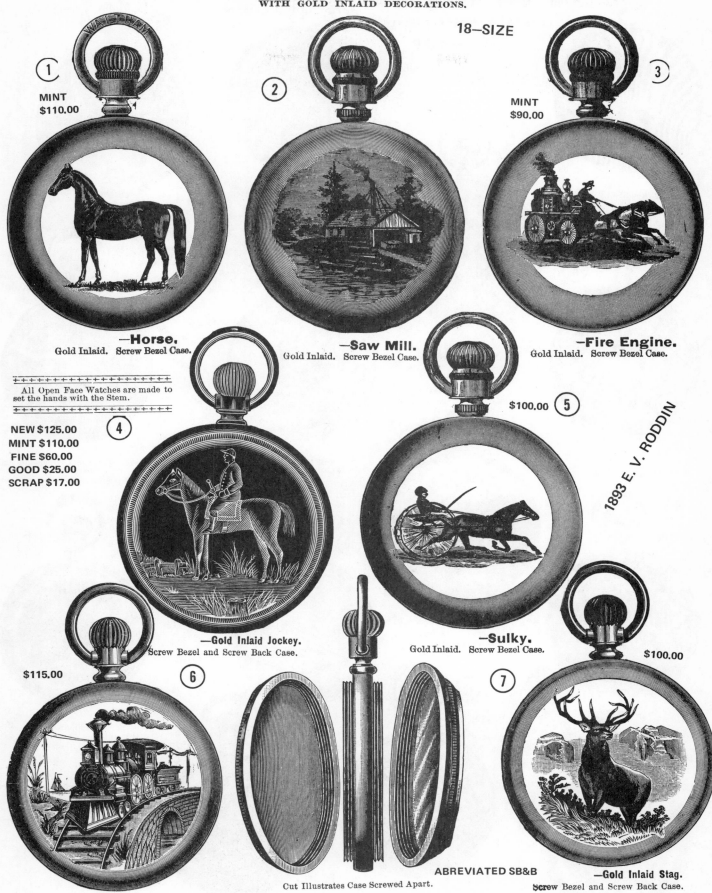

① MINT $110.00

—Horse.
Gold Inlaid. Screw Bezel Case.

—Saw Mill.
Gold Inlaid. Screw Bezel Case.

③ MINT $90.00

—Fire Engine.
Gold Inlaid. Screw Bezel Case.

+++++++++++++++++++++
All Open Face Watches are made to
set the hands with the Stem.
+++++++++++++++++++++

NEW $125.00
MINT $110.00
FINE $60.00
GOOD $25.00
SCRAP $17.00

④

$100.00 ⑤

1893 E. V. RODDIN

—Gold Inlaid Jockey.
Screw Bezel and Screw Back Case.

—Sulky.
Gold Inlaid. Screw Bezel Case.

$115.00 ⑥

⑦ $100.00

ABREVIATED SB&B

Cut Illustrates Case Screwed Apart.

—Gold Inlaid Stag.
Screw Bezel and Screw Back Case.

89

SOLID GOLD
Ladies' Stem Winding Watches.
IN 14 CARAT HUNTING CASES.
6—SIZE

These Cases are made perfectly *dust proof* and are *warranted* to be full *14 Carat fine*, precisely as represented.

1 $200.00

Corrugated Shell Pattern. 14 Carat. 25 Dwt.

2 $300.00

Raised Colored Gold Ornaments. Enameled Flowers. 14 Carat. 22 Dwt.

3 $450.00

Raised Colored Gold Ornaments and Engraved. 8 Real Diamonds. 14 Carat. 23 Dwt.

4 $200.00

Full Engraved. 14 Carat. 24 Dwt

5 $250.00

Full Engraved. Enameled in Colors. 14 Carat. 20 Dwt.

6 BOX $250.00

All Cases on this page have plain space or shield on opposite side for engraving name, initials or monogram. We also furnish a fine plush case with each watch without extra charge.

Full Engraved. 14 Carat. 22½ Dwt.

7 $400.00

Raised Colored Gold Ornaments and Engraved. 5 Real Diamonds. 14 Carat. 23 Dwt.

1893 E. V. RODDIN

8 $200.00

Scalloped, Full Engraved. 14 Carat. 21 Dwt.

9 $250.00

Enameled in Colors. 14 Carat. 22 Dwt.

10 MINT $200.00 EX FINE $150.00 FINE $100.00 SCRAP $100.00

Full Engraved. 14 Carat. 20 Dwt.

11 $250.00

Satin Engraved. 11 Real Diamonds and 5 Rubies. 14 Carat. 20 Dwt.

12 $275.00

Satin Engraved. 7 Real Diamonds. 14 Carat. 20 Dwt.

13 $325.00

Raised Colored Gold Flowers and Ornaments, Richly Engraved. 1 Real Diamond. 14 Carat. 19 Dwt.

14 $275.00

Satin Engraved. 5 Real Diamonds and 2 Rubies. 14 Carat. 20 Dwt.

ALL CASES MUST BE MINT 0-Size AND 6-Size ARE WORTH ABOUT THE SAME. 0-Size IS MORE DESIRABLE AND EASIER TO SELL.

90

SOLID GOLD
Ladies' Stem Winding Watches.
IN 14 CARAT HUNTING CASES.

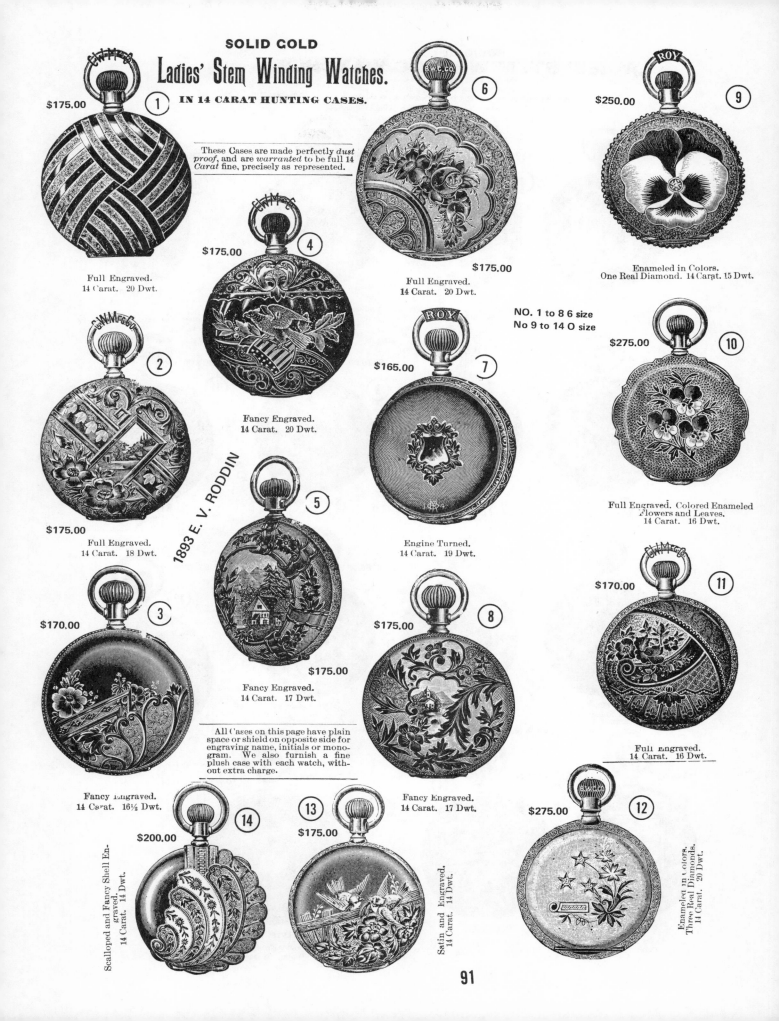

These Cases are made perfectly *dust proof*, and are *warranted* to be full 14 *Carat* fine, precisely as represented.

1 — $175.00
Full Engraved. 14 Carat. 20 Dwt.

4 — $175.00
Fancy Engraved. 14 Carat. 20 Dwt.

6 — $175.00
Full Engraved. 14 Carat. 20 Dwt.

9 — $250.00
Enameled in Colors. One Real Diamond. 14 Carat. 15 Dwt.

2 — $175.00
Full Engraved. 14 Carat. 18 Dwt.

7 — $165.00
Engine Turned. 14 Carat. 19 Dwt.

NO. 1 to 8 6 size
No 9 to 14 O size

10 — $275.00
Full Engraved. Colored Enameled Flowers and Leaves. 14 Carat. 16 Dwt.

5 — $175.00
Fancy Engraved. 14 Carat. 17 Dwt.

1893 E. V. RODDIN

3 — $170.00
Fancy Engraved. 14 Carat. 16½ Dwt.

8 — $175.00
Fancy Engraved. 14 Carat. 17 Dwt.

11 — $170.00
Full Engraved. 14 Carat. 16 Dwt.

All Cases on this page have plain space or shield on opposite side for engraving name, initials or monogram. We also furnish a fine plush case with each watch, without extra charge.

14 — $200.00
Scalloped and Fancy Shell Engraved. 14 Carat. 14 Dwt.

13 — $175.00
Satin and Engraved. 14 Carat. 14 Dwt.

12 — $275.00
Enameled in Colors. Three Real Diamonds. 14 Carat. 20 Dwt.

91

SOLID GOLD
LADIES' STEM WINDING WATCHES.
PENDANT SETTING.
(Styles referred to on page 24.)
IN 14 AND 10 CARAT HUNTING CASES.
The Smallest and most Complete Ladies' Watch Made in America.

O—SIZE

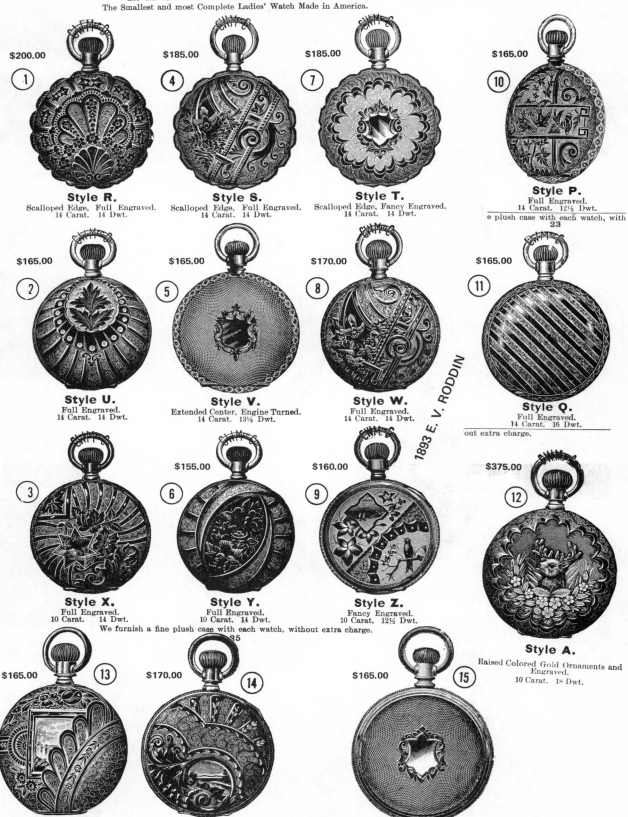

$200.00 — ①

Style R.
Scalloped Edge, Full Engraved.
14 Carat. 14 Dwt.

$185.00 — ④

Style S.
Scalloped Edge, Full Engraved.
14 Carat. 14 Dwt.

$185.00 — ⑦

Style T.
Scalloped Edge, Fancy Engraved.
14 Carat. 14 Dwt.

$165.00 — ⑩

Style P.
Full Engraved.
14 Carat. 12½ Dwt.
e plush case with each watch, with
23

$165.00 — ②

Style U.
Full Engraved.
14 Carat. 14 Dwt.

$165.00 — ⑤

Style V.
Extended Center, Engine Turned.
14 Carat. 13½ Dwt.

$170.00 — ⑧

Style W.
Full Engraved.
14 Carat. 14 Dwt.

$165.00 — ⑪

Style Q.
Full Engraved.
14 Carat. 16 Dwt.
out extra charge.

1893 E. V. RODDIN

$165.00 — ③

Style X.
Full Engraved.
10 Carat. 14 Dwt.

$155.00 — ⑥

Style Y.
Full Engraved.
10 Carat. 14 Dwt.

$160.00 — ⑨

Style Z.
Fancy Engraved.
10 Carat. 12½ Dwt.
We furnish a fine plush case with each watch, without extra charge.
35

$375.00 — ⑫

Style A.
Raised Colored Gold Ornaments and
Engraved.
10 Carat. 18 Dwt.

$165.00 — ⑬

Style D.
Fancy Engraved.
10 Carat. 16 Dwt.

$170.00 — ⑭

Style G.
Fancy Engraved.
10 Carat. 15 Dwt.

$165.00 — ⑮

Style H.
Engine Turned.
10 Carat. 15 Dwt.

Ladies' Stem Winding Watches.

In "Boss" Patent Gold Filled Cases. Warranted to Wear for 20 Years.

6—SIZE

All have Solid Gold Crowns, Bows and Thumb Pieces.

$120.00 ① Fancy Engraved.

$120.00 ② Fancy Engraved, Scalloped Edge.

$100.00 ③ Fancy Engraved.

$120.00 ④ Full Engraved, Scalloped Edge.

$100.00 ⑤ Fancy Engraved.

$200.00 ⑥ Raised Colored Gold Ornaments.

$100.00 ⑦ Fancy Engraved.

$100.00 ⑧ Fancy Engraved.

$110.00 ⑨ Fancy Engraved.

$110.00 ⑩ Full Engraved.

$200.00 ⑪ Raised Colored Gold Ornaments and Engraved. 10 Carat. 18 Dwt.

$100.00 ⑫ Fancy Engraved, Satin Finished. 10 Carat. 17 Dwt.

$85.00 ⑭ Fancy Engraved. 10 Carat. 17 Dwt.

$85.00 ⑬ Diagonal Engraved. 10 Carat. 15 Dwt.

NOTE.—The above cases have the appearance and finish of solid gold, and, in addition to our personal Guarantee, are all warranted by Special Certificate from the manufacturers to wear for 20 years. We furnish a fine plush case with each watch, without extra charge.

1893 E. V. RODDIN

93

Ladies' Stem Winding Watches.

In "Crown," "Monarch" and "Boss" Patent Gold Filled Cases.

All have Solid Gold Crowns, Bows and Thumb Pieces.

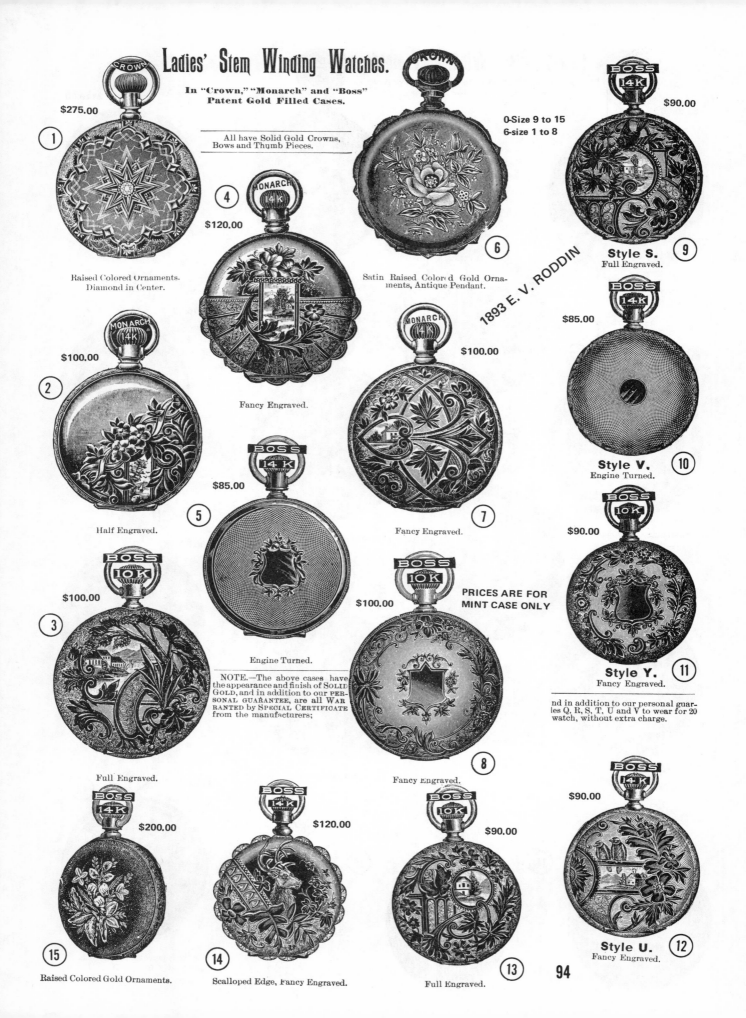

$275.00

(1) Raised Colored Ornaments. Diamond in Center.

(4) **$120.00** Fancy Engraved.

0-Size 9 to 15
6-size 1 to 8

(6) Satin Raised Colored Gold Ornaments, Antique Pendant.

$90.00 **Style S.** Full Engraved. (9)

$100.00 (2) Half Engraved.

$85.00 (5) Engine Turned.

$100.00 (7) Fancy Engraved.

$85.00 **Style V.** Engine Turned. (10)

1893 E. V. RODDIN

$100.00 (3) Full Engraved.

NOTE.—The above cases have the appearance and finish of SOLID GOLD, and in addition to our PERSONAL GUARANTEE, are all WARRANTED by SPECIAL CERTIFICATE from the manufacturers;

$100.00 (8) Fancy Engraved.

PRICES ARE FOR MINT CASE ONLY

$90.00 **Style Y.** Fancy Engraved. (11)

nd in addition to our personal guarles Q, R, S, T, U and V to wear for 20 watch, without extra charge.

$200.00 (15) Raised Colored Gold Ornaments.

$120.00 (14) Scalloped Edge, Fancy Engraved.

$90.00 (13) Full Engraved.

$90.00 **Style U.** Fancy Engraved. (12)

94

1929
C.A. KIGER

ELGIN
THE WATCHWORD FOR
ELEGANCE AND EFFICIENCY

MINT $125.00
EX FINE $100.00
FINE $75.00

THESE ELGIN RR CASES AND OTHER CASED WATCHES SHOWN IN THIS 1929 SECTION WERE MADE BY THE LEADING U.S. CASE MAKERS. THE CASES WERE SENT TO THE WATCH COMPANIES – ELGIN – ILLINOIS – HAMILTON – ROCKFORD – WALTHAM – HOWARD – SOUTH BEND ETC. AND WERE CASED BEFORE LEAVING THE FACTORY. THESE CASES WILL HAVE THE NAME OF THE WATCH COMPANY IN THEM ALSO AND ARE VERY DESIRABLE BY COLLECTORS.

14 karat white or green gold filled
701—White . . . . .List Price, $70.60
702—Green . . . . .List Price, $70.60
Shipped direct from factory on order from wholesaler.*

10 karat yellow gold filled case with rigid bow.
703 . . . . .List Price, $63.30
704—With Wind. Indicator . .List Price, $70.30
Shipped direct from factory on order from wholesaler.*

A WORD OF CAUTION ABOUT FACTORY CASED WATCHES – – ALL EXCEPT THE STANDARD 16 SIZE AND 18 SIZE RAILROAD WATCHES ARE ODD SIZE AND NO OTHER WATCH EXCEPT THE MOVEMENT THE CASE WAS MADE FOR WILL FIT IT. EXAMPLES ARE HAMILTON 922 - 918 - 904 - 902 - 912 – WALTHAM COLONIAL – HOWARD 10 AND 12 SIZE PERIOD WATCHES ILLINOIS – ILLINI – AUTOCRAT ECT. ELGIN ARE FOR THE MOST PART STANDARD. HTC MEANS "HARD TO CASE" AND APPLYS TO THE ABOVE WATCHES.

MINT
CASE $65.00
MVT $135.00
DIAL $50.00

12 karat yellow gold filled case with winding indicator.
705 . . . . .List Price, $70.30
706—Without Wind. Indic . . .List Price, $63.30
Shipped direct from factory on order from wholesaler.*

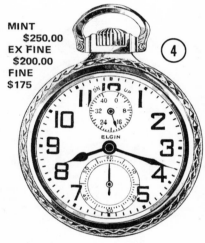

MINT
$250.00
EX FINE
$200.00
FINE
$175

14 karat white or green gold filled, with winding indicator.
707—White . . . . .List Price, $77.60
708—Green . . . . .List Price, $77.60
Shipped direct from factory on order from wholesaler.*

All models supplied, if desired, with Montgomery dial. No extra charge.

*The railroad watches indicated are shipped direct to the jeweler, on order from the wholesaler. We reserve the right to accept or reject any order for any model or models so shipped.

The Elgin Railroad Watch, B. W. Raymond, has 21 Jewels, and is 16 Size Lever set, with 8 Adjustments (5 of them position). Double roller escapement. Each part, embracing features of proven value, is designed by experts who give the best results in this exacting service. The B. W. Raymond Watch is very easy to regulate because the regulator is extremely positive and responds to the slightest move and holds its position without change.

Cases are heavy gold-filled, specially designed screw cases, non-pull-out bow with new improved dust-proof features. Cased and carefully regulated by experts in the Elgin factory, and comply with the requirements of all railroads.

Elgin Watches, as shown, are cased in cases approved by the Federal Trade Commission

"Accuracy First"

When Time means lives . . . and seconds safety . . . the significance of Elgin railroad watches comes to the fore. They must be . . . and are . . . accurate to the split second—and will serve faithfully day and night through the years. Here are five handsome conceptions in railroad watches.

WATCH, DIAL AND CASE MUST BE MINT

① $300.00
$250.00
$125.00

② $310
$225
$130
$130

*727—A new Railroad watch with a 23 jewel movement, 9 adjustments, 6 to position, lever set. Fitted in a 10 Karat yellow gold filled engraved case. With winding indicator. **$70.00**
*734—Same as above with a 21 jewel movement, 8 adjustments, 5 to position, lever set. With winding indicator. **$65.00**
*735—Same as above with a 21 jewel movement, 8 adjustments, 5 to position, lever set. Without winding indicator. **$60.00**

Railroad Watch, 14 karat white or green gold filled case. With Winding Indicator. 16 size B. W. Raymond movement, has 21 jewels, 8 adjustments, lever set.
707—White.........................$70.00
708—Green............................ 70.00
701—White, without Winding Indicator. 65.00
702—Green, without Winding Indicator.. 65.00

③ $300
$250
$125

④ $280
$240
$120

⑤

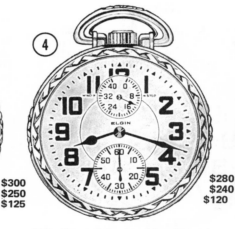

*724—A new, attractive Railroad watch. Has a 23 jewel movement with 9 adjustments, 6 to position, lever set and is fitted in a 14 Karat white gold filled case. With winding indicator. **$75.00**
*728—Same as above with a 21 jewel movement, 8 adjustments, 5 to position, lever set. Winding indicator. **$70.00**
*729—Same as above with a 21 jewel movement, 8 adjustments, 5 to position, lever set. Without winding indicator. **$65.00**

*725—This new Railroad watch has a 23 jewel movement with 9 adjustments, 6 to position, lever set and is fitted in a 14 Karat white gold filled engraved case. With winding indicator. **$75.00**
*730—Same as above with a 21 jewel movement, 8 adjustments, 5 to position, lever set. With winding indicator. **$70.00**
*731—Same as above with a 21 jewel movement, 8 adjustments, 5 to position, lever set. Without winding indicator. **$65.00**

*726—New model Railroad Elgin. Has a 23 jewel movement with 9 adjustments, 6 to position, lever set, fitted in a 10 Karat yellow gold filled plain case. With winding indicator. **$70.00**
*732—Same as above with a 21 jewel movement, 8 adjustments, 5 to position, lever set. With winding indicator. **$65.00**
*733—Same as above with a 21 jewel movement, 8 adjustments, 5 to position, lever set. Without winding indicator. **$60.00**

⑥ $350.00

⑦ $200.00

⑧ $65.00

722—Pilot's and Flight Operator's watch. Has a 21 jewel 8 adjustment 16 size B. W. Raymond movement. Yellow gold filled case of a new alloy, with friction silver dial printed to give maximum visibility. **$65.00**

723—Railroad Watch. 16 size B. W. Raymond movement fitted in a nickel chromium plated case. Has 21 jewels—8 adjustments, lever set. With Winding Indicator. **$55.00**

96

717—Transportation watch. 16 size 17 jewel movement, with 6 adjustments, lever set. Fitted in a yellow gold filled case, enamel Railroad type dial. **$35.00**

Produced especially for interurban railway and bus service where accuracy is necessary.

ELGIN

12 SIZE COMBINATIONS

① $140.00

512—14 karat white gold case. 17 jewels, 3 adjustments. Embossed dial. This is an unusually good value. *Retail Price $60.00*

② $100.00

504—12 size 17 jewel movement with 6 adjustments, fitted in a 14 karat white gold filled case. Bezel decorated with green and black hard enamel. Center and bow handsomely engraved. *Retail Price $65.00*

③ $110.00
$120.00

507 (white) **515** (green)—12 size 17 jewel movement with 3 adjustments. Thin model with 14 karat white or green gold cap case. *Retail Price $75.00*

516 (white) **517** (green) with G. M. Wheeler movement—17 jewels, 6 adjustments. *Retail Price $100.00*

1929 C. A. KIGER

**COMPLETE WATCH MUST BE
MINT AND RUNNING**

④ $150.00

506—12 size 17 jewel movement with 6 adjustments. Cushion shaped case of 14 karat white gold. *Retail Price $100.00*

⑤ $150.00

505—12 size 19 jewel movement with 8 adjustments. Sterling silver raised figure dial. Fitted with very heavy 14 karat white gold cap case. *Retail Price $150.00*

⑥ $150.00

521—12 size 19 jewel movement with 8 adjustments. Extremely thin model. Fitted in a 14 karat green gold engraved case. *Retail Price $150.00*

**ELGIN'S
PRESTIGE
WATCH**

⑦ $200.00

501—12 size 21 jewel movement—8 adjustments. Sterling silver raised figure dial. Wind at six model. 14 karat white gold case. Plain back and bezel. Engraved center. *Retail Price $175.00*

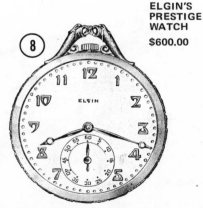

⑧ $600.00

503—12 size 19 jewel C. H. Hulburd movement —8 adjustments. Sterling silver raised figure dial. 18 karat white gold case. *Retail Price $350.00*

⑨ $750.00

502—12 size 19 jewel C. H. Hulburd movement —8 adjustments. Extremely thin model. Sterling silver dial with raised figures. 10% Iridium platinum case. *Retail Price $650.00*

12 SIZE COMBINATIONS

ELGIN
THE WATCHWORD FOR ELEGANCE AND EFFICIENCY

MINT $75.00
EX FINE $50.00
FINE $30.00
GOOD $10.00

$75.00 ①

$75.00 ③

②

508—14 karat white gold filled case. Raised figure dial. 17 jewel movement, 3 adjustments, extremely thin model.
Retail Price $40.00

509 (white) **513** (green)—14 karat white or green gold filled case. This is an unusual model due to the face below the bow. Raised figure dial. 17 jewels, 3 adjustments.
Retail Price $40.00

510 (white) **514** (green)—14 karat white or green gold filled case—engraved border on back and bezel. 17 jewels, 3 adjustments. Embossed dial. *Retail Price $43.00*

$85.00 ⑤

$85.00 ④

$65.00 ⑥

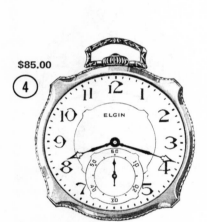

520—This rectangular pocket watch has a 12 size 17 jewel movement, with 3 adjustments. Fitted in a 14 karat white gold filled engraved case of modernistic design. Special dial with plated figures. *Retail Price $47.50*

511—Fitted in a 14 karat white gold filled cushion shaped case. 17 jewels, 3 adjustments. Friction silvered dial. *Retail Price $50.00*

*518—14 karat white gold filled case. 12 size. 17 jewel movement with 3 adjustments. Roman numerals set in bezel in hard black enamel. *Retail Price $47.50*

⑦ $125.00

COMPLETE WATCH MUST BE MINT AND RUNNING

519—Combination pocket and desk watch. This 17 jewel movement with 3 adjustments is fitted in a 14 karat white gold filled, engraved and oxidized case. Raised figure, luminous dot dial and luminous hands. *Retail Price $50.00*

*Watch to be released on or about June 1st.

HAMILTON WATCH

The Railroad Timekeeper of America

$150.00 ①

The Famous Hamilton 992 in Railroad Model Cases

Sturdily wrought from gold filled stock, these specially constructed Railroad model cases are designed by Hamilton to properly protect the famous 992 movement.

$160.00

Of rugged beauty and sturdy construction, all models incorporate special dust proof features. All models are timed in the case by Hamilton workmen.

③

Railroad Model No. 2
Featured by special pendant construction with connecting bar which makes it impossible for bow or crown to come out. 14K gold filled green or white, $65.00.
List, $72.90
10K gold filled yellow, $60.00.
List, $66.60
B. M. dial. **No extra charge**

Railroad Model No. 5
Hamilton's very newest contribution to beauty in Railroad watches. 14K gold filled green or white, $65.00.
List, $72.90
10K gold filled yellow, $60.00. *List, $66.60*
H. G. Dial. **No extra charge**

② $130.00

Railroad Model No. 4
A rigid bow features this particular model together with rich decoration on the bezel. 14K gold filled green or white, $65.00.
List, $72.90
10K gold filled yellow, $60.00
List, $66.60
Numerical dial. **No Extra charge**

⑥

④ $200.00

No. 950 Open Face, 16 size $85.00
White Gold Finish, Bridge Movement, Lever Set, 23 Extra Fine Ruby and Sapphire Jewels in Gold Settings, Patent Motor Barrel, Gold Train, Escapement Cap Jeweled, Steel Escape Wheel, Double Roller Escapement, Sapphire Pallets, Breguet Hairspring, Micrometric Regulator, Compensation Balance, Friction Set Roller Jewel, Double Sunk Dial, Adjusted to Temperature, Isochronism, and Five Positions.
List, $103.00

16 Size and 18 Size Movements

$50.00

**1929
C.A. KIGER**

⑤

$50.00

18 SIZE MOVEMENT
No. 940 Open Face $45.00
Nickel, 21 Extra Fine Ruby and Sapphire Jewels in Gold Settings, Patent Motor Barrel, Adjusted to Temperature, Isochronism, and Five Positions, Double Roller Escapement, Steel Escape Wheel, Breguet Hairspring, Compensation Balance, Patent Micrometric Regulator, Double Sunk Dial, Gilt Lettering, Beautifully and Elegantly Damaskeened.
List, $54.50

No. 992 Open Face, 16 size $48.50
Nickel, ¾ Plate Movement, Lever Set, 21 Extra Fine Ruby and Sapphire Jewels in Gold Settings, Double Roller Escapement, Sapphire Pallets, Gold Center Wheel, Steel Escape Wheel, Micrometric Regulator, Breguet Hairspring, Friction Set Roller Jewel, Double Sunk Dial, Compensation Balance, Beautifully Damaskeened. Adjusted to Temperature, Isochronism and Five Positions.
List, $57.70

⑦

⑧

$1000.00

**HAMILTON
TRAFFIC
SPECIAL**

A new complete 16 size Hamilton case of filled white or yellow gold fitted with Hamilton's 16 size 974, **17** jewel adjusted movement, $35.00.
List, $37.20
Dial No. 16-97.
No extra charge

**Hamilton 36 size
in Chronometer Mounting**

Closely adjusted 21 jewel movement, key wind and key set. In regulation chronometer mounting, swung in gimbals. All metal fittings nickel finish. Three section mahogany box 5″ x 5″ x 5¼″.
List, $160.00

$60.00

Hamilton Watch
The Railroad Timekeeper of America

1929 C. A. KIGER

Illinois Railroad Grades
IT'S THE RESERVE POWER THAT COUNTS

THE combination of the Illinois Superior Motor Barrel together with other outstanding features of construction makes possible the use of an unusually thin mainspring, which gives Illinois Railroad models their 60 hour run, from one winding.

It is for these reasons that the Bunn Specials and the

Plant of The ILLINOIS WATCH, Springfield, Illinois

next 24 hours and then will continue to run for 12 hours more.

This extra power is more important if it is held in reserve by winding regularly every 24 hours. Thus the mainspring maintains practically a uniform tension at all times and furnishes the most fundamental kind of compensation for the variation

Sangamo Special are guaranteed to run 60 hours from one winding. They will, if not wound after the first 24 hours, maintain the accuracy of the average railroad watch for the in tension of the usual mainspring. In addition, the Sangamo Special and Bunn Specials are adjusted to six positions instead of the usual five that is required for railroad time inspection.

The Sangamo Special
The 60 Hour 6 Position Watch

THIS CASE IS REALLY LOOKED FOR BY ILLINOIS RR COLLECTORS AND IS BY FAR THE MOST DESIRABLE OF ALL RAILROAD CASES

Mint
14KSG $500
14KGF $350

The Sangamo Special is an extremely high grade, 23 jewel, 16 size, complete watch, adjusted to 6 positions and is guaranteed to run 60 hours on one winding. This watch is considered by the makers as the "last word" in railroad watches.

All material used in the construction of this watch is of the highest quality and made as accurate as human skill and the latest improved machinery can produce. Each part is individually fitted, one to the other, into the watch it is intended for.

$190.00

(1)

(3)

(2)

Special designed case by Wadsworth, extra heavy and durable with stationary bow. Furnished in either 14K white, green or yellow gold filled, or 14K white, green or yellow solid gold. Also, furnished in 14K white or yellow gold filled, screw bezel and back case.

The dial on model shown above is double sunk, glass enamel. Heavy Gothic figures. Also furnished with Butler center, silver dial, Railroad figures.

Fitted in 14K filled white, green or yellow gold.................. $90.00
List $100.00

Fitted in 14K extra weight, white, green or yellow solid gold.... $150.00
List $185.00

SPECIFICATIONS
23 jewels; nine adjustments; solid gold raised jewel settings; hardened and tempered compensating balance; Breguet hairspring; double roller escapement; hardened and tempered beveled and polished steel escape wheel; positive micrometric screw regulator; safety recoil click; Illinois Superior Jeweled Motor Barrel with 60 hour mainspring.

Special designed case by Wadsworth, extra heavy and durable with stationary bow. Furnished in either 14K white, green or yellow gold filled, or 14K white, green or yellow solid gold. Also furnished in 14K white or yellow gold filled, screw bezel and back case.

The dial on model shown above is double sunk, glass enamel Heavy Arabic figures. Also furnished with either Montgomery or Butler center, silver dial, Railroad figures.

Fitted in 14K filled white, green or yellow gold.................. $90.00
List $100.00

Fitted in 14K extra weight, white, green or yellow solid gold.... $150.00
List $185.00

Prices Subject to Change Without Notice

1929 C. A. KIGER

The 23 Jewel Bunn Special
60 Hours - 6 Positions - Motor Barrel

FOR more than a quarter of a century, Illinois watches have been leaders in railroad service, owing to their durability and accurate time keeping qualities. ¶The 23 jewel, Bunn Special is the perfected railroad watch and is the last word in timing the trains. It so far exceeds railroad requirements that it will meet all service demands of the future. It is our opinion that this watch cannot be surpassed for satisfactory and dependable railroad service, and constitutes the best value in timepieces ever produced. ¶The extra quality sapphire jewels for bearings of both pivots of the going arbor of the motor barrel in the 23 jewel Bunn Specials, greatly reduces friction and adds to the perfection of the construction of these exceptionally fine railroad watches.

$275.00

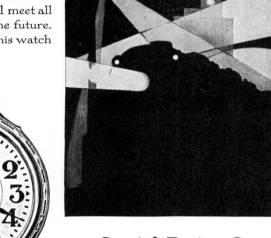

(1)

Above model furnished in 14K white or green gold filled also green center with white back and bezel Keystone case. Dial is double sunk, glass enamel with Heavy Arabic figures.
Retail $75.00
List $81.50

Special Design Case

THE 23 Jewel Bunn Special cases were designed by Keystone especially for this model. They are very unique in design, showing strength of character in every line. They have been termed by many as the mos attractive Railroad cases of recent manufacture. The cases are screw bezel and back. The bows are absolutely non-pull-out, while the pendant, in fact the entire case, is dust proof.

$275.00

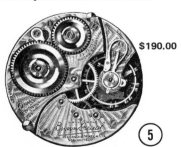

(2)

Above model furnished in 14K white or green gold filled also green center with white back and bezel Keystone case. Montgomery double sunk, glass enamel dial, heavy Arabic figures also furnished with Butler center silver dial, Railroad figures.
Retail $75.00
List $81.50

The 23 Jewel Bunn Special Movement

16 Size   23 Jewels   Three-Quarter Plate Model
Adjusted to 6 positions and heat, cold and isochronism; raised gold jewel settings; spring tempered compensating balance with solid gold screws; polished gold beveled train wheels; double roller escapement and entire escapement cap jeweled, steel escape wheel; Breguet hairspring; concaved and polished steel winding wheels; positive micrometric screw regulator; safety recoiling click; *Illinois Superior Jeweled Motor Barrel.*

$275.00

(3)

Above model furnished in 10K yellow gold filled Keystone case. Dial is double sunk, glass enamel Heavy Arabic figures.
Retail $70.00
List $74.50

$190.00

(5)

Price, Movement Only
Retail $58.00   List $65.50

$275.00

(4)

Above model furnished in 10K yellow gold filled Keystone case. Montgomery double sunk, glass enamel dial, Heavy Arabic figures. Also furnished with Butler center silver dial, Railroad figures.
Retail $70.00
List $74.50

Prices Subject to Change Without Notice

1929 C. A. KIGER

The 21 Jewel Bunn Special
60 Hours - 6 Positions - Motor Barrel

THE 21 Jewel Bunn Special, 16 size, high grade railroad watch is standard for railroad service. Its Superior Motor Barrel permits the use of a longer, thinner mainspring which drives the watch 60 hours from one winding—a tremendous factor of safety, since the watch will maintain its even, accurate rate for more than 48 hours. It is a watch that is giving railroad men everywhere complete satisfaction in every way. For more than a quarter of a century the Bunn Special has been recognized for its superior timekeeping qualities. Its sturdy mechanical construction, together with the most modern improvements, consisting of the Illinois Superior Motor Barrel and the 60 hour running feature, has made it a leader in its line.

$175.00

$175.00

$175.00

$175.00

(1)
Above model furnished in 14K white or green gold filled Wadsworth case. Dial, double sunk, glass enamel, Heavy Arabic figures.

Retail $65.00
List $72.00

(2)
Above model furnished in 14K white or green gold filled Wadsworth case, with Montgomery double sunk, glass enamel dial. Also furnished with Butler center silver dial, Railroad figures.

Retail $65.00
List $72.00

Special Design Case

THE cases, designed by Wadsworth, are the result of their years of experience in the making of fine watch cases. These movements are fitted, timed and rated in their cases at the factory. Both styles of cases are made with screw back and bezel, the metal used being much thicker than is usually found in standard 16 size cases. The bows are absolutely non-pull-out, and pendant contains a special dust-proof feature, making it impossible for dust or dirt to work through into the movement.

The 21 Jewel Bunn Special Movement

16 Size   21 Jewels   Three-Quarter Plate Model
21 selected ruby and sapphire jewels; 9 adjustments; 6 for positions and 1 each for heat, cold and isochronism; solid gold raised jewel settings; hardened and tempered compensating balance with Breguet hairspring; double roller escapement; hardened and tempered beveled and polished steel escape wheel; positive micrometric screw regulator; safety recoil click; Illinois Superior Motor Barrel with 60 Hour mainspring.

$100.00

(3)
Above model furnished in 10K yellow gold filled Wadsworth case. Dial, double sunk, glass enamel, Heavy Arabic figures.

Retail $60.00
List $65.00

(5)
Price, Movement Only
Retail $50.00   List $56.00

(4)
Above model furnished in 10K yellow gold filled Wadsworth case. Montgomery double sunk, glass enamel dial. Also furnished with Butler center silver dial Railroad figures.

Retail $60.00
List $65.00

Prices Subject to Change Without Notice

1929 C. A. KIGER

Commercial Grade Movements

THE movements illustrated or described on this page are all high-grade accurate and dependable timepieces. They are not sold as complete watches, but may be readily fitted in standard cases of any design by wholesalers or retailers, thus affording an unlimited assortment of cases to choose from.

$30.00

$40.00

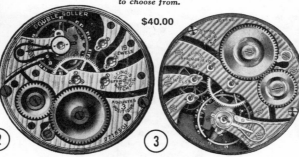

$30.00

706   17 JEWELS   16 SIZE
Open Face
Retail $27.50   List $30.00

17 jewels; polished settings; adjusted to temperature and four positions; hardened compensating balance; polished gold top center wheel; tempered and polished steel escape wheel; Breguet hairspring; safety pinion; micrometric screw regulator; concaved winding wheels; recoil click; double sunk or fancy silver dial.

707   19 JEWELS   16 SIZE
Open Face   Lever Set
Retail $32.50   List $33.00

19 jewels; adjusted to temperature and three positions; spring tempered compensating balance; double roller escapement; sapphire jewels; steel escape wheel; rounded arm train wheels; gold center wheel; Breguet hairspring; patent regulator; recoil click; double sunk or fancy silver dial.

307   19 JEWELS   16 SIZE
Open Face   Pendant Set
Retail $32.50   List $33.00

19 jewels; adjusted to temperature and three positions; spring tempered compensating balance; double roller escapement; sapphire jewels; steel escape wheel; rounded arm train wheels; gold center wheel; Breguet hairspring; patent regulator; recoil click; double sunk or fancy silver dial.

305   17 JEWELS   16 SIZE
Open Face
Retail $24.00   List $25.20

17 jewels; polished settings; adjusted to temperature; hardened compensating balance; double roller escapement; steel escape wheel; rayed center wheel; Breguet hairspring; patent micrometric screw regulator; safety pinion; rayed winding wheels; safety recoil click; white enamel or fancy silver dial.

---

410   23 Jewels   12 Size   Open Face   Retail $60.00   List $75.00

$9.00

23 ruby and sapphire jewels; gold settings; adjusted to temperature, six positions and isochronism; spring tempered compensating balance; beveled steel escape wheel; double roller; entire escapement cap jeweled; conical pivots; beveled and polished gold strata train wheels; Breguet hairspring; micrometric screw regulator; recoil click safety pinion; Illinois Superior Jeweled Motor Barrel; double sunk dial.

A. LINCOLN   21 Jewels   12 Size   O.F.   Retail $47.50   List $53.00

21 ruby and sapphire jewels; gold settings; adjusted to temperature, five positions and isochronism; hardened and tempered compensating balance, double roller escapement; sapphire roller and pallet jewels; beveled steel escape wheel; entire escapement cap jeweled; gold strata center wheel; patent micrometric screw regulator; Breguet hairspring; safety pinion; concaved and polished winding wheel; double sunk dial.

$40.00

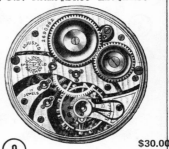

$55.00

279, 21J., 12 Size, O.F.   Retail $38.00   List $41.00

21 jewels; oreide settings; adjusted to temperature; compensating balance; double roller escapement; steel escape wheel; sapphire jewels; gold strata, beveled and polished center wheel; Breguet hairspring; patent regulator; safety pinion; concaved and polished winding wheels; recoil click; damaskeened in bright striped pattern.

407   19 J.   12 Size   Open Face
Retail $32.50   List $33.80

19 jewels; adjusted to temperature and three positions; spring tempered compensating balance; double roller escapement; sapphire jewels; steel escape wheel; rounded arm train wheels; gold center wheel; Breguet hairspring; patent regulator; recoil click; fancy silver dial.

405, 17J., 12 Size, O.F.   Retail $24.00   List $24.50

17 jewels; oreide settings; adjusted to temperature; spring tempered compensating balance; double roller escapement; steel escape wheel; sapphire jewels; rayed center wheel; Breguet hairspring; patent micrometric screw regulator; safety pinion; rayed winding wheels; safety recoil click; damaskeened in bright striped pattern.

$45.00

$30.00

Strap Watch Movements

No. 907   19 Jewels   6/0 Size
Bridge Model   Open Face   Pendant Setting

$10.00

19 ruby and sapphire jewels in settings; compensating balance with timing screws; steel escape wheel; double roller escapement; Breguet hairspring; concaved and polished ratchet and winding wheels; recoil click; escape pinion cap jeweled.

No. 905   17 Jewels   6/0 Size
Bridge Model   Open Face   Pendant Setting

No. 903   15 Jewels   6/0 Size
Bridge Model   Open Face   Pendant Setting

The description of above models is the same as No. 907 with exception of jewels.

	Retail	List
No. 903.	$25.00	$29.00
No. 905.	$30.00	$34.50
No. 907.	$35.00	$40.00
No. 24.	$25.00	$26.00

Prices Subject to Change Without Notice

No. 24   17 Jewels   3/0 Size
Bridge Model   Hunting   Pendant Setting

17 ruby and sapphire jewels in settings; compensating balance with timing screws; steel escape wheel; Breguet hairspring; micrometric screw regulator; rayed center wheel; safety screw center pinion; safety recoil click; rayed ratchet and winding wheels; damaskeened in a circular striped pattern.

$10.00

HTC

Extra Thin 12 Size

The Illini

21 Jewels 8 Adjustments

THE beautiful Illini was especially designed and made for the man who demands an attractive durable and accurate timepiece in an extra thin watch. It is the highest grade thin model made by Illinois and is unequalled in quality and style at the price. ¶The movement contains 21 extra quality large ruby and sapphire jewels; special tempered compensating center arm balance; is adjusted to heat, cold, isochronism and five positions. The Illinois Superior Motor Barrel, with both pivots of barrel staff operating in sapphire jewels, is one of its special features. This exceptionally fine movement is supplied only in exclusive and distinctive designed 14K and 18K solid gold cases.

$190.00

$225.00

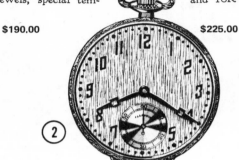

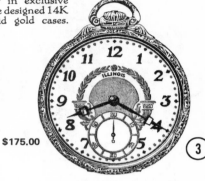

$175.00

(1)

(2)

(3)

Retail $175.00 :: List $190.00
14K solid extra heavy white gold hand carved case with inlaid black enamel decoration; Butler back with sterling silver dial with 18K applied figures.

Retail, 18K case, $200.00 :: List $230.00
Solid white gold, engraved Empire case; special raised figure dial with choice of 18K applied or steel figures.

Retail $160.00 :: List $176.00
14K solid white gold, extra heavy hand carved case; Butler or etched back. Etched dial with figures in relief.

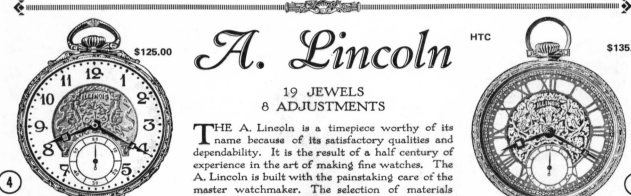

$125.00

A. Lincoln

HTC

$135.00

19 JEWELS
8 ADJUSTMENTS

THE A. Lincoln is a timepiece worthy of its name because of its satisfactory qualities and dependability. It is the result of a half century of experience in the art of making fine watches. The A. Lincoln is built with the painstaking care of the master watchmaker. The selection of materials used in the construction of this watch is based upon knowledge gained through years of specialization in the manufacture of high grade timepieces—such is the assurance of its quality.

There is a mark of refinement in the selection of the cases which are furnished in either solid or 14K gold filled.

(4)

(5)

PIONEER MODEL
Retail $75.00 :: List $86.00
14K filled green or white gold, full chased inside cap case, special etched center dial.

BARRISTER MODEL
Retail $100.00 :: List $120.00
14K green or white solid gold, full chased center and bezels, inside cap case, new process etched dial with ancient Roman figures in relief.

$120.00

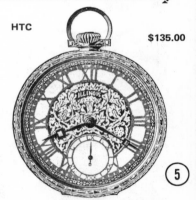

SPECIFICATIONS

19 ruby and sapphire jewels, raised settings; adjusted to temperature, five positions and isochronism; special quality hardened and tempered center arm compensating balance; double roller escapement; sapphire roller and pallet jewels; beveled steel escape wheel; gold center wheel; conical pivots; patent micrometric screw regulator; best quality Breguet hairspring; recoil click; Illinois Superior Jeweled Motor Barrel; concaved and polished winding wheels; damaskeened in bright striped pattern; black enamel lettering.

(6)

(7)

ACORN MODEL
Retail $75.00 :: List $84.00
14K filled green or white gold inside cap case, silver etched or embossed raised figure dials.

Prices Subject to Change Without Notice

MOVEMENT VIEW

HTC

1929 C. A. KIGER

The Marquis
The Aristocrat of Watches

12 SIZE
THIN MODEL

17 JEWELS
6 ADJUSTMENTS

THE Marquis-Autocrat was designed and built to meet the demand for a thin, attractive, high grade and dependable watch at a reasonable price. It is constructed of the best materials throughout and has many superior features not usually found in watches selling within its range of price. This watch can be depended upon to give satisfactory and faithful service.

The Marquis-Autocrat contains 17 selected ruby and sapphire jewels, in settings; is adjusted to three positions, heat, cold and isochronism, has special quality tempered and hardened compensating balance; double roller escapement; steel escape wheel; gold center wheel; Breguet hairspring; patent regulator adjustment; concaved and polished winding wheels; Illinois Superior Motor Barrel and safety recoil click.

The Marquis-Autocrat is supplied in a beautiful plush and satin lined box, making it an ideal watch for gift or presentation.

① $70.00

CUSHION MODEL
Retail $55.00
List $61.00

Furnished in either plain or engraved oxidized, 14K white gold filled case.

$90.00
$100.00

$55.00

② **CAMBRIDGE MODEL**
Retail, Queen Case, $75.00
List, " " $86.00
Retail, Inside Cap case, $85.00
List, " " $98.00
14K green or white solid gold case. Special etched, lined or Butler back. Sterling silver inlaid enamel, raised figure or etched center dial.

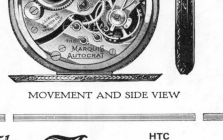

MOVEMENT AND SIDE VIEW

③ **ETON MODEL**
Retail $50.00
List $56.00

14K filled green or white gold, chased case. Etched, Butler finish or lined back. Embossed raised figure dial.

$50.00

④ Retail $43.50
List $46.00

Fitted in chased green or white 14K gold filled case. Raised figure, luminous, engraved or special Moire dial.

The Autocrat
HTC

17 Jewels, Adjusted to Temperature and Isochronism

THIS extremely popular model has been produced to meet the demand for an attractive, dependable timepiece at a moderate price. It is guaranteed by the makers to be reliable and give satisfactory service.

The Shrine Special

THE beautiful dial on the Shriner's Special is of Sterling silver, the numerals of which are raised and finished in gold. The outer section beneath the numerals is of a satin finish. The center highly polished. The emblem is engraved and filled with enamel, giving a touch of color on a beautiful back-ground of solid silver. These dials are supplied only on complete Autocrat movements.

Prices Subject to Change Without Notice

$50.00

⑤ Retail $43.50
List $46.00

Fitted in chased green or white 14K gold filled case. Raised figure Shrine Dial.

1929 C. A. KIGER
H.T.C

All watches are
gold filled,
mint and running

17J $80.00
19J $90.00
21J $100.00

① Keystone Extra

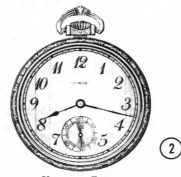

② Keystone Extra

No.		Retail	List
1295	17J White or Green	$ 75	$ 90
1595	19J White or Green	100	120
1495	21J White or Green	125	150

Supplied with Butler or Engraved back.

No.		Retail	List
1295	17J White or Green	$ 75	$ 90
1595	19J White or Green	100	120
1495	21J White or Green	125	150

Supplied with Butler or Engraved back.

THE HOWARD 10 SIZE watch is the latest achievement of the Howard horologists. It is an outstanding example of the life-long precision and distinction which everyone has come to expect of any watch bearing the name Howard.

The movement is manufactured on new principles combining simplicity and accuracy.

The second hand can be set to the exact second from the stem, without opening the case and stopping the movement. This is one of many exclusive features and refinements of construction.

The 10 size movement is made in three grades: 17J adjusted to 3 positions; 19J adjusted to 5 positions; 21J adjusted to 5 positions.

The compactness of this movement permits graceful casing not possible with larger movements.

o   o   o

Every Howard movement is fitted and timed in its own case at the factory.

Dials are of sterling silver or finest quality enamel.

③

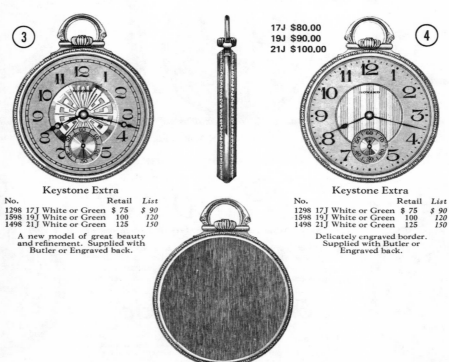

17J $80.00
19J $90.00
21J $100.00

④

Keystone Extra

No.		Retail	List
1298	17J White or Green	$ 75	$ 90
1598	19J White or Green	100	120
1498	21J White or Green	125	150

A new model of great beauty and refinement. Supplied with Butler or Engraved back.

Keystone Extra

No.		Retail	List
1298	17J White or Green	$ 75	$ 90
1598	19J White or Green	100	120
1498	21J White or Green	125	150

Delicately engraved border. Supplied with Butler or Engraved back.

Made by KEYSTONE WATCH CASE CORPORATION, *Riverside, New Jersey*

1929 C.A. KIGER

The small, thin dimensions of the 10 size Howard movement make possible the noticeably superior grace of this octagonal model.

The No. 07 model illustrated below is one of the latest Howard creations, a dignified and distinctive timepiece.

Keystone 14K Gold
Sterling Silver Dial with 18K Solid Gold Applied Numerals

No.			Retail	List	
1206	17J	White only, Butler	$125	$150	**$110.00**
1506	19J	White only, Butler	150	180	**$120.00**
1406	21J	White only, Butler	175	210	**$130.00**

Keystone 14K Gold

No.			Retail	List	
1205	17J	White or Green	$100	$120	**$100.00**
1505	19J	White or Green	125	150	**$110.00**
1405	21J	White or Green	150	180	**$120.00**

Supplied with Butler or Engraved back.

Keystone 14K Gold

No.			Retail	List	
1207	17J	White only, Butler	$100	$120	**$100.00**
1507	19J	White only, Butler	125	150	**$110.00**
1407	21J	White only, Butler	150	180	**$120.00**

Keystone 14K Gold

No.			Retail	List
1245F	17J	Wh. or Gr., Cap	$125	$150
1545F	19J	Wh. or Gr., Cap	150	180
1445F	21J	Wh. or Gr., Cap	175	210

Supplied with Butler or Engraved back.

Howard Applied Numeral Dial

This sterling silver dial with 18K solid gold applied numerals can be supplied on any 10s. model at an extra charge

$10 extra retail; $12 extra list.

Made by KEYSTONE WATCH CASE CORPORATION, *Riverside, New Jersey*

1929 C. A. KIGER
DORIC

H.T.C.

The Howard 12 size 17 Jewel Period Watches take their inspiration from the great historic art motifs and appeal particularly to those who appreciate fine things.

17 selected sapphire and ruby jewels. Train and balance have olive hole-jewels. Double roller escapement and steel escape wheel. Adjusted to 3 positions, temperature and isochronism.

Keystone Extra

No.		Retail	List	
765	Doric 17J White or Green, Cap	$65	$78	**$100.00**

Supplied with Butler or Engraved back.

IONIC

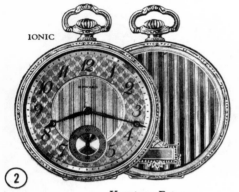

TUSCAN

Keystone Extra

No.		Retail	List	
795	Ionic 17J White or Green	$60	$72	**$100.00**

A most attractive and very popular model.
Supplied with Butler or Engraved back.

Keystone Extra

No.		Retail	List	
798	Tuscan 17J White or Green	$60	$72	**$100.00**

A new model of great distinction.
Supplied with Butler or Engraved back.

TUDOR

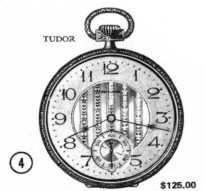

$125.00

VICTORIAN

$100.00

Keystone 14K Gold

No.		Retail	List
705	Tudor 17J Wh. or Gr.	$100	$120

Supplied with Butler or Engraved back.

Keystone Extra
Yellow or Green

No.		Retail	List
755	Victorian 17J, Cap	$65	$78

Made by KEYSTONE WATCH CASE CORPORATION, *Riverside, New Jersey*

C. A. KIGER
Montgomery
dials
supplied on
railroad watches
on request
without
extra charge

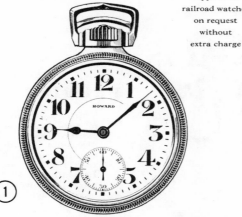

(1)

(2)

HOWARD RAILROAD STANDARD
Keystone Extra Case

	No.		Retail	List	
$200.00	1095	21J White Screw Butler	$90	$108	
$200.00	1095	21J Gr. Screw Butler or P. P.	90	108	
$375.00	95	23J White Screw Butler	125	150	
$375.00	95	23J Gr. Screw Butler or P.P.	125	150	

HOWARD RAILROAD STANDARD
Open Face Jointed-Inside Cap, 14K Yellow Only

No.		Retail	List	
1035	21J 14K Gold P.P.	$135	$162	**$300.00**
35	23J 14K Gold P.P.	170	204	**$475.00**

Howard railroad watches were developed for railroad men, field engineers and others who demand time-keeping accuracy under the most severe conditions.

The Howard Railroad Chronometer, is a 16 size, 21 Jewel lever set movement, closely adjusted to 5 pos., temperature and isochronism.

All pivots running in extra hard Rubigust olive-shaped bearings. Pallet stones, impulse pin and endstones of Rubigust. Howard Bi-metallic balance wheel especially hard tempered, proof against jar and vibration.

Howard Railroad Watches are fitted in the famous Keystone Railroad Case with many special features. The pendant is spun on the center. Heavy stock, long thread on the screws. Narrow bezel with bead gives more hand room under the glass. Dust Proof Nut Pendant, *Nonpull-out Bow*

The 23 Jewel movement and the 21 Jewel Series No. 10 movement have selected rubies and sapphires with oriental sapphire pallet stones and banking pins. Train and balance have olive hole-jewels. Recessed steel escape wheel. Closely adjusted to 5 pos., temperature and isochronism.

(3)

Note thin edge view

HOWARD
RAILROAD
CHRONOMETER

Jas. Boss 10K Gold Filled

No.		Retail	List	
1195A	21J Yellow Screw P.P.	$70	$80	**$200.00**

Keystone Extra

No.		Retail	List
1195	21J White Screw Butler	$80	$96
1195	21J Gr. Screw Butler or P.P.	80	96
1195	21J Yellow Screw P.P.	80	96

Made by KEYSTONE WATCH CASE CORPORATION. *Riverside, New Jersey*

WALTHAM
COLONIAL WATCHES
C. A. KIGER —1929

16—Size

$2200.00

PREMIER MAXIMUS

No. 500   *Price* $610.00

PRESENTATION WATCHES

What Presentation Piece could be more fitting than one of the distinguished Waltham Watches illustrated on this page? Its beauty will be appreciated daily ... its dependable time-keeping service a source of lifetime satisfaction.

WALTHAM'S PRESTIGE WATCH

PREMIER MAXIMUS

This is Waltham's finest Watch; a superb movement magnificently cased. The Premier Maximus is recognized as the crowning triumph of the watch-maker's art; an unsurpassed Presentation Piece whose bestowal recognizes supreme achievement.

Movement: — 23 Jewels — fine Diamonds, Rubies, and Sapphires. Winding Indicator. Adjusted to Isochronism, changes in Temperature and 6 Positions.

Case: — Heavy hand-made of 18K solid Gold—White, Green, or Yellow. Invisible Joint. Plain or Hand-Carved.

Dial:—Enamel Hand-Painted or Fine Silver with Applied Numerals of 18K Gold.

Delivered from the Factory in a Special Leather Presentation Box with two extra Mainsprings and Crystal.

Box $200.00

Silver Box $400.00

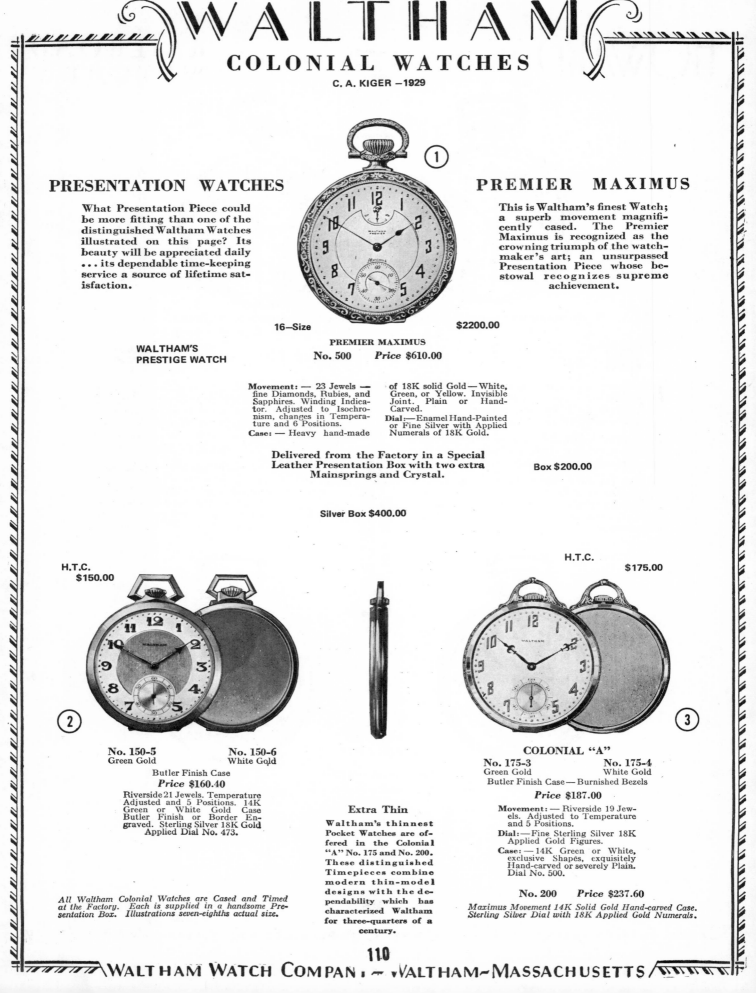

H.T.C. $150.00

H.T.C. $175.00

No. 150-5 Green Gold   **No. 150-6** White Gold

Butler Finish Case

***Price* $160.40**

Riverside 21 Jewels. Temperature Adjusted and 5 Positions. 14K Green or White Gold Case Butler Finish or Border Engraved. Sterling Silver 18K Gold Applied Dial No. 473.

All Waltham Colonial Watches are Cased and Timed at the Factory. Each is supplied in a handsome Presentation Box. Illustrations seven-eighths actual size.

Extra Thin

Waltham's thinnest Pocket Watches are offered in the Colonial "A" No. 175 and No. 200. These distinguished Timepieces combine modern thin-model designs with the dependability which has characterized Waltham for three-quarters of a century.

COLONIAL "A"

No. 175-3 Green Gold   **No. 175-4** White Gold

Butler Finish Case—Burnished Bezels

***Price* $187.00**

Movement: — Riverside 19 Jewels. Adjusted to Temperature and 5 Positions.

Dial:—Fine Sterling Silver 18K Applied Gold Figures.

Case: — 14K Green or White, exclusive Shapes, exquisitely Hand-carved or severely Plain. Dial No. 500.

No. 200   *Price* $237.60

Maximus Movement 14K Solid Gold Hand-carved Case. Sterling Silver Dial with 18K Applied Gold Numerals.

WALTHAM WATCH COMPANY — WALTHAM—MASSACHUSETTS

WALTHAM
COLONIAL WATCHES

1929 C. A. KIGER

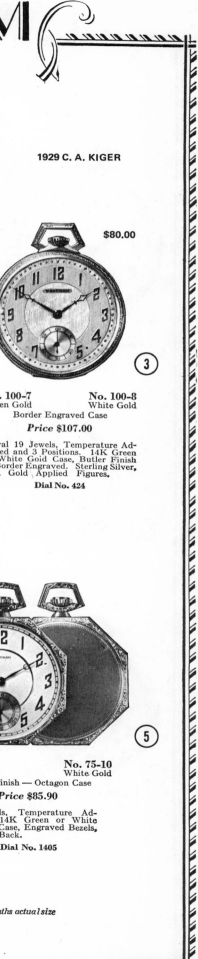

$100.00

$80.00

(1)

No. 100-9   **No. 100-10**
Green Gold   White Gold
Butler Finish — Octagon Case
Price $107.00

Royal 19 Jewels, Temperature Adjusted and 3 Positions. 14K Green or White Octagon Case, Engraved Bezels, Brushed Back. Sterling Silver, 18K Applied Gold Figures.
Dial No. 473

Waltham Colonial "A" Watch No. 175 in Presentation Box

(2)

No. 100-7   **No. 100-8**
Green Gold   White Gold
Border Engraved Case
Price $107.00

Royal 19 Jewels, Temperature Adjusted and 3 Positions. 14K Green or White Gold Case, Butler Finish or Border Engraved. Sterling Silver, 18K Gold Applied Figures.
Dial No. 424

(3)

Waltham Colonial Watches are Cased and Timed at the Factory. Each is supplied in a handsome Presentation Box.

$75.00

No. 60R-15   **No. 60R-16**
Green Gold   White Gold
Butler Finish — Cushion Case
Price $64.10

Royal 19 Jewels, Temperature Adjusted and 3 Positions. 14K Filled Green or White Cushion Case, Engraved Bezels.
Dial No. 1407

$85.00

(4)

No. 75R-13   **No. 75R-14**
Green Gold   White Gold
Engraved Center Case
Line Finish Back
Price $85.90

Royal 19 Jewels, Temperature Adjusted and 3 Positions. 14K Green or White Gold Case, Engraved Center, Burnished Bezels.
Dial No. 727

$55.00

(6)

(5)

No. 75-9   **No. 75-10**
Green Gold   White Gold
Butler Finish — Octagon Case
Price $85.90

17 Jewels, Temperature Adjusted. 14K Green or White Octagon Case, Engraved Bezels, Brushed Back.
Dial No. 1405

Illustrations seven-eighths actual size

WALTHAM WATCH COMPANY ~ WALTHAM ~ MASSACHUSETTS

WALTHAM
COLONIAL WATCHES

Waltham Colonial Watches are
Cased and Timed at the Factory.
Each is supplied in a handsome
Presentation Box.

1929 C. A. KIGER

$55.00

① **No. 60-19** Green Gold
No. 60-20 White Gold
Butler Finish Case
Price $64.10
Dial No. 727

$50.00

② **No. 60-13** Green Gold
No. 60-14 White Gold
Line Finish Case
Price $64.10
Dial No. 727

$65.00

③ **No. 45-15** Green Gold
No. 45-16 White Gold
Butler Finish — Cushion Case
Price $51.20
Dial No. 1407

No. 60   *Price $64.10*
17 Jewels, Temperature Adjusted. 14K Green or White Gold, Brocaded or Butler, Engraved Center, Burnished Bezels. Etched, Engraved or Butler Finished Dials.

No. 45   *Price $51.20*
17 Jewels, Temperature Adjusted. 14K Filled Green or White Cushion Case, Engraved Bezels.

No. 40   *Price $45.70*
17 Jewels, Temperature Adjusted. 14K Filled Green or White. New Designs. Etched Figures, Hand-engraved or Butler Dials.

$50.00

④ **No. 60-25** Green Gold
Plain Bassine Case
Price $64.10
Dial No. 2

$55.00

$50.00

⑤ **No. 40-17** Green Gold
No. 40-18 White Gold
Butler Finish Case
Price $45.70
Dial No. 1401

No. 40-26 Green Gold
No. 40-27 White Gold
Straight Line — Etched Panel Case
Price $45.70
Dial No. 1408

⑥ **No. 40-28** Green Gold
No. 40-29 White Gold
Etched Finish Case
Price $45.70
Dial No. 727

$50.00

Illustrations seven-eighths actual size

⑦

WALTHAM WATCH COMPANY ～ WALTHAM ～ MASSACHUSETTS

WALTHAM
RAILROAD WATCHES

Waltham Railroad Watches will pass the inspection of any railroad in the world. At Waltham they are subjected to the most exacting tests known to watchmakers. Over a period of sixty days they are adjusted to extremes of temperature, also in each position that a watch can be subjected to in railroad service.

Mint without indicator $135.00
Mint indicator $275.00

1929 C. A. KIGER

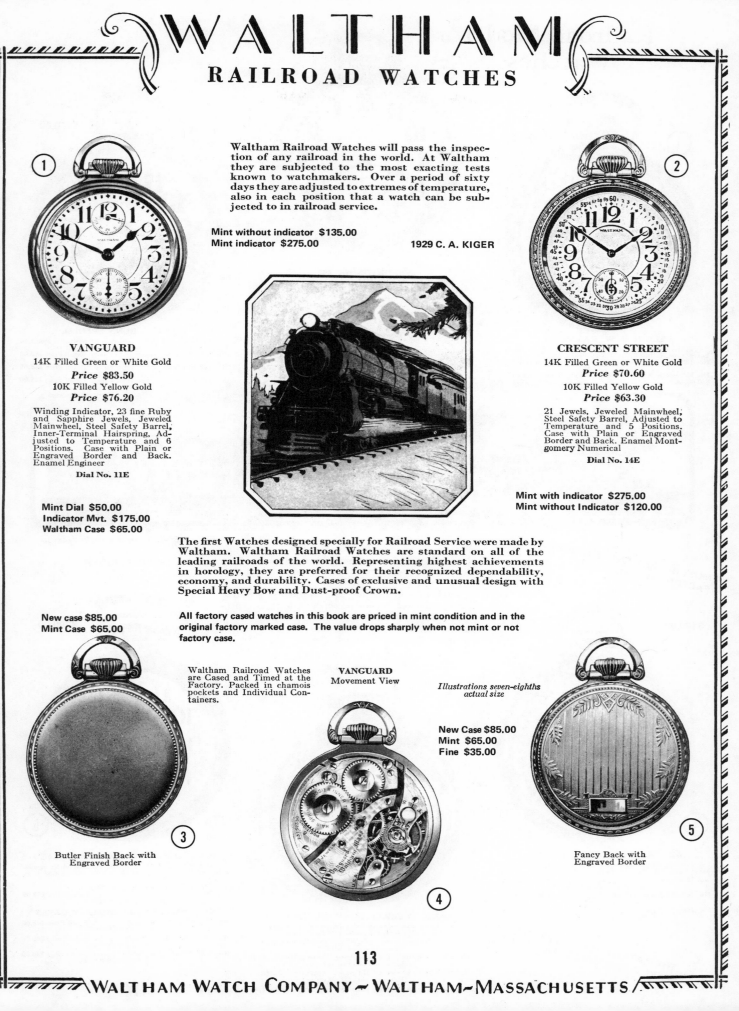

VANGUARD

14K Filled Green or White Gold
Price $83.50
10K Filled Yellow Gold
Price $76.20

Winding Indicator, 23 fine Ruby and Sapphire Jewels, Jeweled Mainwheel, Steel Safety Barrel, Inner-Terminal Hairspring, Adjusted to Temperature and 6 Positions. Case with Plain or Engraved Border and Back. Enamel Engineer

Dial No. 11E

Mint Dial $50.00
Indicator Mvt. $175.00
Waltham Case $65.00

CRESCENT STREET

14K Filled Green or White Gold
Price $70.60
10K Filled Yellow Gold
Price $63.30

21 Jewels, Jeweled Mainwheel, Steel Safety Barrel, Adjusted to Temperature and 5 Positions. Case with Plain or Engraved Border and Back. Enamel Montgomery Numerical

Dial No. 14E

Mint with indicator $275.00
Mint without Indicator $120.00

The first Watches designed specially for Railroad Service were made by Waltham. Waltham Railroad Watches are standard on all of the leading railroads of the world. Representing highest achievements in horology, they are preferred for their recognized dependability, economy, and durability. Cases of exclusive and unusual design with Special Heavy Bow and Dust-proof Crown.

New case $85.00
Mint Case $65.00

All factory cased watches in this book are priced in mint condition and in the original factory marked case. The value drops sharply when not mint or not factory case.

Butler Finish Back with Engraved Border

Waltham Railroad Watches are Cased and Timed at the Factory. Packed in chamois pockets and Individual Containers.

VANGUARD
Movement View

Illustrations seven-eighths actual size

New Case $85.00
Mint $65.00
Fine $35.00

Fancy Back with Engraved Border

WALTHAM WATCH COMPANY ~ WALTHAM ~ MASSACHUSETTS

Railroad Model Watches

① $125.00

ELGIN B. W. RAYMOND
21 jewel, adjusted to 5 positions, cased in special heavy type Railroad model gold filled cases.
No. 755—10 Karat Yellow Gold Filled. Retail Price **$60.00**
(Keystone List $63.30.)
No. 756—14-K White or Green Gold Filled. (Keystone List $70.60.)..................Retail Price **$65.00**

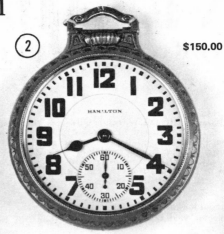

② $150.00

HAMILTON No. 992
21 jewel, adjusted to 5 positions, cased in special heavy type Railroad model gold filled cases.
No. 758—10 Karat Yellow Gold Filled. Retail Price **$60.00**
(Keystone List $66.60.)
No. 759—14 Karat White Gold Filled. Retail Price **$65.00**
(Keystone List $72.90.)
No. 760—14 Karat Green Gold Filled. Retail Price **$65.00**
(Keystone List $72.90.)

③ $175.00

ILLINOIS BUNN SPECIAL
21 jewel, 60-hour, adjusted to 6 positions, cased in special heavy type Railroad model gold filled cases.
No. 761—10 Karat Yellow Gold Filled. Retail Price **$60.00**
(Keystone List $65.00.)
No. 762—14 Karat White Gold Filled. Retail Price **$65.00**
(Keystone List $72.00.)
No. 763—14 Karat Green Gold Filled. Retail Price **$65.00**

(Photo by courtesy of Atchison, Topeka & Santa Fe Railroad.)

MUST BE MINT AND IN ORIGINAL FACTORY MARKED CASE.

All of these master timepieces are cased in specially designed heavy duty cases, and have all passed rigid timing tests before leaving the factories.

These watches are guaranteed to pass the severe timing tests made by railroad time inspectors and to pass inspection for use on any railroad in the United States.

Montgomery minute numerical dials can be supplied on any of these watches at no extra cost.

1929 C. A. KIGER

$120.00

④

WALTHAM CRESCENT STREET
21 jewel, adjusted to 5 positions, cased in special heavy type Railroad model gold filled cases.
No. 764—10 Karat Yellow Gold Filled. Retail Price **$60.00**
(Keystone List $63.30.)
No. 765—14 Karat White Gold Filled. Retail Price **$65.00**
(Keystone List $70.60.)
No. 766—14 Karat Green Gold Filled. Retail Price **$65.00**
(Keystone List $70.60.)

THE WATCHES ON THIS PAGE MAKE A FINE COLLECTION.

$275.00

⑤

THE 23 JEWEL BUNN SPECIAL
23 jewel, 60-hour, adjusted to 6 positions, cased in special heavy type Railroad model gold filled cases.
No. 767—10 Karat Yellow Gold Filled. Retail Price **$70.00**
(Keystone List $74.50.)
No. 768—14 Karat White Gold Filled. Retail Price **$75.00**
(Keystone List $81.50.)
No. 769—14 Karat Green Gold Filled. Retail Price **$75.00**
(Keystone List $81.50.)

$200.00

⑥

HOWARD RAILROAD CHRONOMETER
21 jewel, adjusted to 5 positions, cased in special heavy type Railroad model Keystone quality gold filled case.
No. 770—Boss 10 Karat Yellow Gold Filled..........................Retail Price **$70.00**
(Keystone List $80.00.)

KEYSTONE EXTRA QUALITY CASES
No. 771—White Screw Butler........Retail Price **$80.00**
(Keystone List $96.00.)
No. 772—Green Screw Butler......Retail Price **$80.00**
(Keystone List $96.00.)
No. 773—Yellow Screw Butler......Retail Price **$80.00**
(Keystone List $96.00.)

(Cuts shown are exact reproductions, photographed directly from the goods.)

New $85.00
Mint $75.00
Fine $70.00
Good $60.00

① 500—White $40.00
501—Green 40.00

Keystone 14k. solid gold case with inside cap, engraved border and back. Open face, snap bezel and hinge back.

$75.00

② 502—White $29.50
503—Green 29.50

Keystone 14k. solid gold case with engraved border and Butler back. Open face, snap bezel and hinge back.

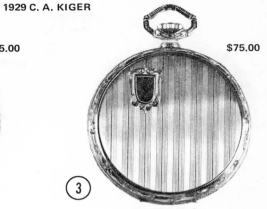

$75.00

③ 504—White $32.00
505—Green 32.00

Keystone 14k. solid gold case with engraved border and back. Open face, snap bezel and hinge back.

New $30.00
Mint $25.00
Fine $10.00
Good $2.00

④ 506—White $15.30
507—Green 15.30

Keystone Boss 14k. gold filled case with engraved center and fancy etched back. Open face, snap bezel and hinge back.

THE 3 GOLD CASES AT THE TOP OF THE PAGE IN 12 SIZE USUALLY WILL NOT SELL FOR ANY MORE THAN THE GOLD IS WORTH. 12 SIZE OPEN FACE WATCHES ARE NOT VERY DESIREABLE COLLECTORS PIECES AT THIS TIME. IN THE PAST 2 YEARS I HAVE BOUGHT MANY OF THESE LITTLE WATCHES FOR LESS THAN THE SCRAP GOLD VALUE. THESE SHOWN WEIGHT 15 to 20 DWT'S.

$25.00

⑤ 508—White $13.30
509—Green 13.30

Keystone Boss 14k. gold filled case with engraved center and plain Butler back. Open face, snap bezel and hinge back.

12 Size 14K Solid Gold and Gold Filled Cases

$30.00

⑥ 510—White $16.00
511—Green 16.00

Wadsworth 14k. gold filled case. Triad shape with engraved center. Plain Butler back, open face, snap bezel and back.

$30.00

⑦ 512—White $18.00
513—Green 18.00

Fahys 14k. gold filled Decagon shape with engraved border and back. Open face, snap bezel and back.

$30.00

⑧ 514—White $18.00
515—Green 18.00

Wadsworth 14k. gold filled case. Triad shape with engraved border and back. Open face, snap bezel and back.

(Cuts shown are exact reproductions, photographed directly from the goods.)

New $30.00
Mint $25.00
Fine $10.00
Good $2.00

① 516—White $15.30
517—Green 15.30

Keystone Boss 14k. gold filled case with engraved center and fancy etched back. Open face, snap bezel and hinge back.

$25.00

② 518—White $15.30
519—Green 15.30

Keystone Boss 14k. gold filled case with engraved center and back. Open face, snap bezel and hinge back.

$25.00

③ 520—White $15.30
521—Green 15.30

Keystone Boss 14k. gold filled case with engraved center and fancy etched back. Egyptian finish. Open face, snap bezel and hinge back.

1929 C. A. KIGER

$25.00

④ 522—White $15.30
523—Green 15.30

Keystone Boss 14k. gold filled case with engraved border and fancy etched back. Open face, snap bezel and hinge back. Rigid bow.

THESE LITTLE 10 AND 12 SIZE WATCHES WILL ONLY BRING A GOOD PRICE WHEN SOMEONE WANTS TO CARRY OR GIVE A MINT ONE AS A GIFT. THE HIGH GRADE 19J AND 23J ARE ABOUT THE ONLY COLLECTABLE WATCHES AT THIS TIME.

$25.00

⑤ 524—White $15.30
525—Green 15.30

Keystone Boss 14k. gold filled case with engraved border and fancy etched back. Open face, snap bezel and hinge back. Rigid bow.

12 Size 14K Gold Filled Cases

$25.00

⑥ 526—White $15.30
527—Green 15.30

Keystone Boss 14k. gold filled case with engraved border and back. Open face, snap bezel and hinge back. Rigid bow.

$25.00

⑦ 528—White $15.30
529—Green 15.30

Keystone Boss 14k. gold filled case with engraved border and back. Open face, snap bezel and hinge back. Rigid bow.

$25.00

⑧ 530—White $15.30
531—Green 15.30

Keystone Boss 14k. gold filled case with engraved border and fancy etched back. Open face, snap bezel and hinge back. Rigid bow.

(Cuts shown are exact reproductions, photographed directly from the goods.)

New $30.00
Mint $25.00
Fine $10.00
Good $2.00

①
532—White $13.30
533—Green 13.30

Keystone Crown 14k. gold filled case with engraved border and back. Open face, snap bezel and hinge back.

$25.00

②
534—White $13.30
535—Green 13.30

Keystone Crown 14k. gold filled case with engraved border and back. Open face, snap bezel and hinge back.

$25.00

③
536—White $11.30
537—Green 11.30

Keystone Crown 14k. gold filled case with engraved border and plain Butler back. Open face, snap bezel and hinge back.

$30.00

④
538—White $13.30
539—Green 13.30

Keystone Crown 14k. gold filled case, with engraved border and back. Open face, snap bezel and hinge back. Rigid bow.

1929 C. A. KIGER

I HAVE VALUED THESE CASES FOR MINT CONDITION WHICH MEANS NO VISIBLE WEAR & WITH MOST OF THE FACTORY LUSTURE. I HAVE SHOWN VALUES FOR NEW—MINT—FINE AND GOOD ON AT LEAST ONE WATCH ON EACH PAGE. THERE ARE STILL A FEW OF THESE NEW OLD STOCK CASES LEFT IN JEWELRY STORES ETC. THESE NEW CASES ARE WORTH A GOOD BIT MORE THAN MINT CASES.

$25.00

⑤
540—White $13.30
541—Green 13.30

Keystone Crown 14k. gold filled case with engraved border and back. Open face, snap bezel and hinge back.

12 Size 14K Gold Filled Cases

$30.00

⑥
542—White $13.30
543—Green 13.30

Keystone Crown 14k. gold filled case with engraved border and back. Open face, snap bezel and hinge back. Rigid bow.

$30.00

⑦
544—White $13.30
545—Green 13.30

Keystone Crown 14k. gold filled case with engraved border and back. Open face, snap bezel and hinge back. Rigid bow.

$30.00

⑧
546—White $11.30
547—Green 11.30

Keystone Crown 14k. gold filled case with engraved border and plain Butler back. Open face, snap bezel and hinge back. Rigid bow.

(Cuts shown are exact reproductions, photographed directly from the goods.)

New $30.00
Mint $20.00
Fine $10.00
Good $3.00

①

548—$10.40

Keystone Boss 10k. yellow gold filled, screw
back and bezel, engraved border and back.

$20.00

②

549—$10.40

Keystone Boss 10k. yellow gold filled, screw
back and bezel. Engraved border and plain
polish back.

$20.00

③

550—$10.40

Keystone Boss 10k. yellow gold filled, screw
back and bezel. Engraved border and back.

1929 C. A. KIGER

$20.00

④

551—$10.40

Star 10k. white gold filled, screw back and
bezel. Engraved border and engraved back.

I THINK THESE LITTLE 10 AND 12
SIZE WATCHES ARE ONE OF THE
MILD SLEEPERS OF TODAY. IF
YOU CAN BUY THEM RIGHT
$10 TO $20 AND CAN AFFORD TO
PUT THEM BACK. I THINK THEY
WILL BE WORTH MUCH MORE IN
10 YEARS THAN A $25.00 SAVINGS
BOND WOULD BE.

$20.00

⑤

552—$10.40

Star 10k. white gold filled, screw back and
bezel. Engraved border and engraved back.

12 Size 10K Gold Filled and Rolled Plate Cases

$20.00

⑥

553—$4.90

Fahys Monarch, rolled plate, white engraved
border and engraved back, cushion shape.

$20.00

⑦

554—$4.20

Fahys Monarch, rolled plate, white, engraved
border and engraved back. Screw back and
bezel.

$20.00

⑧

555—$4.90

Fahys Monarch, rolled plate, white engraved
border and engraved back. Octagon shape.

(Cuts shown are exact reproductions, photographed directly from the goods.)

12 Size Keystone Victory Quality Cases

New $20.00
Mint $15.00
Fine $5.00
Good $2.00

(1) 556—White $6.50
557—Green 6.50

Keystone Victory quality, screw back and bezel case, with engraved border and back.

$15.00

(2) 558—White $6.50
559—Green 6.50

Keystone Victory quality, screw back and bezel case, with engraved border and back.

$15.00

(3) 560—White $5.80
561—Green 5.80

Keystone Victory quality, screw back and bezel case, with engraved border and plain Butler back.

1929 C. A. KIGER

$20.00

(4) 562—White $6.50
563—Green 6.50

Keystone Victory quality, screw back and bezel case, with engraved border and back. Rigid bow.

MOVEMENT PRICES

Price List of 12 Size Movements Suitable for These Cases:

7 Jewel Elgin or Waltham	$14.90
15 Jewel Elgin or Waltham	21.30
17 Jewel Elgin or Waltham	23.90
17 Jewel Illinois, Adjusted	24.50
17 Jewel Elgin or Waltham, Adjusted	25.80
19 Jewel Waltham, Adjusted	33.80
19 Jewel Illinois, Adjusted	33.80
21 Jewel Waltham, Adjusted 5 Positions	53.00
21 Jewel Illinois A. Lincoln, Adjusted 5 Positions	53.00
23 Jewel Illinois, Adjusted 6 Positions	75.00

Extra Charge for Fancy Metal Dials as Follows:

Raised Figure, Elgin or Waltham	$4.50
Moire Center, Illinois	2.50
Raised Embossed Figure, Illinois	4.00
Luminous	4.50

$15.00

(5) 564—White $6.50
565—Green 6.50

Keystone Victory quality, screw back and bezel case, with engraved border and back.

$20.00

(6) 566—White $6.50
567—Green 6.50

Keystone Victory quality, screw back and bezel case, with engraved border and back. Rigid bow.

$20.00

(7) 568—White $6.50
569—Green 6.50

Keystone Victory quality, screw back and bezel case, with engraved border and back. Rigid bow.

$20.00

(8) 570—White $5.80
571—Green 5.80

Keystone Victory quality, screw back and bezel case, with engraved border and plain Butler back. Rigid bow.

(Cuts shown are exact reproductions, photographed directly from the goods.)

New $10.00
Mint $7.50
Fine $5.00

① 615—$2.50

Keystone nickeloid, 12 size screw back and bezel case with engraved border and back.

1929 C. A. KIGER

② 616—$2.50

Keystone nickeloid, 12 size screw back and bezel case, with engraved border and plain Butler back.

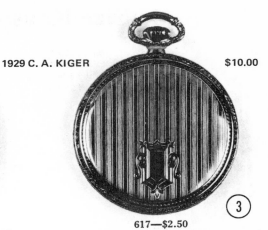

$10.00

③ 617—$2.50

Keystone nickeloid, 12 size screw back and bezel case, with engraved border and back.

Mint $20.00
New $30.00

④ 618—$3.80

Keystone Crescent nickeloid, 16 size, swing ring dust-proof pendant, with gilded reflector. Plain polish case.

THERE IS STILL A LOT OF THESE NEW NICKELOID CASES AROUND AND I THINK THE STAR WATCH CASE COMPANY AT LUDINGTON, MICHIGAN IS STILL MAKING THEM IN 10—12 AND 16 SIZE. BE CAREFUL ABOUT BUYING NEW CASES THAT TAKE A SWISS STYLE STEM. YOU CAN IDENTIFY THEM BY THE FACT THAT THEY DO NOT COME WITH A STEM. THE STEM IS PART OF THE WATCH AND IS RELEASED WITH A DENTENT SCREW. ALL OF THE CASES SHOWN IN THIS BOOK FIT STANDARD SIZE AMERICAN MOVEMENTS.

New $30.00
Mint $20.00
Fine $10.00
Good $2.00

⑤ 619—$2.00

Keystone nickeloid, 18 size screw back and bezel, plain polish case.

12 and 16 Size Keystone Nickeloid Cases

Mint $20.00

⑥ 620—$2.50

Keystone nickeloid, 16 size screw back and bezel case, with engraved border and back.

New $30.00
Mint $20.00
Fine $10.00
Good $2.00

⑦ 621—$3.80

Keystone nickeloid, 16 size heavy duty screw back and bezel, knurled border, plain polish case.

Mint $20.00

⑧ 622—$2.50

Keystone nickeloid, 16 size screw back and bezel case, with engraved border and plain Butler back.

(Cuts shown are exact reproductions, photographed directly from the goods.)

New $65.00
Mint $40.00
Fine $15.00
Good $3.00

①

572—White $18.00
573—Green 18.00

Keystone Boss 14k. gold filled screw back and
bezel case with engraved border and fancy
etched back.

Mint
$40.00

②

574—White $18.00
575—Green 18.00

Keystone Boss 14k. gold filled screw back and
bezel case with engraved border and fancy
etched back.

Mint $40.00

③

576—White $18.00
577—Green 18.00

Keystone Boss 14k. gold filled screw back and
bezel case with engraved border and fancy
etched back.

C. A. KIGER — 1929

New $75.00
Mint $50.00
Fine $20.00
Good
$3.00

④

578—White $19.10
579—Green 19.10

Keystone Boss 14k. gold filled screw back and
bezel, dust proof. Heavy railroad model case
with knurl bezel and back. Fancy etched.

COLLECTORS OF RAILROAD
WATCHES ARE LOOKING HARD
FOR MINT AND FACTORY NEW
CASES FOR THEIR PRIZE MOVE-
MENTS. THESE CASES SHOWN
IN THIS 1929 SECTION ARE
HIGH QUALITY AND ARE TRULY
BEAUTIFUL. MORE OFTEN
THAN NOT THE CASE IS WORTH
MORE THAN THE MOVEMENT
THERE ARE ACTUALLY
HUNDREDS OF MOVEMENTS
THAT COULD BE MADE TO
RUN THAT ARE NOT IN CASES.

Mint
$50.00

⑤

580—White $19.10
581—Green 19.10

Keystone Boss 14k. gold filled screw back and
bezel, dust proof. Heavy railroad model case
with knurl bezel and back. Fancy etched.

Mint $50.00

⑥

582—White $19.10
583—Green 19.10

Keystone Boss 14k. gold filled screw back and
bezel, dust proof. Heavy railroad model case
with knurl bezel and back. Fancy engraved.

$50.00

⑦

584—White $17.70
585—Green 17.70

Keystone Boss 14k. gold filled screw back
and bezel, dust proof. Heavy railroad model
case with knurl bezel and back. Engine turned.

$50.00

⑧

586—White $16.40
587—Green 16.40

Keystone Boss 14k. gold filled screw back and
bezel, dust proof. Heavy railroad model case,
with knurl bezel and back. Plain Butler finish.

(Cuts shown are exact reproductions, photographed directly from the goods.)

NEW $65.00
Mint $40.00
Fine $15.00
Good $3.00

$40.00

$40.00

①

②

③

588—$11.70

Keystone Boss 10k. yellow gold filled, screw back and bezel case, with engraved border and back.

589—$11.70

Keystone Boss 10k. yellow gold filled, screw back and bezel case, with engraved border and back.

590—$11.70

Keystone Boss 10k. yellow gold filled, screw back and bezel case, with engraved border and back.

1929 C. A. KIGER

New $75.00
Mint $50.00
Fine $20.00
Good $3.00

$50.00

ANY 16 SIZE SOLID 14K GOLD CASE LIKE THE ONE SHOWN ON THIS PAGE WOULD BE WORTH $150.00 to $250.00. MORE THAN GOLD FILLED DEPENDING ON WEIGHT AND CONDITION. MOST ANY 16S OF RR CASE IN SOLID GOLD MINT CONDITION IS NOW WORTH ABOUT $200.00 to $300.00

④

591—$13.70

Keystone Boss 10k. yellow gold filled, screw back and bezel, dust proof case, with knurl bezel and engraved back. Heavy railroad model.

⑤

592—$13.70

Keystone Boss 10k. yellow gold filled, screw back and bezel, dust proof case, with knurl bezel and engraved back. Heavy railroad model.

$50.00

$50.00

$50.00

⑥

593—$13.70

Keystone Boss 10k. yellow gold filled, screw back and bezel, dust proof case, with knurl bezel and engraved back. Heavy railroad model.

⑦

594—$13.00

Keystone Boss 10k. yellow gold filled screw back and bezel, dust proof case. Heavy railroad model, with knurl bezel and back. Engine turned.

⑧

595—$11.70

Keystone Boss 10k. yellow gold filled screw back and bezel, dust proof case. Plain polish and Butler back, with knurl bezel and back. Heavy railroad model.

(Cuts shown are exact reproductions, photographed directly from the goods.)

16 Size Keystone Victory   Quality Cases

New $35.00
Mint $20.00
Fine $10.00
Good $2.00

①

596—White $7.10
597—Green 7.10

Keystone Victory quality screw back and bezel case, with engraved border and back.

$20.00

②

598—White $7.10
599—Green 7.10

Keystone Victory quality screw back and bezel case, with engraved border and back.

$20.00

③

600—White $6.50
601—Green 6.50

Keystone Victory quality screw back and bezel case, with engraved border and plain Butler back.

$20.00

④

602—White $7.10
603—Green 7.10

Keystone Victory quality screw back and bezel case, with engraved border and back.

I HAVE USED THESE 1929 C. A. KIGER CO, KC MO. CATALOG PAGES BECAUSE IT BEST REPRESENTS THE 1915 TO 1950 COMMON UNITED STATES OPEN FACE POCKET WATCH DESIGNS USED FOR THAT PERIOD. MANY OTHER COMPANIES MADE AND SOLD GOOD HIGH QUALITY CASES DURING THIS PERIOD AND WOULD BE WORTH ABOUT THE SAME MONEY.

$20.00

⑤

604—White $7.10
605—Green 7.10

Keystone Victory quality screw back and bezel case, with engraved border and back.

1929 C. A. KIGER

New $45.00
Mint $25.00
Fine $10.00
Good $3,00

⑥

606—White $7.80
607—Green 7.80
608—Yellow 7.80

Keystone Victory quality screw back and bezel case. Heavy dust-proof pendant, with engraved border and back.

$25.00

⑦

609—White $7.80
610—Green 7.80
611—Yellow 7.80

Keystone Victory quality screw back and bezel case. Heavy dust-proof pendant, with engraved border and back.

$25.00

⑧

612—White $7.10
613—Green 7.10
614—Yellow 7.10

Keystone Victory quality screw back and bezel case. Heavy dust-proof pendant, with engraved border and Butler back.

(Cuts shown are exact reproductions, photographed directly from the goods.)

By permission of Mr. William L. Scolnik I have reproduced exactly, without any additions or deletions, his current watch catalog of today 1-6-76. Mr. Scolnik is a very well known rare watch dealer and is a very busy man engaged every day in all aspects of buying, selling and appraising collectible watches, and would welcome a call or visit from you. "PLEASE" do not call him to find out the identity of your watch or how much it is worth.

ROY EHRHARDT

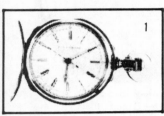

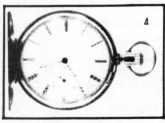

S-1. ELGIN HUNTING CASED SWEEP SECOND WATCH. 16s. 4th model, 3/4 plate movement #926459. Ca. 1881. Gold/Gold filled box case. Sweep center seconds movements are rare in American watches. $175.

S-2. GOLD HUNTING CASED MINUTE REPEATER. High quality fully jewelled movement, 46mm. Slide repeat, Swiss, stemwind/set. 14Kt case. $975.

S-3. SILVER CASED MINUTE REPEATER. Very attractive engraved Art Nouveau case. 45mm Swiss movement, lever set. Extremely attractive. $865.

S-4. GOLD HUNTING CASED WATCH BY ALFRED JURGENSEN. 35mm (6s) extremely high quality movement. Case, movement and dial signed. Engine turned 18KT case. $265.

S-5. WOMAN'S GOLD QUARTER REPEATER. 29mm, keywind/keyset Swiss movement. Cuvette signed A. Montandon. 18KT case beautifully engraved. With a small gold lapel chain. An extremely small and attractive repeater $975.

S-6. SILVER REPOUSSE PAIR CASED HALF QUARTER REPEATER. 18th C. English inner case, pierced and engraved. 32mm movement signed *Valentin*. Strikes half quarters on a bell or will dumb repeat by means of a button in the bezel. Pierced outer case. $985.

S-7. GOLD AND ENAMEL HUNTING CASED WATCH. 35mm Geneva bar movement. Cuvette signed *E. Favre Perret, Locle*. Keywind/keyset. 18KT case in new, mint condition. Split stem. Exceptionally attractive. $525.

S-8. MINIATURE GOLD HUNTING CASED WATCH. 20mm (14/0s) movement. Stemwind pinset. Gold hands, 18KT engraved case. An exceptionally small hunting cased watch. Excellent condition. $325.

NOT ILLUSTRATED

S-9. AN UNUSUAL 5 MINUTE SILVER HUNTING CASED REPEATER. A small button on the rim of the case activates, when pushed, a clockwatch type train causing the repeater to operate. A very clever, unusual repeating arrangement. 3/4 plate jewelled, good quality movement. $885.

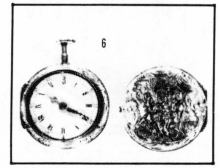

A CATALOG OF
WATCHES

WILLIAM L. SCOLNIK
ANTIQUARIAN HOROLOGIST

FOR SALE

WHEN VISITING NEW YORK CITY, PLAN TO STOP AND SEE ME. THE SHOP IS LOCATED AT 1001 SECOND AVENUE AT 53rd STREET, NEW YORK, N.Y. 10022

SHOP HOURS
TUESDAY THROUGH SATURDAY 12 - 5
SATURDAY AND MONDAY BY APPOINTMENT

MAIL ADDRESS
36 Paramus Road
Paramus, N.J. 07652

TELEPHONES:
(201) 843-2610
    AFTER 7pm & WEEKENDS
(212) 355-1160
    WEEKDAYS UNTIL 6pm

A SUPERB PATEK PHILIPPE PERPETUAL CALENDAR, SPLIT SECOND CHRONOGRAPH, MINUTE REPEATING WATCH, WITH MOON PHASES AND CHRONOGRAPH REGISTER. Described by Patek Philippe as the "Grande Complication", it is generally conceded by collectors that these watches represent the height of modern horological practice.

This watch is in new condition and is accompanied by a letter stating that the piece was started in December of 1921 and finished in October 1927, almost 6 years later. The movement is 19 ligne, 39 jewels, and the 18KT gold case weighs over 81 grams.

A complicated Patek watch is perhaps the finest and most satisfying horological investment one can make, and this exceptional piece would enhance any collection.

AN UNUSUAL GOLD DISAPPEARING AUTOMATON WATCH. When the pendent is pressed, two articulated silver cherubs appear on either side of the father time figure, and beat out the hours and the quarters on his scythe and staff. When they are finished, they swiftly disappear to the side.

The 58mm movement is a continental, full plate verge fusee type. The dial is gold with an offset enamel chapter and enamel numerals set on a guilloche centre. Automaton watches are found with much less frequency in today's market, and this is an unusually interesting one.

125

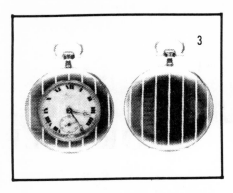  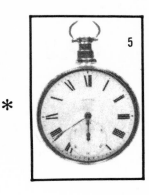

3. GOLD AND ENAMEL ART DECO WATCH. 18KT case engraved with small diamond pattern, and enamelled with white thin stripes. High quality Swiss movement. Very thin case tapering at the edges. Stemwind, stemset move ment. A very elegant watch. $325

4. EARLY 18th CENTURY GOLD REPOUSSE PAIR CASED WATCH. The heavy outer gold case in fine condition. The inner case of gold also, with a 35mm verge/fusee movement signed *Hen(ton) Brown, London*. Silver, diamond capped balance cock. In mint condition.

5. 18KT GOLD PAIR CASED RACK LEVER WATCH. 45mm fusee movement with maintaining power. Large window jewels in the plates. Jewelled pallets with counter balance. Steel balance. Movement signed *Alexander and Co., London*. Ca. 1820. In fine condition. An exceptional example of the rack lever movement. $835.

6. 18th CENTURY REPOUSSE PAIR CASED WATCH WITH CHATELAINE. Silver gilt cases. 42mm movement, verge/fusee, signed *Jn. May, London*. Movement profusely engraved. Bridged balance cock. With an attractive gilt chatelaine. $685.

7. 18th CENTURY PAIR CASED COACH WATCH. Oversize 90mm movement, verge/ fusee, signed *Wm. Mould, London*. Center seconds. Eccentric chapters showing hours and minutes and date. Outer case set with brilliants surrounding the dial, and with a multi colored enamel on the back. Exceptionally attractive. $3600.

8. MULTI-DIAL 8 DAY WATCH. Hebdomas type visible escapement 41mm movement. Center seconds. Three dials showing time in three different cities. Pinset. $385.

9. HUNTING CASED CHINESE DUPLEX. Keywind, keyset. 47mm jewelled duplex movement. Gilt case (marked 18KT!) Signed *L. Breting, Geneva* on the cuvette. Silvered, profusely engraved movement. Center seconds. Duplex movements in closed cases are unusual.

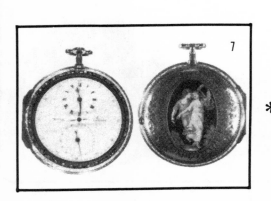 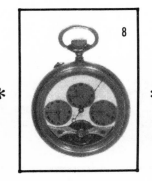 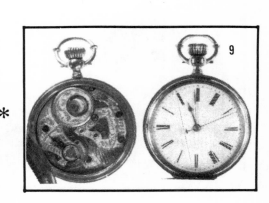

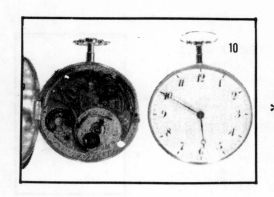  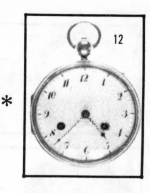

10. GOLD QUARTER REPEATING MUSICAL WATCH. 48mm movement, chased and engraved. Polished steel repeating work is exposed on the back plate (!). An exceptionally well made piece with disc type musical movement playing automatically on the hour or at will. Unusual automatic music governor speed compensation. Cuvette signed *Dubois & Comp.* and dated 1822. $3375.

11. SWISS ENAMEL REPEATER WITH CHRONOGRAPH. Silver gilt case with enamels front and back set with pearls. 45mm quarter repeating jewelled lever movement. Signed on the cuvette, *Jack Watch Factory, Chaux-de-Fonds.* Center sweep flyback chronograph with subsidiary constant seconds. Exhibition back. $2250.

12. SILVER HOUR REPEATING CLOCKWATCH. Two train 51mm verge. Continental type full plate movement. Automatically striking the hours and half hours. The repeat train can be activated by a button set in the pendent. Dial and cuvette signed *Breguet et Fils a Paris.* $1975.

13. GOLD OPEN FACE MINUTE REPEATER BY PATEK PHILIPPE. 38mm movement with 31 jewels and 8 adjustments. Signed on the cuvette and movement *Patek Philippe #156949.* 18KT gold Patek case with concealed hinge. An exceptionally fine piece. $2200.

14. LADIES SIZE GOLD DEMI HUNTER MINUTE REPEATER. Highly jewelled 27mm movement, probably Patek, signed *Tiffany & Co.* on the dial, cuvette and movement, dated 1885. 18KT case. Black enamelled outer case chapter ring. This watch is in new condition. $3875.

15. GOLD GRUEN MINUTE REPEATER. A rare American Market repeater made for the Gruen Watch Co. 27 jewel movement with 6 adjustments. 14KT case and gold double sunk dial marked *Gruen Watch Co. #50584.* Subsidiary seconds. $1750.

16. GOLD DUDLEY MASONIC WATCH. Beautifully engraved 18KT case with exhibition back, displaying the gilt movement laid out in the form of Masonic Emblems. Raised silvered bible. 19 jewel movement #4841. In new condition. $1075.

* * *

ALL OF THE WATCHES IN THIS CATALOG ARE GUARANTEED TO BE AS DESCRIBED. ALL WATCHES HAVE BEEN REPAIRED WHERE NECESSARY AND ARE RUNNING. I DON'T SELL WATCHES AS IS UNLESS I SPECIFICALLY STATE SO.

17. GOLD HUNTING CASED QUARTER REPEATER WITH CHRONOGRAPH. 18KT case. Jewelled 44mm move· ment. Slide repeat, button activated chronograph. Stem wind, lever set. $735.

18. GOLD HUNTER CASED WATCH BY ASSMAN. 18KT case. Gold double sunk dial signed *J. Assman, Glashutte I / Sachsen*. Movement 41mm fully jewelled with diamond end cap on the cock. #21230. A superb watch in mint condition.

19. GOLD HUNTING CASED QUARTER REPEATER BY HENRY CAPT. Extra heavy 18KT case. Movement and case signed, #31429, and marked *demi chronometre*. 31 jewel, 45mm Swiss movement of the highest quality. Exhibition back under the back cover. $2550.

20. GOLD OPEN FACE ENAMEL LADIES WATCH. Fully jewelled Swiss anchor movement, 21mm. Stemwind, pinset. 18KT case beautifully enamelled and set with stones. In mint condition. $425.

21. MINIATURE GOLD DEMI HUNTER 18th CENTURY VERGE WATCH. 22mm Continental fusee movement. 18KT case, original gold hands. Rare small size. $645.

22. SWISS WATCH WITH MOCK PENDULUM. 44mm lever movement. Exhibition back over movement. Mock pendulum is seen moving in an aperture below the dial. Attractive multi color dial. Stemwind, pinset. Late 19th Century. $375.

23. GOLD HUNTING CASED ENAMELLED LADIES WATCH. 25mm jewelled Swiss movement. Front is enamelled with a child holding a hoop and a bird flying through it, surrounded with enamel flowers set with brilliants. $325.

24. GOLD HUNTING CASED LADIES ENAMELLED WATCH. Stemwind, pinset 29mm jewelled cylinder movement by *Vacheron, Geneve*. 18KT gold engraved case with black enamelled covers set with brilliants in a flower pattern. Extremely attractive. $395.

24A. LADIES SIZE GOLD HUNTING CASED MINUTE REPEATER. Highest quality fully jewelled movement. 18KT case. Dial, movement and case marked *Tiffany & Co*. 28mm (3/o) movement probably by Patek Philippe. An extremely nice piece in a rare size. $2775.

* * *

A TELEPHONE CALL WILL RESERVE YOUR PURCHASE.
(212) 355-1160 DAYS ☀ (201) 843-2610 EVENINGS

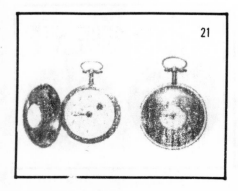

25. GOLD OPEN FACE 5 MINUTE REPEATER. 40mm Swiss jewelled lever movement. 14 kt. case. Slide repeat. Dial marked Geneva. Stemwind, stemset movement. A late attractive repeater. $685.

26. 18KT GOLD OPEN FACE 19TH CENTURY SWISS WATCH. Gold engraved dial. Beautifully engraved case and bow. Jewelled lever movement, 43mm. Cuvette signed *James Guedin, Geneva*. Keywind, keyset. An extremely nice watch. $345

27. GOLD OPEN FACE ENGLISH LADIES WATCH. Attractively engraved case. 33mm full plate movement signed *W. Potts and Sons, London*. 18kt. case. $235

28. UNUSUAL SKELETONIZED WATCH. Swiss 45mm fully jewelled lever movement completely and very delicately skeletonized, including the silver dial. Silver plated case. Stemwind, pinset movement, late]9th Century. Pieces of this type are most unusual and were produced generally by very skilled Swiss watchmakers at home as "extra" work. $425.

29. GOLD HUNTING CASED MINUTE REPEATER WITH CHRONOGRAPH. 47mm Swiss lever movement. Stemwind lever set. Button activated chronograph. 18kt smooth case. Silent repeat work governor. $1285.

30. GOLD HUNTING CASED MINUTE REPEATER BY LONGINES. Highest quality fully jewelled 46mm movement with wolfs tooth winding. Very heavy engine turned case. Cuvette and dial signed *Longines*. Stemwind, lever set. In fine condition. $2375.

31. SILVER AND TORTOISE SHELL CANE HANDLE WATCH. An early 19th Century verge watch specially made to fit a cane handle. The movement is laid out in a long and narrow manner. The watch is wound by turning the heavy engraved silver handle. It is set by a rather unusual arrangement on the tortoise shell body. An extremely interesting piece. $385.

31A. FINE GOLD HUNTING CASED CALENDAR WATCH. Heavy 18kt case. Exhibition back. Extremely high quality lever movement. Large ruby jewels in settings. Wolfs tooth winding. 50mm movement. Extra large compensated balance. Dials indicate day, date and seconds, with the month showing through an aperture at the top. A very elegant watch. $975.

* * *

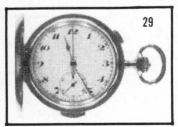

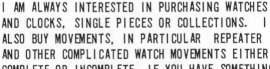

I AM ALWAYS INTERESTED IN PURCHASING WATCHES AND CLOCKS, SINGLE PIECES OR COLLECTIONS. I ALSO BUY MOVEMENTS, IN PARTICULAR REPEATER AND OTHER COMPLICATED WATCH MOVEMENTS EITHER COMPLETE OR INCOMPLETE. IF YOU HAVE SOMETHING TO SELL, PLEASE CONSIDER ME. I WILL TRAVEL TO BUY.

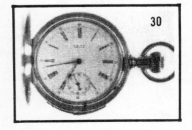 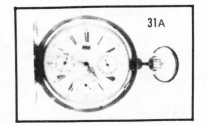 

32. 23 JEWEL WALTHAM VANGUARD. Stemwind, leverset, 16s movement adjusted to 6 positions. #25340418. 30 hour up/down indicator at 12. In a special exhibition case engraved Waltham Watch Company around the bezels front and back. $285.

33. GOLD HUNTING CASED AMERICAN WALTHAM WATCH. Crisp engine turned case with black monogram shield. 16s Hillside movement #1,739,777. Woerd's patent. $235.

34. GOLD OPEN FACE 23 JEWEL HOWARD WATCH. 14KT keystone case. 16s movement #1218960 adjusted to 5 positions and temperature. Porcelain dial marked *Howard*. In fine condition. $265.

35. GOLD HUNTING CASED WALTHAM WATCH. Heavy crisp engine turned case with blank monogram shield. 17 jewel movement #21839800. 14KT case. Dial marked *Waltham, USA*. Subsidiary seconds. $325.

36. WATERBURY LONGWIND TOURBILLON. Made by Benedict and Burnham, the movement rotates as the watch runs. Duplex escapement. Completely original throughout. $295.

 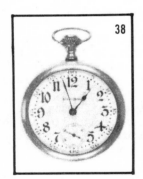   

37. GOLD HUNTING CASED ELGIN WATCH. 18s. G.M. Wheeler movement #2571048. Heavy, 14KT case profusely engraved. Blank monogram shield. An extremely attractive watch. $325.

38. 24 JEWEL BUNN SPECIAL. 18s damaskeened movement adjusted to 6 positions and temperature, #2019549. Double sunk dial marked *Illinois Watch Co.* Outer seconds chapter in red. Stemwind, lever set. Gold filled case. $475.

39. GOLD HUNTING CASED WALTHAM WATCH. Beautifully engraved 14KT case in fine condition. 16s Waltham 17 jewel movement #14007447. Stemwind, stemset. $245.

40. 21 JEWEL RAILROAD WATCH WITH UP/DOWN INDICATOR. Elgin 21 jewel. B. W. Raymond movement adjusted to 5 positions. G. F. case. 40 hour up/down indicator, subsidiary seconds. $290.

41. GOLD HUNTING CASED GERMAN WATCH. Fully jewelled high quality movement. 14KT case exquisitely engraved and engine turned. Stemwind, lever set. Subsidiary seconds dial. 18s movement. Cuvette marked *System Glashutte*. $325.

42. GOLD OPEN FACE WATCH BY VACHERON & SONSTANTINE. 21 jewel 38mm movement adjusted to 8 positions. 14KT case. Wolfs tooth winding. Dial and movement signed. Movement of extremely high quality. $335.

43. GOLD OPEN FACE CHRONOGRAPH BY AGASSIZ. An extremely high quality fully jewelled 42mm movement. Flyback chronograph, button activated. Constant subsidiary seconds. Gold dial. In new condition. $325.

44. HAMILTON RAILROAD WATCH. 21 jewel 18s movement adjusted to 5 positions. Model 992. $115.

45. WALTHAM MULTICOLOR GOLD CASED WATCH. 15 jewel 16s movement. Attractive 10KT gold case with raised 14KT multicolor overlay with stag head motif and flowers. Nice condition, showing some wear. $235.

46. BALL RAILROAD WATCH. 18s movement, 21 jewels adjusted to 5 positions. Marked "Official RR Standard" #B251179. Original ball open face case. In fine condition. $175.

47. SWISS CALENDAR WATCH. 45mm jewelled lever movement stemwind, pinset. Dial indicates day, date, month and moon phase. Subsidiary seconds. Blued steel case, gilt hands. $235.

47A SILVER PAIR CASED RACK LEVER WITH CALENDAR. Early 19th Century beautifully executed movement with a rack lever escapement. Large oversize jewels with diamond cap on the cock. Concentric calendar chapter. Dial & Movement are marked *Diego Helsby & Co. Liverpool.* A fine example! $365.

*

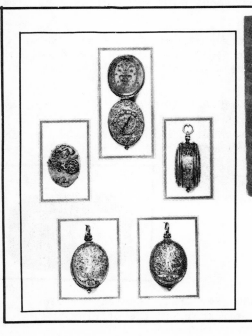

48. AN ORIGINAL COPY OF THE "CATALOGUE OF COLLECTION OF WATCHES, THE PROPERTY OF J. PIERPONT MORGAN.

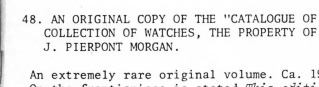

An extremely rare original volume. Ca. 1912. On the frontispiece is stated *This edition printed on hand-made paper consists of 45 copies, and is for private circulation only. This is copy #24.*

This copy is in mint original condition with the original slipcase. Over 300 pages of text and over 90 full page illustrations. $3875.

ONE OF THE NUMEROUS FULL PAGE HIGHLY DETAILED PLATES OF WATCHES IS SHOWN ILLUSTRATED ON THE LEFT.

  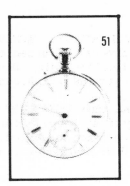  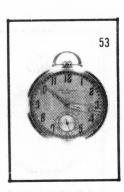

49. OVERSIZE CALENDAR WATCH WITH A SILVER REPOUSSE CARRYING CASE. 57mm jewelled lever movement with an exhibition back. Attractive decorated dial showing day, date, moon phase month and seconds. Stemwind, pinset. Blued steel case. $335.

50. GOLD O.F. WATCH BY JULES JURGENSEN. 41mm movement fully jewelled and of extremely high quality. Silvered dial with applied numerals. White gold case. Ca. 1920. $185.

51. GOLD O.F. QUARTER REPEATER. High quality fully jewelled movement with wolfs tooth winding. Stemwind, pinset. Cuvette signed *Allard Rousseau a Roubaix, 1864*. Slide repeat. A very high quality repeater. $675.

52. SILVER CASED ENGLISH LEVER WITH UP/DOWN INDICATOR. Fusee lever movement of excellent quality. 30 hour up/down indicator at 12, subsidiary seconds at 6. Dial and movement signed *James Gilchrist, Irvine*. Keywind, keset movement. Heavy silver case. Ca. 1860. Fusee lever watches with indicators are quite rare. $385.

53. GOLD O.F. WATCH BY JULES JURGENSEN. Fine quality stemwind, stemset movement, 12s, 21 jewels adjusted to 10 (!) positions. Plain 18KT Jurgensen case. Silver dial with applied gold numerals. Ca. 1920. Matching case and movement numbers. In fine condition with the original Jurgensen box. $335.

54. SILVER JUMP HOUR, RETROGRADE MINUTE WATCH. Stylized art case. Silvered dial with an aperture for the hour, and the minute chapter running from 9 to 3. When the minute hand reaches 60 it flys back to 0 as the hour changes. Subsidiary seconds at 6. Jewelled Swiss lever movement, stemwind pinset. $390.

55. SILVER HUNTING CASED 5 MINUTE REPEATER WITH AN UNUSUAL REPEAT MECHANISM. A button on the rim of the watch at the 12 position activates, when pushed, a clockwatch like train causing the repeater to operate. The repeat mechanism is wound when the watch is wound. It is a very clever, unusual repeating arrangement. Crisp engine turned case. 3/4 plate jewelled lever movement of good quality. $875.

S4. GOLD O.F. WATCH IN ITS ORIGINAL TORTOISE SHELL CASE. Key wind, key set jewelled movement, very thin. Engraved back and bow. 43mm. movement. In the original attractive octagon shaped box with the spare crystal. 18KT case. $275.

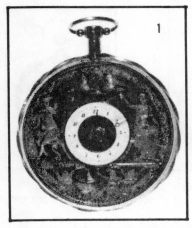

1. ELEGANT GOLD SKELETONIZED AUTOMATON WATCH. Quarter repeating on 3 gongs. Three gold figures strike bells with the repeat. Fancy 18kt gold case with large engraved sunburst back. Verge/fusee movement, 53mm. Cuvette signed *Breguet N. 3865*. Double glass front. $3875.

2. AN EXCEPTIONAL PERPETUAL CALENDAR, MINUTE REPEATING, SPLIT SECOND CHRONOGRAPH WITH REGISTER. Signed *Audemar* in two places on the movement. Heavy gold 18kt case. Full perpetual calendar with Moon Phase. The movement is fully jewelled and beautifully finished. A fine watch in every respect.

3. A RARE, GOLD, GRUEN MINUTE REPEATER. 41mm movement. 14kt O.F. case marked *Gruen Watch Co. #50584*. Movement with 27 jewels and 6 adjustments engraved Gruen Watch Co. Gold double sunk dial marked Gruen. Subsidiary seconds. Excellent condition. $1975.

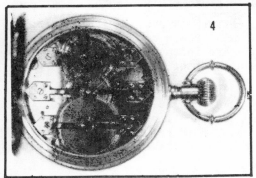

4. AN EXCEEDINGLY UNUSUAL GOLD HUNTING CASE WATCH BY *GIRARD PERREGAUX*. Three bar movement with a Tourbillon Detent escapement. In fine condition. Cuvette signed *Girard Perregaux*, *Chaux de Fonds*, Chronometre Tourbillon.

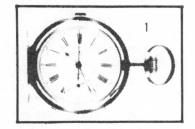
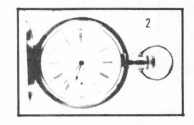

S1. GOLD HUNTING CASED MINUTE REPEATING CHRONOGRAPH. Heavy 18KT engine turned case showing no wear! Highly jewelled 48mm movement, beautifully finished. Wolfs tooth winding. Dial and cuvette signed *Qte. Salter*. Blank monogram shield. Stemwind, lever set. This watch is in exceptional condition. $1975.

S2. GOLD HUNTING CASED WATCH BY VACHERON & CONSTANTIN. 43mm movement of the highest quality. Heavy 18KT case. Dial and movement both signed. Exhibition back under the gold cuvette. Stem wind, lever set. Ca. 1884. A superior watch in every respect. $775.

S3. GOLD HUNTING CASED WATCH. English half plate movement with jewels in settings. Stem wind, pinset movement, 43mm. Movement and dial signed *J. W. Benson*, *Special Warrents to the Queen & The Prince of Wales*. Smooth 18KT case. A fine English Watch. $275.

S5. SILVER CASED O.F. QUARTER REPEATER. 49mm. verge/fusee key wind key set movement. Silver engraved dial. Movement signed *Berthoud* on the cuvette. $575.

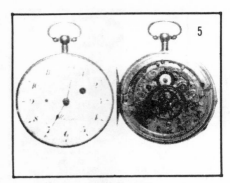

5. 18TH CENTURY GOLD QUARTER REPEATER. 18kt engine turned case with reeded sides. 46mm verge/fusee movement. Steel polished cock, blued regulator. Dial, movement and cuvette signed *Meuron*. $985.

6. BEAUTIFULLY ENGRAVED GOLD HUNTING CASE CHRONOMETER. Movement with helical hairspring and detent escapement, of very high quality. Crisp, heavy engraved case in mint condition. An excellent piece in every respect. $1225.

7. GOLD O.F. MINUTE REPEATER. Extremely high quality fully jewelled movement. 18kt case. 36mm movement. Cuvette and dial signed *Haas, Neveux & Co., Geneva*. Mint condition. $1800.

8. IVORY CASED QUARTER REPEATER. 18th Century, 36mm verge/fusee movement signed *Ch. Moricand, Geneva*. Push repeat on a single gong. With a matching ivory chain carved from one piece. Extremely unusual. $885.

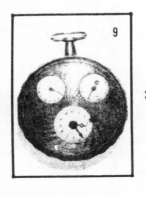

9. SILVER CONTINENTAL VERGE/FUSEE CALENDAR WATCH. 47mm movement. Silver case. Silver Guilloche dial set with 3 enamel chapters showing day, date and time. Mid 18th century. $565.

10. SILVER CAPTAINS WATCH. The outer Turkish dial indicates time by the long set of Hands, the inner Roman dial showing time on the smaller set of Hands. Hands are independently set. Jewelled Swiss lever movement. An unusual form of the double time watch. $375.

11. A FINE GOLD INDEPENDENT SECONDS WATCH. The cuvette signed *E. & F. Droz, Locle*. Two train detached lever 23 jewel movement with an unusual layout. 18kt case, gold engraved dial. Jumping seconds. Gold and enamel cuvette! An extremely fine, high quality watch. $590.

11a. INGERSOLL PARIS EXPOSITION WATCH. Attractive multicolor dial bearing the portraits of 12 famous personages of 1900 in place of the numbers. Dial marked *"Souvenir Exposition Universelle, Paris 1900, Ingersoll & Bro."*. Fully engraved back restates the same information. With the original silver repousse and leather travelling case. $275

*

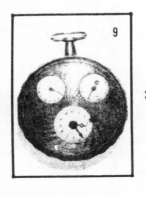
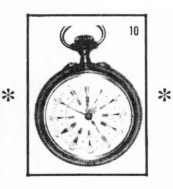

12. SILVER ENGLISH WORLD TIME WATCH. Late 19th Century, Superb quality, 3/4 plate lever movement, 48mm. Keywind, keyset. 24 hour porcelain dials showing the time (day/night) in 43 cities including all of the major U.S. cities. Sweep center seconds. Heavy sterling case. Center procelain dial rotates. Extremely attractive and unusual. $985.

13. 19TH CENTURY AUTOMATON REPEATER WATCH WITH EROTIC SCENE. Silver gilt case. Signed on the movement and dial *Breguet & fils*. Keywind/set, verge/fusee movement. Under the back cover, set into the cuvette, the gold figures of a man and woman in the traditional (?) positions are set in motion by the repeat train. Absolutely original! $1725.

14. GOLD CONTINENTAL MUSICAL QUARTER HOUR REPEATER. Early 19th Century. Disc type musical movement plays automatically on the hour or at will. Push pendant repeat on two gongs. 55mm movement. In excellent condition. $2650.

15. TIFFANY & CO. SPLIT SECOND CHRONOGRAPH. 18kt heavy gold case marked Tiffany as is the movement and dial. 45mm movement of the very highest quality. Double timing hands, constant seconds dial. This watch is in new condition. Ca. 1910. $450.

16. ORNATELY SKELETONIZED GOLD QUARTER REPEATER. Gold and enamel scalloped chapter ring. The entire movement including the top plate is skeletonized and engraved exposing all of the repeat work and the time train. 46mm verge/fusee movement. Gold hands. 18kt case. In fine condition. $1700.

17. SILVER PAIR CASED QUARTER REPEATER. Outer case of silver and tortoise shell. Inner case of silver, pierced and chased. Gold hands. Verge/fusee movement striking on a single bell. Mid 18th century. German.

18. SILVER WATCH WITH VISIBLE CENTER BALANCE. A very unusual 19th century French watch signed *L'Abeille*. The balance is visible in the center of the dial. Hands move on rings around the balance. Pinset, stemwind. Very unusual. $485.

* * *

I AM ALWAYS INTERESTED IN PURCHASING WATCHES AND CLOCKS, EITHER SINGLE PIECES OR COLLECTIONS. I ALSO BUY MOVEMENTS, IN PARTICULAR REPEATER AND OTHER COMPLICATED WATCH MOVEMENTS COMPLETE OR INCOMPLETE. PLEASE CONSIDER ME IF YOU SHOULD HAVE SOMETHING TO SELL. I WILL TRAVEL TO BUY.

19. GOLD HUNTING CASED ASTRONOMICAL QUARTER REPEATER. Smooth 18kt case. Full calendar indicating Day, Date, Month and Moon Phase. Button activated chronograph, lever set. 47mm jewelled lever movement. $1725.

20. GOLD HUNTING CASED AUTOMATON QUARTER REPEATER. 14kt case. Two striking jacks in two color gold on the face hit bells when the repeater is activated. 24 hour dial with subsidiary seconds. Jewelled lever 52mm movement with exhibition back under the gold cuvette. Fine condition. $2945.

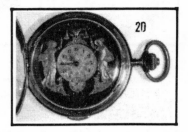

21. GOLD HUNTING CASED MINUTE REPEATER. Smooth heavy 18kt case. Dial, cuvette, and movement signed *Henry Sandoz, Le Locle* No. 731. Very high quality half plate silvered movement. Secret silver fraternal emblem on movement. 46mm. $1875.

22. DUPLEX CAPTAINS WATCH WITH VISIBLE PENDULUM. Keywind, keyset English duplex 45mm movement. Two independently set time dials. Second jumping center seconds. Moving pendulum visible in the lower portion of the dial. Dial and cuvette marked *Chronometer*. Silver gilt case. $625.

23. 19TH CENTURY SILVER GILT COMPASS WATCH. Marked on the dial and cuvette *Patent Compass Time Keeper, Jewelled in 23 (!) actions, Joseph French & Co., Liverpool.* Subsidiary seconds at 8, compass at 4. Keywind/set. 46mm lever movement. $165.

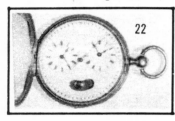

24. EARLY 19TH CENTURY REPOUSSE HUNTING CASED WATCH. Verge/fusee movement. French silver case with repousse scenes on both sides. Unusual bezel-less arrangement. 36mm movement. $235.

25. RARE MINIATURE CARIATIDE CASED CARRIAGE CLOCK. Beautifully cast and elaborately chased gilt case. In near mint condition with matching cariatide key. A fine example of a rare case style. $1125.

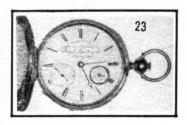

CHAINS & WATCHKEYS

K1. Large flat engraved gold filled key with rope edging. $35.

K2. Gold filled ratchet key set with a stone in the top. $30.

K3. Gold filled stone set key. $30.

K4. 18KT Gold filled ratchet key set with a caged stone. Excellent condition. $55.

K5. 18KT Gold and steel swivel key. Fair condition. $35.

K6. 18KT Gold swivel key. Engraved star top. Excellent condition. $55.

K7. 20KT Gold engraved stone set key. Excellent condition. $50.

K8. 18KT Gold ratchet key. $45.

K9. Heavy stone set gold filled key. $35.

K10. 14KT Gold stone set key. $45.

K11. 12KT Gold ratchet key. $45.

K12. Silver key with chain. Key flat engraved with Mason symbols. Late 18th Century. $95.

K13. Stone set, engraved gold filled swivel key. $30.

K14. Elaborately made gold filled key, engraved, with handle motif. Excellent. $50.

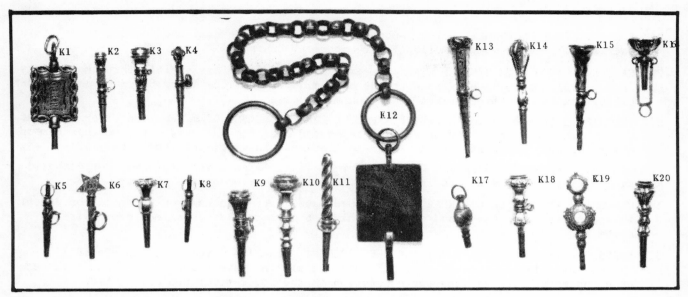

K15. Gold filled swivel key, uncut. With mounted stone. Good condition. $45.

K16. 18KT Gold key with double swivel elaborately engraved with large stone set in crown. $55.

K17. Gold filled ratchet type key. $35.

K18. Elaborate stone set, engraved key. $40.

K19. Two color gold key elaborately engraved, swivel type. $60.

K20. Stone set gold filled key very beautifully worked. $45.

K22. 13" 18KT Gold chain with enamelled Mason's emblem. Shows some wear. 15 dwt. $105.

K23. A beautiful double albert rope type 18KT chain. Excellent. 19 dwt. $145.

K26. 14KT Half albert. Excellent condition. Close link. 18 dwt. $125.

K27. Elaborate large link pinchbeck metal chain. Rope links with engraved studs on each link. 21" long. $135.

K30. 18KT Close link chain, smooth links, 12" long, 40 dwt. Excellent condition. Extremely attractive. $245.

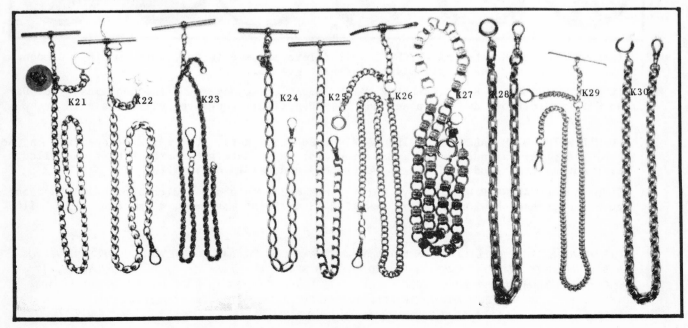

26. 8 DAY VISIBLE ESCAPEMENT WATCH. Subsidiary dials indicate date and seconds (which turn backwards!). Swiss 43mm jewelled lever movement. Gun metal case. $245.

27. CALENDAR WATCH WITH UNUSUAL DIAL. The day, date and month are visible thru small slots in the dial. Moon phase visible at the bottom. Good jewelled lever Swiss movement under exhibition back. Attractive gilt and gun metal case. $245.

28. OVERSIZE CALENDAR WATCH IN SILVER REPOUSSE CARRYING CASE. 57mm Jewelled lever movement with exhibition back. Attractive gilt decorated dial showing day, date, month and moon phase. Pinset, stemwind. Blued case. Repousse case in excellent condition. $345.

29. SILVER CASED CALENDAR WATCH. Good quality 15 jewel Swiss movement, 42mm. Perfect dial with automatic day and date indications. Subsidiary seconds at 6. Pinset. $185.

30. UNUSUALLY ATTRACTIVE CALENDAR WATCH. Blued case. Day, date and month indication appear in apertures. Moon phase and seconds dial at 6. 45mm pinset Jewelled lever Swiss movement. $215.

31. SWISS CALENDAR WATCH WITH "MYSTERY" ESCAPEMENT. Jewelled lever movement. Solid (!) balance visible in cutout at 6. Subsidiary dials indicate seconds and date. Balance wheel operates with no apparent connection to the movement. Blued case. $145.

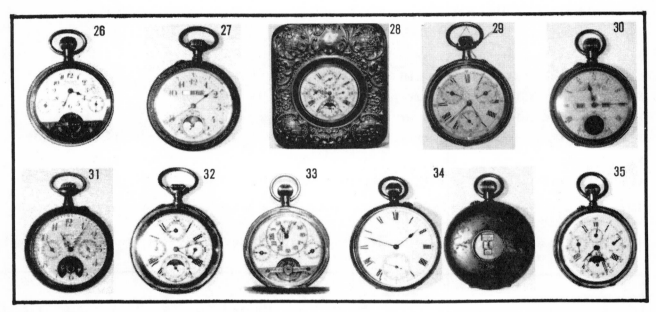

32. SILVER CASED SWISS CALENDAR WATCH. Jewelled lever movement. Day, date, month and moon phase indications. Heavy silver case. Pinset. $225.

33. SILVER HUNTING CASED 8 DAY CALENDAR WATCH. Visible escapement of the Hebdomas type. Day and date indications and sweep seconds (!). Beautifully engraved silver case in crisp condition. $365.

34. UNUSUAL WATCH WITH CALENDAR ON THE BACK. Blued steel case. Thru a glazed aperture on the back, a digital calendar gives indications for day, date and month. Pinset. Jewelled lever movement of good quality. An extremely unusual layout. $285.

35. SILVER CASED CALENDAR WATCH. Day, date, month and moon phase indications. Dial has some age cracks, case shows some wear. Jewelled lever Swiss movement. 43mm. Runs well. $165.

* * *

36. CONTINENTAL VERGE REPOUSSE CALENDAR WATCH. Early 19th Century. Keywind/ set fusee movement. Silver repousse case with scene of an erupting volcano on the back. Concentric calendar chapter on the dial. $265.

37. GOLD WALTHAM HUNTING CASED WATCH. 14KT keystone case. 15 jewel, 16 size movement #18899608. Beautifully engraved case. Excellent. $300.

38. OVERSIZE SILVER CASED CHINESE LEVER WATCH. Profusely engraved ornately cut bridges. Balance wheel with devils. Sweep center seconds. Nickeled top plate shows off movement beautifully. 60mm highly jewelled quality movement. $425.

39. OVERSIZE CALENDAR WATCH. Unusual dial layout. Moon phase and seconds bit at 3. Moon rises behind painted miniature village scene. Heavy nickel case. Swiss jewelled lever movement. Blue and gilt decorated dial. $290.

40. EXTREMELY RARE AMERICAN SILVER WATCH CHATELAINE. Central part pierced and engraved with horse and flowers. Containing two ornate silver keys (one uncut) and matching silver seal. Early 19th century. $650.

41. GOLD KEYWIND O. F. LADIES WATCH. Beautifully engine turned and engraved case. 29mm movement. Elegant and attractive. In mint condition. $235.

42. SILVER HUNTING CASED SPLIT SECOND CHRONOGRAPH. Highly jewelled, high quality 41mm movement. Heavy silver case. Pinset, stemwind. Two subsidiary dials indicate 30 minute register and constant seconds. $265.

43. SILVER LADIES RING WATCH. Jewelled Swiss lever movement. Stemwind, stemset. Set with brilliants around dial. Ca. 1900. $245.

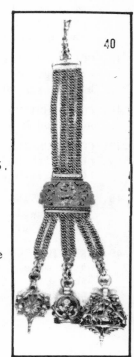

43A. A WALTHAM MULTICOLOR GOLD CASED WATCH. 16 S movement, 15 jewels. Attractive three color case with stag head motif on one side and flowers on the other. Nice condition showing slight wear. $235.

* * *

I AM PARTICULARLY INTERESTED IN PURCHASING STRIKING CARRIAGE CLOCKS, OR CARRIAGE CLOCKS WITH DECORATIVE CASES, ENAMELLED PANELS, OR UNUSUAL ESCAPEMENTS.

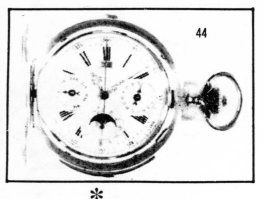 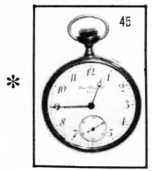 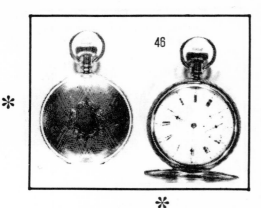

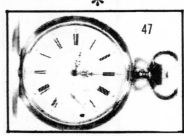 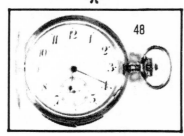

44. HIGH QUALITY GOLD HUNTING CASED ASTRONOMICAL MINUTE REPEATER. Fully jewelled 47mm Swiss movement of extremely high quality. 18Kt gold engine turned, heavy hunting case. Button activated chronograph. Subsidiary dials indicate day, date and moon phase with an aperture at 12 showing the month. Cuvette and movement signed *Clinton Ultra*. An extremely fine and attractive watch. $2650.

45. GOLD OPEN FACE PATEK PHILIPPE WATCH. 42mm movement of the highest quality. Wolfs tooth winding. Movement and dial signed *Patek Philippe & Co*. Heavy 14KT case with exhibition back. Exceptionally clean. $545.

46. GOLD HUNTING CASED E. HOWARD WATCH. Heavy crisp engine turned Howard 14KT case. Dog adjusted N size movement #221281. Near mint condition. $665.

47. GOLD HUNTING CASED CHRONOMETER. 14KT Engine turned case. 48mm Swiss chronometer movement with helical hairspring and detent escapement. Large window jewels in settings. Lever set. Subsidiary seconds. $785.

48. GOLD HUNTING CASED QUARTER REPEATER. Heavy 14KT case. Highest quality Swiss movement fully jewelled and with wolfs tooth winding. Slide repeat. 47mm movement. Smooth case with monogram. An exceptionally nice piece. $725.

49. SKELETONIZED SHELL WATCH BY GIRARD PERREGAUX. An attractive skeletonized watch made for the Shell Oil Co.in the 30's and lubricated with Golden Shell Oil. Black chapter ring with white roman numerals. An interesting and unusual advertising watch. $175.

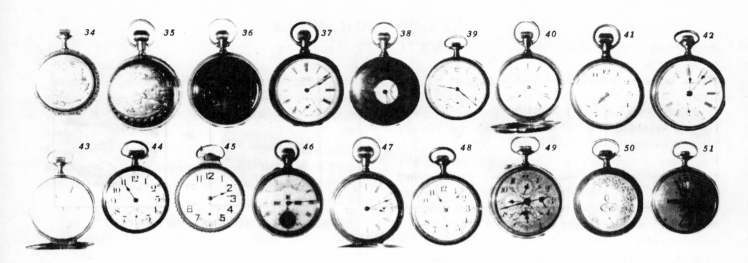

34. GOLD HUNTING CASED WALTHAM. 16s, 17 jewel movement #14007447. Crisp engraving, exceptionally clean watch. $295.

35. GOLD HUNTING CASED ILLINOIS. Heavy 14kt engraved case. 18s Full plate movement #1197290. Clean, completely original. $375.

36. GOLD HUNTING CASED WALTHAM. Heavy 14kt engraved case. 18s full plate movement #5950352, P.S. Bartlett. Lever set, near mint condition. $385.

37. RARE U.S. WATCH CO., WALTHAM, MASS. 18s, 3/4 plate, raised plate movement #5024. Woerd's Patent. Silver O. F. U.S. Watch Co., case. $245.

38. GOLD DEMI HUNTER WALTHAM. 18s. 14kt, heavy case. Numerals engraved around case opening. Clean. $340.

39. O. F. GOLD FILLED HAMILTON. 17 jewel movement, adjusted, Style 910. 12s, #1783131. Swing out case. $85.

40. GOLD HUNTING CASED WALTHAM. 17 jewel P.S. Bartlett movement, 16s #10544087. Heavy engine turned case, still crisp. $290.

41. SILVER O. F. WALTHAM. 16s movement #22990215. Gold inlaid locomotive on back, not worn. $90.

42. O. F. WALTHAM. 15 jewel, 18s full plate movement. #8611940. 20 year case. $75.

43. GOLD HUNTING CASED WALTHAM. 17 jewel, 16s movement #16842758. 14kt smooth case. $225.

44. WALTHAM O. F. WATCH. 21 jewel Riverside Maximus movement #9532873. Double sunk dial. G. F. case. $110.

45. ELGIN RAILROAD WATCH. 21 jewel, B. W. Raymond movement #27900046. O. F. gold filled railraod case. Invar balance. $115.

46. UNUSUAL CALENDAR WATCH. Day, date and month indications appear in apertures. Moon phase and seconds dial at 6. Swiss jewelled lever movement. Pinset 45mm. Gun metal case. $215.

47. GOLD HUNTER CASED PATEK PHILIPPE. 45mm movement of the highest quality. Engine turned 18kt case. Wolf's tooth winding. $700.

48. O. F. ROCKFORD. Gold filled 20 year case. 18s, 17 jewel movement #750824, beautifully finished. $105.

49. SWISS O.F. CALENDAR WATCH. Pinset 47mm movement. Exhibition back. Day, date, month and moon phase indications. Silvered dial, nickel case. $185.

50. SILVER CASED O.F. DIGITAL WATCH. 44mm Swiss movement. Attractively engraved case. Apertures showing jump hour and linear minutes. Subsidiary seconds dial. $245.

51. JUMPING HOUR, RETROGRADE MINUTE WATCH. The minute hand travels only in the upper half of the watch moving from "9" to "3" and then jumps back. The hour appears in an aperture. Jewelled lever movement marked Modernista. Silver gilt case. Curious and unusual. $310.

A CLEARING HOUSE FOR
WATCH NAMES

Watch manufacturers and importers, as well as distributors, make use of names instead of stock numbers to indicate particular styles. The names of these companies, together with their addresses and the key number assigned to each are listed below.

On pages 96 to 117 are arranged alphabetically the basic watch model names together with the key number which will identify the manufacturer, importer or distributor using this name. Two or more numbers following a name, indicate that it is in use by two or more different concerns.

In some cases certain names are used by various concerns both alone and also prefixed by the name of the

company or one of its general lines. Because of the tremendous number of names in the list, it was deemed advisable to eliminate these duplications, and show only the basic name. However, the following sixteen words, although used as prefixes, are not company or brand names but are an essential part of the basic names, and therefore, two-word names appear in the list under these prefixes:

American	Flying	Golden	King
Lady	Lord	Miss	National
Princess	Queen	Royal	Sky
Time	Ultra	Uncle Sam	Worlds

Key	Company Names and Addresses
1	Ace Watch Co., 10 W. 47th St., New York, N. Y.
2	Adams Watch, Inc., 150 Lafayette St., New York, N. Y.
3	Adels, L., Co., 64 W. 48th St., New York, N. Y.
4	Aeolian Watch Co., 93 Nassau St., New York, N. Y.
5	Aisenstein, Louis, & Bros., 630 Fifth Ave., New York, N. Y.
6	Akron Watch Co., 125 Canal St., New York, N. Y.
7	Alwin Watch Co., Inc., 154 Nassau St., New York, N. Y.
8	Americus Watch Co., 220 Bagley Ave., Detroit, Mich.
9	Aristo Import Co., 630 Fifth Ave., New York, N. Y.
10	Aristocrat Clock Co., 245 Fifth Ave., New York, N. Y.
11	Bayer, Pretzfelder & Mills, Inc., 15 Maiden Lane, New York, N. Y.
12	Becken, A. C., Co., 29 E. Madison St., Chicago, Ill.
13	Belmar Watch Co., 1015 Chestnut St., Philadelphia, Pa.
14	Benrus Watch Co., 200 Hudson St., New York, N. Y.
15	Blank, Henry, & Co., 19 Liberty St., Newark, N. J.
16	Blumstein, A, 37 W. 47th St., New York, N. Y.
17	Braude, Emil, & Sons, Inc., 29 E. Madison St., Chicago, Ill.
18	Brenet Watch Co., 266 W. 40th St., New York, N. Y.
19	Bulova Watch Co., 630 Fifth Ave., New York, N. Y.
20	Chase Watch Corp., 68 Nassau St., New York, N. Y.
21	Clinton Watch Co., 29 E. Madison St., Chicago, Ill.
22	Concord Watch Co., 10 W. 47th St., New York, N. Y.
23	Cornell Watch Co., 580 Fifth Ave., New York, N. Y.
24	Crawford Watch Co., 15 Maiden Lane, New York, N. Y.
25	Croton Watch Co., 48 W. 48th St., New York, N. Y.
26	Crysler Watch & Jewelry Co., 580 Fifth Ave., New York, N. Y.
27	Cypres Watch Co., 72 Bowery, New York, N. Y.
28	De Frece Watch Co., Inc., 48 W. 48th St., New York, N. Y.
29	Doric Watch Co., 580 Fifth Ave., New York, N. Y.
30	Ducummon, M., Co., 580 Fifth Ave., New York, N. Y.
31	Easton Watch Co., Baltimore & Liberty Sts., Baltimore, Md.
32	Ebel Watch Co., 665 Fifth Ave., New York, N. Y.
33	Elgin National Watch Co., Elgin, Ill.
34	Eterna Watch Co. of America, 580 Fifth Ave., New York, N. Y.
35	Evkob Watch Co., 41 Maiden Lane, New York, N. Y.
36	Goldin, Sidney S., 5 S. Wabash Ave., Chicago, Ill.
37	Goldsmith, Robert, 210 Post St., San Francisco, Cal.
38	Gotham Watch Co., Inc., 29 W. 47th St., New York, N. Y.
39	Gothic Jar Proof Watch Corp., 10 W. 47th St., New York, N. Y.
40	Graef, Jean R., Inc., 9 Rockefeller Plaza, New York, N. Y.
41	Gruen Watch Co., Time Hill, Cincinnati, Ohio.
42	Gsell, R., & Co., Inc., 15 W. 37th St., New York, N. Y.
43	Hampden Watch Co., 29 E. Madison St., Chicago, Ill.
44	Hamilton Watch Co., Lancaster, Pa.
45	Harman Watch Co., 22 W. 48th St., New York, N. Y.
46	Harvel Watch Co., 630 Fifth Ave., New York, N. Y.
47	Helbros Watch Co., 6 W. 48th St., New York, N. Y.
48	Hiller Jewelry Co., 304-09 Godchaux Bldg., New Orleans, La.
49	Hirsch, Emile S., 3 Maiden Lane, New York, N. Y.
50	Horwitz, H., Co., 36 S. State St., Chicago, Ill.
51	Horowitz & Son, Inc., 48 W. 48th St., New York, N. Y.
52	Hudson Watch Co., 17 John St., New York, N. Y.
53	Ingersoll-Waterbury Co., Division of Waterbury Clock Co., Waterbury, Conn.
54	Ingraham, E., Co., Bristol, Conn.
55	Invicta-Seeland, Inc., 580 Fifth Ave., New York, N. Y.
56	Jardur Import Co., 21 W. 19th St., New York, N. Y.
57	Jurgensen, Jules, Corp., 630 Fifth Ave., New York, N. Y.
58	Katz & Ogush, Inc., 33 W. 60th St., New York, N. Y.
59	Kelbert Watch Co., 608 Fifth Ave., New York, N. Y.
60	Klein Bros Co., 617 Vine St., Cincinnati, Ohio.
61	Kocher, Walter, 9 Rockefeller Plaza, New York, N. Y.
62	Lashof, Samuel, & Co., 700 Sansom St., Philadelphia, Pa.
63	Lauret Watch Co., 48 W. 48th St., New York, N. Y.
64	Lehman, Arthur, Watch Co., 209 Post St., San Francisco, Cal.
65	Lenga & Co., Inc., 9 Maiden Lane, New York, N. Y.
66	Lesse, S., & Sons, Inc., S. E. Cor. Chestnut & 8th Sts., Philadelphia, Pa.
67	Levitz, M., & Co., 133 N. Pearl St., Albany, N. Y.
68	Longines-Wittnauer Watch Co., 580 Fifth Ave., New York, N. Y.
69	Lorna Watch Co., Inc., 22 W. 48th St., New York, N. Y.
70	Louis Watch Co., Inc., 580 Fifth Ave., New York, N. Y.
71	Madison Watch Co., 99 Canal St., New York, N. Y.
72	Maire, O., Inc., 45 Lispenard St., New York, N. Y.
73	Manhattan Novelty Co., 263 Canal St., New York, N. Y.

Key	Company Names and Addresses
74	Manheimer, Louis, & Bros., Inc., 608 Fifth Ave., New York, N. Y.
75	Manheimer Watch Co., 55 E. Washington St., Chicago, Ill.
76	Marvin Watch Co., 580 Fifth Ave., New York, N. Y.
77	Masin Watch Co., Inc., 15 Maiden Lane, New York, N. Y.
78	Mead, M. A., & Co., 58 E. Washington St., Chicago, Ill.
79	Mehler, Erich W., 542 Fifth Ave., New York, N. Y.
80	Meylan, A. R. & J. E., 264 W. 40th St., New York, N. Y.
81	Micron Watch Corp., 9 Rockefeller Plaza, New York, N. Y.
82	Mido Watch Co. of America, 665 Fifth Ave., New York, N. Y.
83	Monarch Watch Co., 1 W. 47th St., New York, N. Y.
84	Morris, Norman M., Inc., 608 Fifth Ave., New York, N. Y.
85	Mt. Vernon Watch Co., Inc., 15 W. 37th St., New York, N. Y.
86	Movado Watch Agency, 610 Fifth Ave., New York, N. Y.
87	Muney, Wm. A., Inc., 52 W. 47th St., New York, N. Y.
88	National Jewelers Co., 155 Canal St., New York, N. Y.
89	Nivada Watch Corp., 599 Fifth Ave., New York, N. Y.
90	Normandie Watch Co., 71 Nassau St., New York, N. Y.
91	Oleet, Harold K., & Bro., 305 E. 47th St., New York, N. Y.
92	Ollendorff Watch Co., Inc., 26 W. 47th St., New York, N. Y.
93	Ostbye & Anderson, 627 First Ave., North, Minneapolis, Minn.
94	Ovis Watch Co., 230 Fifth Ave., New York, N. Y.
95	Parker Watch Co., 580 Fifth Ave., New York, N. Y.
96	Pastor Stop-Watch Co., 43 E. Main St., Waterbury, Conn.
97	Patek, Philippe & Co., 630 Fifth Ave., New York, N. Y.
98	Pathe Watch Co., 155 Nassau St., New York, N. Y.
99	Pierce Watch Co., Inc., 22 W. 48th St., New York, N. Y.
100	Plaut, Joseph M., 505 Walnut St., Cincinnati, Ohio.
101	Pond, A. H., Co., Inc., 214 S. Warren St., Syracuse, N. Y.
102	Racine, Jules, & Co., 20 W. 47th St., New York, N. Y.
103	Reliable Watch Co., 116 Nassau St., New York, N. Y.
104	Rima Watch Co., 15 Maiden Lane, New York, N. Y.
105	Rodman, Harry, 64 W. 48th St., New York, N. Y.
106	Rodman, S., Sons, 64 W. 48th St., New York, N. Y.
107	Rolex Watch Co., Inc., 580 Fifth Ave., New York, N. Y.
108	Rosen, Harry, 9 Maiden Lane, New York, N. Y.
109	Rosenthal, E. M., Jlry. Co., 702 H St., N.W., Washington, D. C.
110	Roxy Watch & Jewelry Co., 12 John St., New York, N. Y.
111	Royce Watch Co., 9 Rockefeller Plaza, New York, N. Y.
112	Sabin, Alexander, & Sons, Inc., 20 W. 47th St., New York, N. Y.
113	Savoy Watch Co., 62 W. 47th St., New York, N. Y.
114	Schein & Engel Co., 170 Broadway, New York, N. Y.
115	Schulz, James, 304 E. 45th St., New York, N. Y.
116	Schwob, L. A., 22 W. 48th St., New York, N. Y.
117	Segal, Ben, Co., 190 N. Well St., Chicago, Ill.
118	Seidman, Nathan, 173 Canal St., New York, N. Y.
119	Seltzer Bros., 80 Nassau St., New York, N. Y.
120	Semca Co., 160 Fifth Ave., New York, N. Y.
121	Sickles, Louis, 1015 Chestnut St., Philadelphia, Pa.
122	Silbert & Wainer, 622 Reynolds Bldg., Winston-Salem, N. C.
123	Silver, J. A., 865 Chapel St., New Haven, Conn.
124	Silverman, S., Co., 525 Walnut St., Cincinnati, Ohio.
125	Solomon, Saul L., 146 N. Prince St., Lancaster, Pa.
126	Soloway, J. M., 21-23 Maiden Lane, New York, N. Y.
127	Spurlock, J. J., 405 S. Hill St., Los Angeles, Cal.
128	Stein & Ellbogen Co., 55 E. Washington St., Chicago, Ill.
129	Stern, Edward L., & Co., Inc., 610 Fifth Ave., New York, N. Y.
130	Sussman & Medney, 65 Nassau St., New York, N. Y.
131	Swan Watch Co., Inc., 64 W. 48th St., New York, N. Y.
132	Tavannes Watch Co., Inc., 608 Fifth Ave., New York, N. Y.
133	Tilmore Watch Co., 134 S. 8th St., Philadelphia, Pa.
134	Tourneau, 431 Madison Ave., New York, N. Y.
135	United States Jewelry Co., 3 N. Liberty St., Baltimore, Md.
136	Vallette, Paul, Watch Co., Inc., 20 W. 47th St., New York, N. Y.
137	Walker Watch Co., 48 W. 48th St., New York, N. Y.
138	Waltham Watch Co., Waltham, Mass.
139	Watch & Jewelry Co., 106 S. Main St., Dayton, Ohio.
140	Weis, David, & Co., 1101 Clark Bldg., Pittsburgh, Pa.
141	Weissman Watch Co., 20 W. 47th St., New York, N. Y.
142	Weksler & Goodman, 5 S. Wabash Ave., Chicago, Ill.
143	Welensky, M., & Co., 36 W. 47th St., New York, N. Y.
144	Westclox Division, General Time Instruments Corp., LaSalle, Ill.
145	Westfield Watch Co., 45 Rockefeller Plaza, New York, N. Y.
146	Wyler Watch Agency, 630 Fifth Ave., New York, N. Y.
147	X-L Watch Co., 170 Broadway, New York, N. Y.
148	Yaeger, Moe M., Co., 730 Hennepin Ave., Minneapolis, Minn.

WATCH NAMES

Name	Key	Name	Key	Name	Key	Name	Key	Name	Key
Chatfield	41	Concordia	41	Dagmar	95	Dorsey	44	Empress Eugenie	14
Chatham	41-92	Concurve	14	Dainty	41-42	Dorsy	19	Emshir	49
Chattel	42	Conga	138	Daisy	42-95	Dot	33	Enchantress	41-92
Chelsea	41	Congress	41	Dale	54	Double Lentile	41	Encore	41-188
Cheltenham	95	Congressman	19	Dalton	145	Douglas	19-41-44-53	Endeavor	33
Cheremay	33	Connecticut Watch Co.	53	Damsel	41	Dover	19	Endicott	44
Cherie	14	Conqueror	19	Danbury	138	Downing	41	Enfield	138
Chermay	33	Coquette	53	Dante	19	Drake	14-19-44-53-92	Engineer	19
Chesterfield	19	Conrad	41	Daphne	19-44-53	Dream	41-92	Enid	95
Chesterton	41	Constance	41-44-92-145	Darien	138	Dressy	42	Ensign	14-19-41-44-53-138
Chevalier	14-138	Constellation	41	Dart	41	Drew	44	Enterprise	33
Cheviot	41	Consuela	41	Dartmouth	41	Drexel	41-44	Envoy	41-138
Chevron	53	Consuelo	95	Darton	138	Driva	59	Epoch	41
Chevy Chase	19-44	Consul	44	Darwin	53	Dryad	92	Equinox	53
Chic	42	Contest	19	Daryll	41	Dryden	14	Equity	138
Chicago Watch Co.	33	Continental	19-41	Date-o-graph	46	DuBarry	14-19-52	Ericsson	44
Chicopee	138	Contour	41-44	Dauphine	19	Dubonnet	41	Ermine	145
Chief	19-33-41-138	Controller	19	Davis	19	Duchess	19-41-42-92-102-138	Erna	41
Chieftain	44-145	Convex	41-53	Dawes	41	Duchess of Alba	14	Ernestine	41
Chilton	41-145	Convoy	41	Dawn	41-92	Dudley	41	Escapade	92
China Clipper	19	Conway	138	Dawson	41	Duke	41-42	Escort	53-92-138
Christina	44	Copperfield	19	Dayton	53-85	Duke of Kent	14	Eska	61
Christine	19	Coq D'Or	47	Daytona	53	Dulcie	145	Esmeralda	95
Churchill	41-138	Coquette	53	Deaconess	41	Dunbar	41	Esquire	41-86
Cincinnati	41	Cora	19-44-138	Dean	19-53	Duncan	19	Essanee	128
Cinderella	95	Coral	41-44-145	Deanna	53-138	Dunkirk	44	Essex	14-41-44
Cirod	29	Cord	79	Dearborn	19-95	Dunn	44	Estelle	19-41
Citadel	41	Cordele	41	Dearden	41	Dunster	138	Esther	41
Claire	41-44-145	Cordelia	41-44	Deauville	41-92	Durham	19	Estine	44
Clara	44	Cordova	44	Debon	11	Duxbury	138	Esty	53
Clara Barton	19	Corinne	44	Deborah	95	Dynasty	41	Eterna	34
Claremont	95	Corinth	41	Debutante	19-41			Ethel	19-41
Clarence	19	Corinthia	19	Decagon	44			Ethelda	41
Clarendon	41	Cornelia	19-95	Deerfield	41	E-Z Vue	19	Eton	14-41-45-145
Claribel	95	Cornell	28-41-95	Defender	41-92-129	Eagle	19-41-63	Eugene	92
Clarice	14	Cornwall	19	Defiance	53	Eagle Wing	95	Eugenia	19
Claridge	14	Corona	19-41	DeFrece	28	Earl	41-44	Eugenie	44-95
Clarion	41	Coronado	41-44	DeKalb	106	Early American	33	Eunice	41
Clarissa	44	Coronation	68	Delano	14	Easel	70	Europa	19
Clark	44	Coronet	19-41-42-53	Delegate	19	Easton	31-185	Eva	44-138
Clarke	44	Corporal	41	Delia	95	Eaton	53	Evalyn	44
Classic	33-41	Corrigan	19	Delight	41	Ebel	32	Evangeline	19-41
Claudette	19-41	Corrine	14-19-41	Della	44-138	Echo	41	Evans	41-78
Claudia	138	Corsair	14	Delma	44	Eclipse	41-53	Eve	41-42
Clay	19	Corsican	33	Delmar	92	Economy	33	Evelyn	19-41
Clayton	41-145	Cort	1	Delmonico	92	Ecstacy	41	Everett	19
Clemente	44	Cortebert	42	Deming	53	Eden	138	Evian Freres	11
Clementine	95	Cortland	22	Demure	41	Edgehill	41	Evington	11
Cleo	41	Cortland Watch Co.	22	Delphi	53	Edgeline	41	Evkob	35
Cleone	19	Cosmopolitan	95	Delphine	19	Edgemere	11	Ewen	44
Cleopatra	19	Cotillion	44	Delta	53	Edgeton	11	Exacto	45
Clermont	41	Counsellor	41	De Luxe	38-41	Edgewater	41	Excel	41
Cleveland	11-44	Count	41	Denise	42	Edgewood	14-44	Exclusive	42
Click	54	Countess	14-41-42	Dennis	19	Edison	145	Executive	41
Clifton	41-145	Country Club	95	Derby	19-41-42-53	Edith	41	Explorer	95
Climax	53	Courier	41-54	Desk	33	Edith Cavell	92-95	Exceltick	138
Clinton	19-21-44-138	Courtney	41	DeSoto	41	Edmond	19	Extra	41
Clipper	19-41-53	Courtship	19	Devon	44-53	Edna	19	Extra Precision	41
Clockometer	138	Covedale	41	Devonshire	41	Edwin	19		
Club	42-53	Coventry	41	Dewey	19-41	Efficiency	19	Fairfax	41-109
Clubman	33	Crafton	145	Dexter	19-41-53	Edgerton	41	Fairfield	41
Clyde	138	Craftsman	19-41-92	Dexter Street	33	Eileen	19-44	Fairhaven	41
Cobalt	41	Cranston	19	Diadem	19-41	Elaine	11-14-19-41	Fairlee	138
Co-ed	19-54	Crawford	24-138	Diamond	33	Elaine W. Co.	11	Fair Maid	42
Colby	41-53	Creighton	41	Diana	19-41-42-138	Elba	55	Fairmaid	85
Cole	44	Cresarrow Watch Co.	15	Diane	44	Elbon	3	Fairmont	44-138
Colebrook	41	Crescent	41	Dickens	44	Eldale	11	Fairview	41
Coleman	41	Crescent St.	138	Dictator	19	Elden	19	Fairway	41
Colfax	41	Crest	41	Dietrich Gruen	41	Eldorado	92	Faith	19-41
Colgate	41	Crest de Luxe	41	Digby	41	Eldridge	41	Falaise	41
Colleen	19-41-138	Creston	138	Dighton	138	Eleanor	19-41	Falcon	41-145
Collegian	41	Crestwood	85	Dinah	41	Electa	102	Fantasy	41-47
Collegiate	14-33-42-85	Cricket	41	Dione	116	Elector	41	Faraday	41
Collette	19	Criterion	53-95	Diplomat	41-92	Elem	94	Fargo	33
Collingwood	14	Crockett	19	Director	19-41-44-53	Eleonore	11	Farragut	19-41-44
Cologne	41	Croix de Guerre	41	Disk	53	Elgin	33	Farwell	33
Colombier	11	Cromwell	14-19-138	Dispatcher	14-44	Elinor	44	Fashion	41
Colonel	41-42	Cronometro Superior	138	Diva	53-138	Elinvar	44	Fashion First	41
Colonial	14-41-138	Cronometro Supremo	138	Dive Bomber	19	Elise	44	Fashions in Time	28
Colonial A	138	Cronometro Victoria	138	Dix	41	Elissa	19-95	Father Time	33
Colonial Lady	14	Cross	38	Dixie	41-54-145	Elite	14-41-92	Favorite	42
Columbia	19-85	Croton	25-51	Dixon	44	Elizabeth	19	Fawn	41
Columbian	53	Croton Aquamatic	25	Dobbs	41	Elkton	145	Fayette	138
Columbus	33	Croton Aquamedico	25	Doctor	42-138	Ella	19	Feather	41
Colorado	19	Crown	24-41-70	Doctor Morton	95	Ellen	41	Federal	74
Combat	19	Croydon	14-41	Dodson	44	Elliott	41-44	Felicia	44-95
Comet	41-138	Cruiser	19	Dodsworth	41	Ellsworth	44	Fellowship	95
Commander	19-41	Crusader	33	Dollar Watch	53	Ellyn	44	Fenton	145
Commander-in-chief	14	Crysler	26	Dolly Madison	19	Eloise	19	Fenway	138
Commando	19-41	Cuff Watch	138	Dolores	19-41-53	Elroy	11	Fenwick	138
Commentator	19	Culver	33-41	Don	19-53	Elsa	138	Ferry, W. H.	33
Commercial	58	Culver, H. C.	33	Donald	19-44	Elsie	44-145	Fidelia	19
Commodore	14-19-41-42	Cumberland	95	Donald Duck	53	Elsine	41	Fiesta	47
Commonwealth	33	Curie	19	Donavan	44	Elson	188	Fifi	95
Community	41	Curtis	41-138	Donna	53-138	Elton	44-53	Fifth Avenue	41-53
Compact	53	Curtiss	19	Dora	19	Elvira	41	Fillmore	19-44
Companion	41-54	Curvette	41	Dorcas	41	Elysee	42	Finessee	138
Compass	53	Curvex	41	Dorchester	41	Embassy	41	Fireman	33
Comptroller	41	Cushion	44	Dorian	44	Emblem	41	First	53
Comrade	33-54	Custer	44	Doric	29	Emel	67	First Lady	14-41-44-54-85
Comus	41	Custodian	19	Dorinda	19	Emerald	138	Fitzroy	95
Conant	138	Cyma	132	Dorine	138	Emerson	44-53-95	Flagman	33
Concert	41	Cynthia	14-19-41	Doris	19-41-44	Emilie	41-145	Flagship	14-53
Concerto	41	Cyprano	19	Dorna	61	Emily	19-44	Flair	138
Concord	19	Cyrano	19	Dorothea	41	Emperor	19-41	Flamingo	41
Concord Watch Co.	22	Cypres	27	Dorothy	19-44	Empire	5-41	Flanders	14
		Czarina	41	Dorset	14-53	Empire State	19	Fleetwing	41
						Empress	19-41	Fleetwood	19-41-85
								Fleur-de-Lis	95
								Fleurette	95

Name	Key
Lido	19-41-114
Lieutenant	19-41-53
Lifetime	19
Liga	61
Lila	95-138
Lille	41
Lillian	41
Lillie	145
Lilliputian	19
Lily	19
Lincoln	19-41-138
Linda	44
Linden	41
Linden Hall	44
Lindon	145
Lindy	19
Linwood	44
Lionel	19
Lipton	145
Lisbeth	95
Lisbon	41
Lister	95
Littleton	138
Livingston	44-145
Lloyd	14
Locarno	41
Locometer	138
Lodge	41
Logan	41
Lola	138
Loma	19
Lombard	31
London	145
Lone Eagle	19
Longacre	41
Long Beach	44
Longchamps	42
Longines	68
Longines Musical Note	68
Longueville	41
Lonville	105
Longville Watch Co.	105
Lois	19-44
Loraine	41
Lord Byron	95
Lord Duquesne	95
Lord Elgin	33
Lord Elgin, 44,000	33
Lord Elgin, 62,500	33
Lord Nelson	14
Lord Springfield	19
Lord Vernon	85
Lord West	113
Lorelei	95
Loretta	92
Lorinda	19
Lorna	19-44-69
Lorraine	15
Lotus	19
Louis	70
Louis XIV	
Louise	19-41-44-92
Lourdes	41
Love Mate	92
Lowell	41-44
Lucerne	41
Lucia	44
Lucian	41
Lucie	145
Lucille	19-44
Lucinda	19-41
Lucretia	19-41
Lucy	19-44
Ludlow	41
Luella	41
Luetta	44
Lugless	75
Lura	138
Lurlene	41
Luster	41
Lydia	19
Lyle	44
Lyman	138
Lynda	95
Lyndhurst	41
Lynne	95
Lyons	41
Lyric	41
Mabel	11
Madeline	19
Madelon	41-42
Mademoiselle	11-41
Madison	19-41-71
Madonna	33-41
Madre-Biel	41
Madretsch	41
Magellan	19
Magnolia	19
Maid of Honor	41
Mainliner	44
Majestic	41-68
Majesty	41
Major	41-42-44-53
Majorette	41
Malcolm	19
Malden	138
Mallory	19
Man-About-Town	92
Manchester	95
Mandalay	41
Manhattan	14-41-92
Manikin	47
Manly	138
Mannequin	11-41
Manon	42
Manor	41
Man O'Service	14
Man-o-time	92
Mansfield	14
Maple Leaf	53
Marathon	41
Marberry	14
Marbury	14
Marcella	14
Marcelle	19-41
Marcene	41
Marchioness	41
Marcia	41-44
Marcus	41
Margaret	19
Margo	19
Margot	41-44
Margy	41
Marian	19-41
Marianne	95
Marie	19-41
Marie Antoinette	14
Marietta	19-41-44
Mariette	95
Marigold	14-19
Marilyn	19-41-42
Marine	41
Mariner	41-47-53
Marion	41-44-138
Marine	124
Marissa	19
Maritza	44-95
Marjorie	19-41
Marksman	14-41
Markton	145
Markwell	14
Marlborough	11
Marlboro	11
Marlene	19-41-42
Marliene	92
Marlow	14
Marlowe	41
Marlton	14
Marlyn	44
Marmon	35
Marquessa	41
Marquette	19-41-53
Marquis	41-44
Marquise	19-41-42
Marshall	41-44
Marston	138
Marta	138
Martha	41-44-145
Martha Washington	19-41
Martin	44-95
Marvel	41-73
Marvelle	19
Marvin	76
Marwood	14
Mary	42-138
Marylin	19-42
Marylyn	14
Mary Lou	19
Mary Todd	44
Mary Tudor	14
Masin	77
Mason	19-44
Master	41-54
Master Bilt	92
Masterpiece	44
Mate	53-138
Mathey-Tissot	84
Maureen	41
Maxim	19-188
Maximus	138
Maxine	44
Maxwell	95
May	19-42
Mayfair	11-14-41-42
Mayfield	41
Mayflower	19-41-42-85
Mayo	41
Mayor	19
Mayview	41
Meadowbrook	14-41-44-116
Medalist	41-44
Medallion	19-41-44
Medical	42
Medical Center	19
Medical Officer	19
Medico	19-92-95
Medley	41
Medwick	44
Melanie	41
Melbourne	41
Melissa	41
Melissande	95
Melita	41
Melodie	44
Melody	41
Melton	41
Melvin	41
Mendon	138
Menton	41
Mentone	41
Mentor	41
Mercedes	41
Mercury	19-41-92-138
Mercy	41
Meriden	129
Meridian	114
Merle	138
Mermaid	19-41
Merrill	41
Merrimac	19
Merritt	44
Merton	145
Mervos	51
Metropolis	92
Meylan, A. R. & J. E.	80
Meylan, C. H.	15
Miami	41-44-72
Micromatic	55
Microthin	55
Mickey Mouse	53
Micron	81
Midas	44
Midget	53
Midinette	19
Midland	85
Mido	82
Midshipman	19
Mignon	19
Mignonette	95
Milburn	14
Mildred	41
Milex	94
Milford	138
Militaire	19
Military	87
Millay	44
Millicent	41
Millis	138
Milos	113
Milton	19-138
Mimo	40
Minerva	19-30-41-92
Minuet	41-138
Minute Man	19-128
Minutes	138
Miranda	95
Miriam	41-44
Miss America	19
Miss Bulova	19
Miss Columbia	95
Miss 5th Avenue	19
Miss Glory	42-85
Miss Hollywood	42-85
Miss Independence	42-85
Miss Ingraham	54
Miss Liberty	14-145
Miss Parker	95
Miss U. S.	19
Miss Universe	19
Mitchell	41
Mite	53
Mitzi	19-41
Moda	138
Mode	41
Mode du Bijou	41
Modern	42
Moderne	19-41
Modiste	41
Mohawk	147
Molly	145
Molly Pitcher	41
Molly Stark	19
Mona	41
Monarch	41-83
Monica	44
Monitor	19
Monogram	19-53-92
Monopol	68
Monroe	41
Monson	138
Montauk	5
Montclair	14
Monte Carlo	41
Monterey	41
Montgomery	33
Monticello	41-44
Montmartre	42
Montour	44
Montrose	41-95
Montross	14
Moonbeam	41
Morgan	41
Moritz	41
Morley	44
Morse	44
Morris	44
Mortimer	19
Morton	36
Motor	92
Moulton	14
Mt. Holyoke	19
Mount Vernon	44-85
Movado	86
Multifort	82
Multimatic	55
Munwill	87
Muriel	19-41-44
Musical Note	68
Musketeer	33-41-92
Myra	138
Myrna	19-41-44
Myron	44
Myrtle	19-44-138
Mysteria	116
Namdor	106
Nancy	19-41-44
Nanette	19-41
Naomi	19
Naples	41
Napoleon	145
Narcissus	95
Narragansett	15
Nassau	8-41
Natalie	19
Nathan Hale	19
Natick	138
National	41-88
National Chief	14
National Park	102
National Watch Co.	33
Nautilus	41
Navarre	41
Navarro	14
Navigator	41
Navy	124
Needham	14
Nelson	44-53
Neptune	19-41-104-138
Newbury	14
Newcomb	14-44
Newport	41-42-44
Newton	19
New Yorker	14-41-44-92
Neyland	14-19
Neysa	19
Nicolet	11
Nicoley	11
Night Hawk	19
Nightingale	19-44
Night Nurse	19
Night-Watch	19
Nimrod	41
Nina	44-95-138
Nita	138
Nobel	44
Nola	44
Nomad	41
Non Stop	53
Nora	19
Noralie	145
Norfolk	44
Norinne	41
Norma	41-92
Norman	19-44
Normandie	41-90
Normis	84
North Shore	11
Northwind	95
Norton	41-138
Norwich	11
Norwood	42-85
Nouvelle	19
Nova	19
No. 348	33
No. 349	33
Nun's	138
Nurse	42-138
Nymph	138
Oakdale	14
Oakley	19
Oakland	19
Oakmont	44
Oakridge	19
Obelisk	11
Observatory	68
Oco	92
Octathin	41
Octavio	41
Officer	19
Ogden, M. D.	33
Ogden, Mat	33
Olcott	95
Old Glory	19
Old Time	33
Oleet	91
Olga	19-44
Olive	19
Oliver	19
Olivia	44
Ollendorff	92
Olympia	19
Olympiad	41
Olympian	14
Olympic	42
Omar	92
Omega	84
On Duty	19
Onset	138
Opera	41-42-138
Operetta	19
Orchid	145
Oriole	41
Orlando	14
Orleans	95
Ormond	41
Orne	41
Oro Reforzado	41
Orville	41
Orvin	42
Osborne	41
Ostende	41
Otis	44-95
Our Flag	53
Overland	19-33
Overland Limited	19
Overture	41
Ovis	94
Oxford	14-19-44-53
Pacer	138
Pacific Clipper	19
Packard	8
Paddock	138
Paige	44
Paillard Non-Magnetic	12
Pal	54
Palace	41
Paladin	41
Palamor	41
Palm Beach	14-19
Palmer	138
Pamela	41
Pan-American	85
Panda	54
Pandora	19
Parashock	99
Paris	42
Parisian	33-41
Parisienne	33
Paris Square	41
Park	42
Parker	95
Parkhurst	95
Park Lane	5-53
ParKurv	95
Parkurve Beau	95
Parla	11
Parlin	138
Parnassos	42-95
Pascal	19
Pasteur	95-145
Pastor	96
Patek, Philippe & Co.	97
Pathe	98
Pathfinder	54
Patricia	14-19
Patrician	41
Patriot	53-138
Patrol	19-47-53-138
Patroness	19-41
Patsy	145
Patten	138
Paula	41-44
Paul Breguette	109
Paul Ditisheim	16
Paulette	41-42-138
Pauline	19-41
Paul Revere	140
Paul Vallette	136
Paxton	138
Payne	41
Peacock	138
Peabody	138
Pear-agon	75
Pearce	41
Pearl	138
Pearl Harbor	19
Pedigree	53-138
Peer	41
Peeress	41
Peerless	19-53
Peggy	41-53-145
Peg O' My Heart	19
Peke	54
Pelham	14
Pemberton	19
Pembroke	19
Pendant	42-53
Pendleton	41
Penelope	14-19-41
Pennant	41
Penrod	14
Pentagon	41
Pentathin	41
Penton	138
Pep	53
Peppy	53
Percy William	19
Perfect	41
Perisphere	19
Perkins	41
Perraux	130
Perroquet	95
Perry	41-44

Name	Key		Name	Key		Name	Key		Name	Key		Name	Key
Pershing	53		Potomac	41		Price	14		Regent	41		Robin Hood	41
Persian	41		Powell	41					Regina	41		Rochelle	41
Pert	53-138		Practitioner	19-41			55		Registerite	41		Rochester	41
Peter Pan	14		Praise	41			44		Regulator	19		Rockland	19
Petite	19-41-42		Precision	41					Reine	42		Rockwood	41
Petrel	19		Prefect	41			19-53		Reinforced	41		Roderick	19
Phaeton	145		Premier	41-138			95		Renaissance	95		Rodney	44
Phantom	19-41		Premo	41			41-42		Rendezvous	19		Roland	41
Phelps	41		Prentice	19		Queen	14		Renee	14		Rolex	41-107
Phillips	19		Prescott	41-44			14-19		Renown	14-41		Romaine	41
Phoebe	19		Presentation	19-33			14		Republic	41		Romance	42-85
Phoenix	19-41		President	19			102		Resilient	138		Romany	41
Phyllis	19		Prestige	41			138		Revere	19-41-128		Romona	41
Physician	19		Preston	138					Reward	138		Rona	19-138
Picadilly	41-44-92		Preview	41			145		Rewco	103		Rondeau	44
Picard, James	11		Pride	54			42		Rex	41		Ronnie	145
Picard, Lucien	15		Prima Donna	14			102		Reynold	19		Rockwood	41
Picard, R., Fils	54		Primrose	95			41		Rhapsody	41		Roosevelt	11-128
Picford	41		Prince	41-54			95		Rhoda	19-44		Rosalie	41-44-145
Pickometer	138		Prince Albert	19			19-41-92		Rhodes	41		Rosalind	19
Picktime	72		Princess				41		Rialto	95		Rosamonde	95
Pickwick	41			11-14-19-41-42-54-92			41		Ribaux	40		Rosanne	19
Piedmont	19		Princess Anne	95			19		Ricardo	41		Rose	145
Pierpont	41		Princess Astrid	95			58		Richard	19		Rosebud	19-53
Pierce	99		Princess Carole	41			95		Richardson	19		Rosella	41
Pierre	41-44-92		Princess Catharine	95			58		Richelieu	41		Roselle	19
Pierrette	19-42		Princess Elizabeth	95			44		Richford	138		Rose Marie	41
Pilgrim	14-41-92		Princess Mary	14-95			33-41		Richmond	41-42-44		Rosemary	41
Pilot	14-19-41-42-47-53-138		Princess Pat	14-19			86		Rickenbacker	41		Rosemond	41
Pinecrest	19		Princess Vanity	41			5-44-95		Rima	104		Rosette	11
Pinehurst	14-41-44		Princess Victoria	95			41-95		Rindge	138		Rosina	41
Pink Lady	92		Princeton	14-19-41			53		Ripple	41		Rosine	108
Pinnacle	41		Princine	19			44		Rist-Arch	53		Roslyn	41
Pioneer	44-53-138		Priora	61			19-41-47		Ristside	41		Ross	44
Piping Rock	44		Priscella	41			41		Rita	19-41-44		Rossel	11
Pittsfield	14		Priscilla	19			41		Ritchie	41		Rossiter	41
Placid	41		Proctor	41			42		Rite-Angle	19		Rotary	92
Plainsman	14		Professional	33-42-54			41		Rite-Time	11		Rothschild	41
Plaisted	138		Promenade	33			33		Ritime	42		Rough Rider	19
Planetarium	70		Protheus	41			138		Rittenhouse	44		Round the World	19
Plaza	41-42		Provence	42-85			44		Ritz	42-53-95		Rowe	138
Plymouth	19-41		Providence	19			41		Riverdale	14-19		Rowenna	44
Pocket Ben	144		Provis	95			138		Riverside	138		Roxanne	14
Pocket Pal	54		Prudence	19-41			116		Riverside Maximus	138		Roxbury	41
Pola	138		Pulitzer	44			95		Riviera	41-42-99		Roxy	110
Polo	42		Pup	54			41		Rivoli	95		Royal	41-53-70-138
Pony	54		Purdue	95			138		Roanoke	41		Royal Beauty	14
Pool	33		Puritan	41			53		Robert	19		Royal Family	95
Poppy	95		Pursuit	47			19		Roberta	19-44-92-138		Royal George	95
Portia	19-41-44		Putnam	44-138			41-138		Robert Morris	44		

(Contd. on page 116)

This copy was not legible on my original.

Name	Key		Name	Key		Name	Key		Name	Key		Name	Key
Van Dyke	95		Vinton	41		Warren	19-41-44		Wheatland	44		World's Fair Grand Prize Watch	68
Vanessa	95		Viola	41-95		Warrenton	41		Wheeler	41		World War Veteran	19
Van Gerard	138		Violet	41-145		Warrington	14		Wheeler, G. M.	33		Worren	11
Vanguard	41-138		Virginia	14-19-41-42-44		Warrior	19-53		Whippet	41		Wright	41
Vanity	41-42		Viscount	41		Wartime	19		Whirl	41		Wrist	53
Vanity Fair	95		Vision	41		Washington	41-53		Whisper	138		Wrist Ben	144
Vant	11		Vivian	14-19-41-44		Wasp	53		Whitehall	41		Wrist-Curve	53
Varga	138		Vivienne	41		Watchdog	53		Whitman	44		Wristfit	54
Varney	138		Vogue	11-41-54-92		Watchman	11		Whitney	44		Wristform	41
Varsity	41-45		Voirol, E.	22		Watch of the Immortals	68		Whittier	19		Wristlite	53
Vassar	14-19-41-42		Volney	14		Watch of Railroad Accuracy	44		Wilkinson	44		Wrist-O-crat	10
Vauchay	11		Volunteer	19-47		Watch Specialties Co.	41		Willard	11		Wrist-Pal	54
Venice	41-42		Vonda	44		Watch Word	33		William Osler	33		Wyco	146
Venita	44		Wachusett	138		Waterbury	53		Willson	44		Wyda	11
Ventura	19		Wadena	44		Waterbury Clock Co.	53		Wilshire	19		Wyler	146
Venus	41		Wadleigh	19		Waterproof	42-158		Wilson	19		Wyman	138
Vera	44		Wafer	53		Watertight	145		Wilton	138		Wynne	53
Vera	138		Wafer-Thin	41		Watertite	92		Wimbledon	19-42		Wynyard	44
Veritas	33		Waferthin	41		Watertite Self-Winder	145		Winchester	19		
Veri-thin	41		Wafer Thin	41		Watson	44		Windsor	14-41-145		X-L	147
Verno	113		Wagner	41		Watt	44		Wingate	138		Xray	138
Vernon	41		Wakefield	41		Waverly	41		Wings	53		
Verona	19		Waldemar	11		Wayne	19-41-44		Winifred	19		Yale	41
Veronica	44		Waldorf	41-92		Weather Meter	53		Winner	42-53		Yankee	53
Versatile	42		Wales	19-41		Webster	19-41-44		Winnie	41		Yankee Clipper	19
Verve	41		Walker	137		Wedgemere	138		Winona	44		Yardley	41-92
Verythin	41		Wallace	138		Weisco	141		Winslow	44		Yarmark	41
Very Veri-Thin	41		Wallie	145		Wellesley	14-19-41-44		Winsome	41-138		Yarmouth	138
Vestoria	19		Wall Street	92		Wellington	14-19		Winston	19-53-138		Yeoman	41
Veteran	19-92		Waltham	138		Welsbro	141		Winthrop	19-44		York	41-122
Viceroy	19-41-53		Waltham Eagle Watch	138		Welson	143		Winton	19-41		Yorktown	95
Victor	41		Walton	145		Wendie	145		Wisp	41		Yorktowne	44
Victoria	19-41-42-44		Waltz	41		Wendy	145		Wisteria	41		Yvette	44
Victory	41-42-92		Wand	41		Wentworth	41		Wittnauer	68		Yvonne	41
Vida	95		Wanda	138		Wesley	44-138		Wollaston	138		
Vigilante	19		Warden	47		Wesleyan	41		Wollcott	44		Zelandia	44
Viking	14-41-145		Wardman	41		Westbury	14		Wonder	11-41		Zelton	19
Vilma	44		Wardman	95		Westchester	11-19-85		Woodbury	138		Zephyr	33-41-93
Vincent	44		Wareham	138		Westfield	145		Woodland	138		Zodiac	97
						Westgate	41		Woodmere	11		Zorina	138
						Westminster	41		Woodside	19		
						Weston	14		World	92		
						Westpoint	41-42-85		World's Champion	14		
						West Pointer	19-113		World's Fair	14		
						Weybourn	19					

(Contd. from page 105)

Name	Key
Royal Lady	14
Royal Prince	92
Royalton	53
Royalty	95
Royce	61-111
Rosel	19
Rubaiyat	19
Rubie	145
Ruby	138
Ruby Queen	14
Rugby	19
Russell	44
Rutgers	41
Ruth	19-41
Rutledge	44
Ruxton	145
Ryerson, J. T.	33
Rythm	41
Rytime	40
Sahara	41
Sagamore	138
Salem	138
Salisbury	14
Sallie	145
Sally	19-42-95
Samaritan	41
Samrod	100
Samson	145
Sandra	19-44
Sanford	138
Sangamo	44
Sapphire	138
Sara	19-44
Saratoga	41-44
Sarazen	14
Sargent	41-44
Satellite	41
Savoy	41
Saxon	145
Saybrook	41
Scarlett	41
Scepter	41
Schulz, J.	115
Schuyler	14
Schwob	116
Scientist	41
Scioto	41
Scott	44
Scout	41-53
Seabury	138
Sea Hawk	40
Seahawk	47
Sea King	19
Sea Scout	40
Seal Tight	116
Seaside	138
Seckron	44
Secometer	44-54
Secontrol	55
Secron	44
Security	102
Seeland	55
Seidma	118
Selbro	119
Selden	138
Selena	44
Selina	41
Self-o-matic	46
Selma	41
Semca	120
Semi Cartouche	41
Semithin	41
Senator	19-53
Seneca	44-53
Senior	33-53
Senorita	19-41-53
Sentinel	41-44
Sentry	41-54
Septer	41
Serena	19
Serenade	41

Name	Key
Seville	41
Sewanee	41
Sexton	19
Seymour	138
Shadow	41
Shand	44
Shawmut	138
Sheffield	41
Sheila	44
Shelburne	138
Sheldon	53
Shelton	41-53
Sheridan	11
Sherman	19-41
Sherwood	41-44
Shield	41
Shipmate	41
Shirley	19-41-42
Shock Proof	38
Shrine	20
Sidney	44
Signet	53
Silhouette	41
Silver Lark	41
Silverex	11
Silver Star	41
Sinclair	41
Sinton	14
Siren	47
Sir Knight	19
Sir Walter Scott	33
Skeleton	138
Skidmore	19
Skipper	41
Sky-chief	14-41
Sky King	14-145
Sky Lark	14
Sky Master	14
Sky Pilot	33
Sky Prince	14
Sky Princess	14
Sky Queen	14
Sky Time	53
Skyway	44
Sleda	3
Slim	19
Slipstream	33
Smart	42
Smart Set	19
Smith	19
Smithfield	41
Snowden	95
Socialite	41
Solachron	37
Solitaire	19
Solvil	16
Solora	61
Somerset	41
Sonata	19-41
Sonia	19
Sonnet	41-138
Sonya	44
Sophie	44
Sophisticate	19
Sophomore	14
Sorority	33-41
Southerner	19
Sovereign	41
Spalding	19
Spare	123
Spartan	41-145
Sparton	138
Specialist	41
Speedway	19-41-44
Sphere	47
Spencer	19
Splendor	41
Sponsor	19
Sport	42-138
Sport King	14
Sport Queen	14
Sportsman	41-99-145

Name	Key
Sportster	52-92
Spring Lark	41
Sprite	41
Spur	41-44
Squadron	14-19
Square B	41
Squire	14-41
Stadium	41
Stag	92
Stalwart	19
Stamford	19
Standish	19-41-53
Stanford	19-41-44
Stanley	41
Stanton	145
Star	41
Stardust	41
Starlight	41
Starling	138
State Street	33
States	33
Stauffer, A. E.	22
Staunton	41
Steelclad	42
Stella	19
Sterling	96-138
Stetson	41
Stevens	44
Stewardess	41
Stewart	41
Stoneleigh	41
Straighline	42
Strand	33
Strasburger, Byron L., & Co.	11
Stratford	41-95
Stratoliner	14
Stratton	138
Streamline	33
Streemcurv	41
Stuart	41
Sturdy	54
Stuyvesant	95
Style Line	33
Style Queen	14
Stylist	41
Sub-Deb	41
Submarine	138
Submersible	138
Suburban	68
Sudbury	138
Suffolk	44
Sultan	138-145
Sultana	19-41
Summit	41
Sumter	41
Sun	11
Sunapee	138
Sun Glo	92
Sungold	19
Super-Automatic	82
Superb	11-41-42
Superbe	41
Superior	53-138
Superior Veri-thin	41
Supervisor	19
Supreme	41
Surgeon	19-41
Surrey	19-41
Susan	19-44
Susanne	95
Sussex	41-51
Sutton	41-44
Suzanne	44
Suzette	95
Swagger	53-138
Swanson	145
Swan Watch Co.	131
Swarthmore	41
Sweatproof	41
Sweatpruf	41
Sweepstakes	19
Sweetbriar	41

Name	Key
Sweetheart	14-92
Sweetheart of the Air	14
Swetpruf	41
Swingster	92
Sybil	95
Sylvia	19-41-44-92-138
Sylvian	44
Symphony	41
Syracuse	41
Tacy	132
Taft	41
Talbot	44
Talisman	41
Talmadge	14
Tango	41
Tank	41
Tanya	44
Taperflow	41
Tara	41
Tavan	132
Tavanco	132
Tavannes	132
Taylor, H.	19-33-41-44
Taylor, H. H.	33
Tear-Drop	92
Teasdale	41
Technician	41
Templar	19
Temple	138
Tempometer	68
Tempor Watch Co.	11
Tempus	126
Tennis	42
Teresa	42-44-85
Tess	19
Texan	41
Thais	95
Thalia	44
Thayer	41
The Age	33
The Alamo	19
The Chicago Watch	33
The "400"	138
Thelma	19-138
Theodora	19
Theodore Roosevelt	128
Theresa	41
Thin Man	19
Thora	138
Thornton	138-145
Thorpe	41
Three Way Contour	44
Thrift	33
Tiara	41
Tibet	99
Ticonderoga	95
Tildon	145
Tilmore	133
Tilton	41
Time and Space	68
Time Award	68
Time Ball	54
Time Hill	41
Time King	19
Time Micros ope	44
Time Omatic	55
Time from the Stars	33
Time Study	116
Time-Teacher	53
Times	92
Times Square	41
Tip Top Timer	11
Titan	14
Titia	44
Token	41
Toledo	19
Tom Sawyer	19
Tonneau	44-138
Topaz	95
Top Notch	54
Topper	53
Topsfield	138
Touchdown	33-41

Name	Key
Touchon & Co.	68
Touraine	44
Tourneau	134
Townley	95
Townsman	44
Townsend	138
Traffic Special	44
Train Timer	19
Trained Nurse	19
Traveler	53-138
Traymore	19
Treasure	42-54
Treasured Album	92
Treasurer	19
Trent	53
Trenton	53-145
Tribune	95
Trident	19
Trilby	44
Trim	53
Trina	138
Triton	41
Triumph	41
Trixie	145
Trojan	145
Trooper	41-138
Trophy	19-44
Tropical	92
Troubador	19
Trouville	41
Trudie	145
Trulee	138
Trump	53
Trutime	11
Trylon	19
Trylon & Perisphere	19
Tsarina	41
Tudor	95
Turner	44
Tuscan	14-19
Tutone	33
Tu-Tone	92
Tux	53
Tuxedo	19-41-53
Twentieth Century	19
Twilight	41
Twin	19
Twinkle	41
Tycoon	53
Tyler	41
Tyson	138
Ultra	41-42
Ultra Quality	41
Ultrathin	41
Ultra Ultrathin	41
Ultra Veri-thin	41
Ultra Vogue	41-42
Uncle Sam	54
Uncle Sam Bomber	54
Union	85
Unique	42
Unit Control	33
United	41-92
Unity	41
Universal	53-138
University	41
Upton	138
Ursula	41
Vaile	44
Valencia	41
Valentine	95
Valeria	41-95
Valerie	41
Valet	53
Valiant	41
Volkyrie	95
Vallette	136
Valley Forge	85
Valor	41
Van Buren	44
Van Cortlandt	95
Vanderbilt	11

FAKE AMERICAN RAILROAD WATCHES

The following is a list of names found on Swiss made, fake American railroad watches. Along with the name you will usually find one or more of the following descriptions: Special - Specially Adjusted - Non Magnetic - Heat & Cold - Interchangable - Direct Transmission - 21 Jewels - 23 Jewels - Positions - Fully Adjusted - Regulator - 3,5,6,8 Adjustments - 543 - 846 - 548 - No. 89 - No. 99 - Specially Adjusted for Railway Service - Double Roller - and other statements that would fool you into thinking you were getting a high grade railroad watch. Some American companies made these watches also: Trenton - Seth Thomas - New York Standard, and maybe others.

Alton Special
Algier
Algona
Bradford Special
Burdicks Special
B. W. Special
B. F. Reymond
Central Express
Central Special
Central Time
Companion
Corona Special
Ed. C. Hall
Engineers Special
Empire Special*
Erie
Frisco Special
Golden State
Girard
Grand Central Chronometer
Grand Central
Great Western
H & A Special
Hartford
Hampton
Helmet Non-Magnetic
H.W. Company Special
Locomotive Special - USA (Trenton)
Malton Special
Marvin
Madison Special
Marmon
Missouri Pacific
Mexican Railway Special
Newport
New Haven
N.H.W. Co. Special
Northern Express

Northern Pacific
Northwestern Special
Pennsylvania*
Pennsylvania Special*
Railway Time Keeper
Railroad Time Keeper
R.R. Special
Railroad Trainmens Special
Railroad Special
Railway Flyer
R.W. Co. Special
Rock Island
Rock Island Special
Rock Island Express
Southern Express
Southern Flyer
Southern Railway Special
Sterling Watch Co. - Springfield
Time Ball Special
Time Service
Train Dispatcher
Trans Atlantic
Trans Pacific
Tribune - USA (American Made)
The Plan
Union Watch Co.
Union National Special
Universal Time Keeper
Victor
Walden
Waldren
Wallingford Watch Co.
Wall Street
Washington
Woldorf
Western Special
Whalen

Swiss made, fake American railroad watches are being collected by some collectors but knowledgable buyers will usually not pay over $35.00 to $50.00, depending on how they are cased. Watch buyers are still being fooled by these, and high prices are reported occasionally. If not running the value drops sharply because they are hard to fix. Some examples are shown on Pages 53 and 54.

IMPORTED FOREIGN WATCH NAMES
(Mostly Swiss)

The following list of watch names was made up from many different sources. Both pocket watch and wrist watch names are included. This is not a complete list. An asterick indicates these names also appear on American made watches.

Aara	Arnould	Bica	Century	Croydon
Abra	Arnould Fils	Bidling Maier	Cervine	Culmina
Accro	Aro	Bijou	Champ	Cupillard
Accro Bond	Arown	Bikoff, Freres	Chancellor	Cycloid
Accuratus	Aurore	Bill W. Co.	Charleton	Cyma
Ace	Arrow	Blanc-Pain	Chase	Dalia
Achievement	Arsea	Blanc-Pain LeCoultre	Chateau-Cadillac	Daisy
Actina	Art	Block	Chatham	Dawes
Adams	A. S.	Blossom	Chaucer	Darax
Adele	Assa	Bonheur	Chezard	Datinell
Admiral	Aster	Bonnet	Chic	Davidson
Aedko	Astor	Bonny	Chirot	Daynite
Agassiz	Atlantic	Bornand	Chopard	Debon
Agora	Aubrey	Boulevard	Chromo	Decimal
Ajax	Aubrey-Cyl	Bourquin	Chronometre	Decorum
Alacris	Aureole	Brac	Chronex	Delego
Albuse	Aurore	Brack	Chrono	De Fond
Alco	Gene Autry	Bradford	Chum	Delemont
A. Lecoultre	Ava	Brandt	Cico	DeBerne
Alere	Avalon	Branmore	Cimier	Delfa
Alexora	Avia	Brehm	Civic	Delia
Alfo	Awoner	Breitling	Clare Fax	Delmar
Algier	Axa	Brenet	Claremont	Delta
Alleman	Axa-Cyl	Brevet	C. L. Guinana	Deluxe
Allsopp	All, N. A.	Brevo	Clemence	Depolier
Alpa	Banner	Bristol	Cleo	Derby
Alparosa	Barclay	Broadway	Clermont	Desa
Alpine	Barlow	Bruen	Clinton	Desired
Alpina	Barbezat Bole	Bruner	Cockburn	Delso
Alpino	Baumgartner	Brunvil	Colgar	Diademe
Alsale	Beacon*	Bryn-Maur	Collegiate	Diana
Altrue	Beaty	Budin	Combine	Didis
Altus	Bedford	Buffalo	Bommodore	Didisheim
Alvera	Beer	Buges	Companion	Dike
Alvin	Begus	Builtrite	Concord	Dila
American Beauty	Beguelin	Bulova	Congress	Diona
American Lady	Beleco	Burdicks	Consistant	Ditis
American Maid	Bella	Buren	Constant	Doret
American Standard *	Bellevue	Burlington	Continental	Dot
Americus	Belmar	Buser	Conway Record	Douglas
Amida	Belmont	Busga	Coneille	Doxa
A. N.	Benott	B. W.	Conicley	Dreadnought
Angelus	Benrus	Cabot	Cornavin	Doroz
Apollo-Timer	Berex	Calame, A.	Corniolex	Dubois
Apont	Berger	Calis	Cortebert	Duchess
Appco	Berkshire	Camden	Court	Dunand
Arcadian	Berling	Capital	Courtland	Duro
Arcola	Berna	Capitol	Crane	Durr
Argo	Berner	Cartier	Crawford	Duval
Aristo	Berthoud	Cathin Aubrey	Crelia	Durowe
Aristocrat	Berwyn	Cattin	Crestline	Eaton
Ariston*	Betina	Celtic	Cretets	Ebel
Ark	Bettlach	Central Time	Critic	Eberes
Arlington	Beverly	Centaur	Croton	Ebosa

Edandem	Farbique Electra	Governor	Home	King
Edelco	Fagot	Grace	Hora	Kino
Edgemere	Fairy	Graef	Howland	Klason
Edgeton	Fairfax	Grana	Hudson	Kleiner
Edys	Favre	Granby	Huguenin	Knickerbocker
Eglantine	Fellicetti	Grand Central	Humair	Knockabout
Eigeldinger	Felsa	Grangin	Humbert	Kocher
Eisler	Fern	Grant	Hurwitz	Krysler
Elbio	Ferrero	Great Northern	H. W. Co.	Kumer
Elaine	Fiat	Great Western	Hyde Park	Kummer Freres
Elba	Fidelis	Grenad	Ibex	Kurth
Elbon	Fidelity	Grossenbacher	Imhof	La Chappelle
Elbra	Fidia	Gruen	Illinois Central	La Cioche
Eldor	Fidola	Guarantee	Imperial	Laco
Election	Finetta	Gubelin	Impetus	Lapena
Electra	Fink	Guinand	Improved	Lador
Elegant	Flat Iron	Gustafson	Indicatum	Lady Alice
Eledem	Fleetwood	Hadorn	Ines	Lady Grant
Elem	Fleur	Haenni Freres	Ingenious	Lady Racine
Elida	Fleurette	Hafis	International	Lady Suffolk
Eligia	Fleurier	Hahn	Inula	Lady Tess
Elliot	Fleury	Hall	Invar	Lady West
Ellis	Fonsinger	Hallmark *	Inventic	Lady of the Lake
Elman	Fontain	Hallwatch	Invicta	Lafayette
Elroy	Fountainemelon	Hampden *	Invieta	Lakeshore
Elsemere	Formosa	Hamis	Ioca	Lamode
Embga	Formosoh	Hamlet	Ipearlham	Lancet
Embsa	Formost	Hamlin	Ira	Lanco
Empire	Fortis	Hammand	Iris	Landeron
Emshir	Galco	Hampton	Isberg Precieuse	Langendorf
Engardine	Gale	Handicap	Ito	Lanovak
Engineer	Gallet	Handlin	Ithaca	Larmin
Enicar	Galmor	Hanlin	Jaccards	LaSalle
Enigma	Garfield	Hanover	Jack	Lassiver
Enterprise	Garland	Harman	Jacona	Latham
Eric	Gasser	Hartford	Jacot	Lauret
Erima	Gast Freres	Harvel	Jaeger	Lavina
Erin	Gem	Harvord	Jagot	LaVogue
Esef	General	Hassler	Jaguy	Lawran
Espirit	Geneva	Hauser	Jay Eff	Leal
Eta	Geneve	Hayne	Jean	LeCoultre
Eterna	Genius	Hebdo	Jeanbrun	Lehman
Ethic	Genot	Hebdomas	Jeanneret	Lemania
Etna	Georgia	Heckler	Jerome Park	Lenora
Eton	Gilgo	Helbein Freres	Jetka	Lenore
Ettienne	Gilomen	Helbros	Jewel	Lenox
Eureka	Gina	Helmet	Jiiga	Leonidas
European	Ginault	Heney	Jockey Club	Leonore
Everbrite	Ginnette	Henex	Jovis	Le Phare
Everett	Girard	Henry	Judex	Lessor
Everest	Girod	Herald	Jule Jurgensen	Leuba
Evington	Glazier	Heuer, Ed. & Co.	Juigar	Liama
Evkob	Globe	Highmere	Juillard	Liberty
Exastus	Glycine	Himalaya	Jules Jurgensen	Lido
Excello	Go Ahead	Hinco	Junghans	Liengme
Excelsior Park	Godat	Hisch	Jura	Liegmo
Exhibition	Goering	Hoff Bros	Jury	Liemo
Expert	Golay	Hoffman	Juvenia	Liga
Express Leader	Gotham	Hofferes	Karo	Lilly
Express Monarch	Gothic	Hoffreres	Kelbert	Lincoln

Linnett
Locarno
Locomotive
Locust
Longeus
Longia
Longines
Lonier
Lonville
Lorna
Looping Alarm
Lorraine
Lotos
Lotus
Louis
Louverne
Luber
Luci
Ludero
Ludwo
Lunesa
Luor
Luther
Luxor
Luzon
Mader
Madewell
Mae
Madison
Maga
Magna
Magnific
Maiden Lady Special
Maine
Maire
Malleray
Malton
Manotoba
Manfred
Manhattan *
Manistee *
Manzoni
Marathon
Marcel
Marcella
Margo
Marine
Marion
Maritime Express
Marksman
Marlboro
Malys
Marmac
Marne
Marnex
Mars
Marshall
Martha
Marvin
Mathey

Mido
Mida
Mignon
Milex
Million
Milora
Milos
Milox
Mimo
Modern
Moeris
Mona
Monarch
Monitor
Monnier
Monopol
Montanden
Montandon
Montauk
Montbrilliant
Montellier
Montgomery
Montilier
Montreaux
Mordin
Mormac
Morningside
Mothier
Movado
Mura
Mutual
Myfair
Mysteria
Namdor
Narcisse
N. Hardin
Nassau
Nation
National Park
Navarre
Nedos
Nelka
Nelton
Nerny
New Haven
Newport
New Tavannes
New York Special
Niagara
Niolay
Nicolet
Nicoli Repeater
Nocollet
Nidor
Nifty
Nimra
Nivia
Nildi
Noldi
Nonesuch

Norco
Nordica
Normal
Normis
North Shore
Norwich
Nouvelle Tavennes
Notserp
Novalis
Numa-Droz
Nuni
Oak Park
Obelisk
Octava
Octa
Octora
Okeh
Olga
Ollendorff
Olympic
O'Maire
Omega
Omina
Ophir
Optima
Ora
Oranco
Orator
Orbit
Oria
Oriental
Orion
Oris
Orlins
Orvin
Ostara
Oxima
Oyster
Paimblanc
Panarama
Pandow
Paradox
Paragon
Paramount
Parfis
Park
Park Alarm
Parkside
Park Timer
Paskar
Pataca
Patek-Philippe
Patria
Patriot
Paul Breton
Pealham
Peerless
Pedos
Peggy
Pennant

151

Pennsylvania *
Perfecto
Perla
Perpetual
Perrenaud
Parrenin
Perrenoud
Perrin
Perrit Fils
Pery
Peseux
Pet
Peter Pan
Phenix
Phinney-Walker
Piaget
Piccolo
Piedmont
Pierce
Piguet
Pioneer
Plan
Pleade
Plymouth *
Poradox
Postala
Precimax
Preciosa
Precision
Precosia
Premo
Pride
Primrose
Princess
Principal
Puritan
P. U. W.
R & R
Racer
Racine
Rado
Railroad Special *
Railway Monarch
Ramle
Ramona
Raymond
Rebberg
Reber
Record
Recta
Rector
Red Feather
Red Wing
Rega
Regal
Regent
Regina
Reid
Relief
Relion

Reminder
Reminder Alarm
Rena
Renard
Renora
Republic *
Revardo
Revela
Revere *
Revil
Renue
Rexo
Reymond
Reynolds
R. I.
Rialto
Riso
Ritta
Rival
Roamer
Robert
Rocail
Rockford *
Rock Island
Roco
Rode
Roger & Co.
Rolex
Rolls Automatic
Roo
Rooster
Roric
Rosalia
Rose
Roseau
Rosemere
Rosetta
Roskoff
Roskopf
Rossel
Rosette
Roxane
Roxy
Royce
Rubaiyet
Russback
Ruth
Rythmos
Rytime
S. F. Q.
Sada
Salco
Salvia
Sandoz-Vuille
Sanor
Saracen
Saranac
Satisfaction
Savillon
Savoy

Saxon
Schild
Schilla
Schlup
Schwab
Schwob
Scilla
Seco
Seeland
Seiko
Select
Selva
Senator
Seneca
Senovak
Septeria
Serona
Seymour
Shell
Sheriden
Sherman
Shrine
Silena
Siris
Sirom
Siva
Slam
Sleda
Soldale
Soleta
Solrex
Solis
Solo
Solomax
Solrex
Solvil
Sonceboz
Sopra
Sorex
Sorority
Southern Express

Spahr
Speck
Speedway
Sphere
Springfield *
Sphink
Stabilis
Stand
Stauffer
Statesman
Steelclad
Stika
Stona
Stowa
Stratford
Stuber
Sturday
Sturtz
Stuyvesant
Suburban
Success
Sun
Sunrite
Supberb
Supreme
Sussie
S.W.C.
Swan
Swiza Clock
Syda
Tacy
Talis
Taresse
Tavannes
Tefar
Telefame
Terrasse
Thiel
Tilden-Thurber
Timemeter

Times
Tirette
Tissot
Toledo
Touchon
Touraine
Tramelan
Tramelon
Tramway
Transit
Transpacific
Travail
Trevail
Tribune
Trinitas
Trinite
Trinity
Triun
Trojan
Trotter
Troy
Truly
Ultra
Ultrathin
Ultus
Union Nat'l Watch
Unique
Unitas
Universal
Utmost
Urania
Urco
Urofa
V. & W. Watch Co.
Vacheron & Constantine
Vaco
Vagda
Valant
Valjoux
Valdez

Valencia
Valengine
Vallette Paul
Vallon
Van Buren
Vanchay
Vanity
Vant
Vanta
Vauchay
Va Vogue
Venus
Vera
Verithin
Vermont
Vermot
Verno
Vernon
Victor
Vigilant
Vilray
Vilroy
Vinca
Vince
Vitalis
Viva
Vivid
Vogt
Vow
Vuille
Vulcain
Vulcan
Waldemar
Wallingford
Walter
Ward
Warwick
Wasa
Watchford
Wearwell

Wega
Weiss
Weldwood
Wellington
Welsa
Welsam
Welsboro
Welta
Weltall
Wenco
Wengia
Westfield
Weston
Westpointer
Wilberco
Wildwood
Wilka
Willard
Winslow
Windsor
Winton
Wittnauer
Wizard
Wolf
Wonder
Woodmere
Woog
Worcester
Wyda
Wyler-Selfwind
Wyss
York
Zadik
Zebra
Zenith
Zeth
Zila
Zinnia
Zodiac

NAME ON WATCH	SOLD BY	MADE BY OR EXAMPLE
Abbott Sure Time	Alter & Co., Chicago, Il.	American Made
Acme Watch Company	Otto Young & Co., Chicago, Il.	Unknown
Advance - USA	Trenton	16 Size, Trenton Watch Co.
American General	Holsman & Co., Chicago, Il.	American Made
Ariston Watch Company, Chicago, Il.	Marshall Field	Illinois
Atlas Watch Company, Chicago, Il.	Louis Manheimer	Elgin
Ball Watch Co., Cleveland, Ohio	Webb C. Ball	Seth Thomas - Hampden - Howard -
Ball Watch Co., Cleveland, Ohio	Webb C. Ball	Swiss - Illinois - Hamilton - Waltham -
Ball Watch Co., Cleveland, Ohio	Webb C. Ball	Elgin - All Sizes
Benjamin Franklin - USA	Oskamp Nolting Co., Cin., Oh.	Illinois
Betsy Ross	Keystone Watch Case Co.	U.S. Watch Co. - Waltham
Boston Watch Co.	Unknown	18 Size - Hampden 211546
Burlington Watch Co., Chicago, Il.	Burlington	Illinois - Mail Order
Calumet - USA	A. C. Becken.	16 Size, Trenton Watch Co.
Canadian Pacific	Unknown	Waltham
Century - USA	Seth Thomas	18 Size, Seth Thomas
Century Watch Co.	S. F. Meyers	Swiss
Clinton Watch Co., Chicago, Il.	Unknown	Swiss
Columbia Watch Co., 1896-1901 Waltham, Mass.	Unknown	Unknown
Columbia - USA	New York Standard	New York Standard Watch Co.
Colorado & Eastern Watch Co.	Unknown	170,965 18 Size Keystone Watch Co.
Corono Watch Co., N.Y., N.Y.	R.R. Fogel Company	Unknown
Crown Watch Company	N. Y. Standard	N. Y. Standard
Dan Patch 1:55	M. W. Savage, Minn., Minn.	New York Standard - New England
Equity Watch Co., Boston	Waltham	Waltham
Excelsior - USA	New York Standard	New York Standard Watch Co.
Federal Watch Co., N.Y.	Louis Manheimer & Bros., N.Y., N.Y.	Unknown
Unknown	Garden City Watch Co., (1892), Chicago	Unknown
Globe Watch Co., N.Y., N.Y.	S. F. Meyers	Unknown
Granger Watch Company, S.F., Ca.	J. W. Tucker	Unknown
Grant - USA	A. C. Becken, Chicago	Chicago, Il. 16 Size, Illinois
Hammond Watch Co. - USA	Unknown	Unknown
Harvard Watch Co. - USA	Alter & Co., Chicago	American Made
Hayword Watch Co. - USA	Unknown	16 Size, 15J, N.Y. Standard 7,909,115
Herald Square	R. H. Macy Co.	Illinois
Hi-Grade - USA	Holsman & Co., Chicago	N. Y. Standard
Hollers Watch Co., Brooklyn, N.Y.	Unknown	18 Size Columbus 341143
Home Watch Co., Boston	Waltham	Waltham
Ideal - USA	N. Y. Standard	N. Y. Standard Watch Co.
Illinois Watch Case Co., Elgin, Il.	Unknown	16 Size, Trenton Watch Co.
Imperial Watch Co., Chicago	Unknown	18 Size Illinois 1,063,283
Iowa City Watch Co., Iowa City, Ia.	Iowa City	Illinois
Keystone Watch Co., Riverside, N.J.	Keystone	Howard & New York Standard
Lady Franklin	Oskamp Nolting Co., Cin., Oh.	Illinois
Lady Martha	A. C. Becken, Chicago	6 Size, Illinois
Lake Shore Watch Co., Fredonia, N.Y.	Lake Shore	Seth Thomas
La-Salle - USA	Alter & Co., Chicago	American Made
Lincoln Park - USA	A. C. Becken, Chicago	18 Size, Illinois
Lincoln - USA	A. C. Becken, Chicago	16 Size, Illinois
Locomotive Special - USA	Trenton	Trenton Watch Co.
Main Line Watch Co., Minn., Minn.	W. M. Stone	Unknown
Marvel Watch Co.	Trenton	Trenton Watch Co., N.J.
Mermod-Jaccard, St. Louis, Mo.	Mermod-Jaccard	Hampden - Hamilton
Monarch Watch Company, Chicago, Il.	Rogers, Thurman Co., Chicago, Il.	Illinois - Seth Thomas
New Era - USA	N. Y. Standard	N. Y. Standard
New Jersey Watch Co.	Unknown	16 Size Tavannes (Swiss)
New York - USA	Mosbacher & Co., N.Y.	Mosbacher & Co., N.Y.

NAME ON WATCH	SOLD BY	MADE BY OR EXAMPLE
Non-Magnetic Watch Co. of America Paillard - Chicago, USA	Non-Magnetic - Paillard	Swiss - Peoria, Illinois - Elgin 16 and 18 Size
Paillard Non-Magnetic Watch Co. - USA	Paillard	Swiss - Elgin - Peoria, Illinois
Pan American - USA	Alter & Co., Chicago	American Made
Perfection - USA	N. Y. Standard	N. Y. Standard
Plymouth Watch Co.	Sears Roebuck	Illinois - Seth Thomas - Rockford
Progress - USA	N. Y. Standard	N. Y. Standard
Providence Watch Co.	Unknown	18 Size, Seth Thomas, 15J
Railroad Watch Co., Cleveland, Oh.	Probably Ball	18 Size 20857 Hamilton
Regent - USA	Holsman & Co., Chicago	American Made
Reliance Watch Co., Chicago - USA	Trenton	16 Size, Trenton
Remington Watch Co.	Unknown	American
Republic - USA	Seth Thomas	6 Size, Seth Thomas, 31054686
Sante Fe Special	Sante Fe Watch Co., Topeka	Illinois
Sante Fe Watch Co., Topeka, Ks.	H. S. Montgomery	Waltham
Solar Watch Company, Chicago, Il.	Louis Manheimer	Elgin
Standard - USA	N. Y. Standard	N. Y. Standard
Stewart Watch Co.	A. W. Sproehnle, Chicago, Il.	12, 16 and 18 Size - Illinois
Suffolk Watch Co., Waltham, Mass.	Unknown	U. S. Watch Co. - Waltham
Sun-Dial, Washington, D. C.	Jason R. Hopkins	Elgin
Toronado Watch Co., Chicago, Il.	Unknown	17J, 12 Size, Seth Thomas, 931,996
Tribune - USA	Alter & Co., Chicago	Seth Thomas - Fake 23J
Tucker Watch, San Francisco, Ca.	John Gordon	Unknown
Veri-Best - USA	Alter & Co., Chicago	N. Y. Standard
Victoria Watch Co., N.Y., N.Y.	R. R. Fogel Co.	Unknown
Washington - USA	A. C. Becken, Chicago, Il.	18 Size - Illinois
Washington Watch Co.	Montgomery Ward	Illinois
Western Watch Co., Chicago, Il. (1880)	Unknown	Unknown
Wyoming Watch Co. - USA	Unknown	Seth Thomas

I WISH TO THANK THE FOLLOWING FINE PEOPLE FOR THEIR HELP

Bernie R. Nickel
  Sugar Creek, Mo.
Al Griner
  Overland Park, Ks.
Paul Graehling
  Polo, Illinois
Arthur Zimmerla
  Los Angeles, Ca.
Billie D. Beck
  Independence, Mo.
Mr. & Mrs. E. H. Parkhurst, Jr.
  Lancaster, Pa.
Dr. C. G. Berger
  Washington, D.C.
Dr. John N. Hoffman
  Washington, D.C.
Dr. Edwin A. Battison
  Washington, D.C.
Steward Dow
  Akron, Ohio
John D. Miller
  Bartlett, Illinois

Theo McCabe
  Manhattan, Kansas
Ron Starnes
  Tulsa, Oklahoma
Bob Coonfield
  Oklahoma City, Ok.
Eugene Fuller
  Sugarland, Texas
William Cheaqui (Photos)
  Kansas City, Mo.
Terry Rhoades
  Miami, Florida
Mike Beam, Jr.
  Lincolnton, N.C.
Jarvis Warren
  Charlotte, N.C.
Paul Wing
  Lanesville, Ma.
Harry Neames
  Baton Rouge, La.
David L. Self
  Lincolnton, N.C.

Paul Morgan
  Decatur, Indiana
Robert G. Williams
  Bailey, Colorado
John J. Yurkus
  East Templeton, Ma.
W. L. Pritchard
  Bethesda, Md.
Shirley Shelley (Art Work)
  Kansas City, Mo.
William L. Scolnik
  New York, N.Y.
Sidney Rosenberg
  Fresh Meadows, N.Y.
Fred Andrews
  Bossier City, La.
Sidney Schimmel
  Los Angeles, Ca.
Douglas Calkins
  Shreveport, La.
Mrs. Bill Bruer
  Kansas City, Mo.

COMMON IMPORTED COMPANY NAMES

Listed below are some of the more common watch company names found on the larger sizes of imported watches that are sometimes thought to be American made. Many of these names will be found on the Swiss made, fake American railroad watches. Most are very low grade 18 Size full plate and look like the 1857 model Waltham. There are collectors for these but usually bring less than $40.00 among collectors who know what they are. *Names also used on American made watches.

Albert Saltzman - Swiss
Albert Vuille - Swiss
Arrow Watch Company - Swiss
Bijou Watch Company - Swiss
Bourquin Family - Swiss
Bradford Watch Company - Swiss
Brighton Watch Company - Swiss
Bristol Watch Company,
  Bristol, Connecticut - Swiss?
Bulova, Small sizes - Swiss
Buren Watch Company - Swiss
Camden Watch Company - Swiss
Charles Latour - Swiss
Chase Watch Company - Swiss
Cleveland Watch Company - Swiss
Climax Watch Company - Swiss
Concord Watch Company - Swiss
Congress Watch Company - Swiss
Corgemont Watch Company - Swiss
Cortland Watch Company - Swiss
Dillon Watch Company - Swiss
Enterprise Watch Company - Swiss
Eterna Watch Company - Swiss
Frederic Nicoud - Swiss
Garfield Watch Company - Swiss
Gebruder-Theil - German
General Watch Company - Swiss
Genius Watch Company - Swiss
Gragin Watch Company - Swiss
Guarantee Watch Company - Swiss
Harney Watch Company,
  Springfield - Swiss
Hartford Watch Company - Swiss

Hebdomas, 8 day - Swiss
Helmet Watch Company - Swiss
Helvetia Watch Company - Swiss
H. Montandon - Swiss
H. W. Company - Swiss
Imperial Watch Company - Swiss
James Nardin Locle - Swiss
Jean Cardot - Swiss
Locust Watch Company - Swiss
Lonville Watch Company - Swiss
Lowiza Watch Company - Swiss
Lucien Sandoz - Swiss
Majestic Watch Company - Swiss
*Manhattan Watch Co. - Swiss
Marvin Watch Company
  Springfield, - Swiss
*Massasoit Watch Company,
  Boston, Mass. - Swiss?
*Melrose Watch Company - Swiss
Melville Watch Company - Swiss
Meriden Watch Company - Swiss
Metropolitan Watch Company,
  New York - Swiss
Meyer & Studelisa - Swiss
Minerva Watch Company - Swiss
Montauk Watch Company - Swiss
Montilier Watch Company - Swiss
N.D.C. Watch Company - Swiss
New Britian Watch Company - Swiss
*New Haven Watch Company - Swiss
Newton Watch Company - Swiss
Nicole Nielsen, London - Swiss
*North American Watch Co. - Swiss

Norwich Watch Company - Swiss
Ohio Watch Company - Swiss
Paul Breton - Swiss
Paul Laval - Swiss
Plan Watch Company - Swiss
*Providence Watch Company - Swiss
Renova Watch Company - Swiss
Roger & Company - Swiss
Romney Watch Company - Swiss
Roskoff-System Watch Co. - Swiss
Sandoz, Car Clocks - Swiss
Star Watch Company - Swiss
*Suffolk Watch Company - Swiss
Superior Watch Company - Swiss
Tavannes Watch Company - Swiss
Tacy Watch Company - Swiss
The Silver Cloud - Swiss
Tiffany & Company - Swiss
Union National Watch Company - Swiss
Universal Watch Company - Swiss
V. Vuillanne - Swiss
Wallingford Watch Company - Swiss
Washington Street Watch Company,
  Chicago, Illinois - Swiss
Western Watch Company,
  Chicago, Illinois - Swiss
Weston Watch Company - Swiss
Windsor Watch Company - Swiss
Winton Watch Company - Swiss
W. W. Watch Company - Swiss
Zentra Watch Company - Swiss

HIGH GRADE IMPORTED WATCH COMPANIES

Agassiz	Borquin	C. L. Guinand	Gruen	Longines	Tissot
A. G. Mathey	Breguet	Dent	H. L. Matile	Omega	Ulysse Nardin
Audemars-Piguet	Breitling	E. Hugenin	International	Patek Phillippe	Vacheron-Constantin
Louis Audemars	C. H. Meylan	Frodsham, Chas.	Jules Jurgensen	Rolex	Wittnauer
					Zenith

This list was made up from old advertisements or actual watches that I either have or have seen. There are no doubt many more, maybe hundreds, of company names. Some of these watch company names were actual manufacturers but most were used only for merchandising purposes and the watches were actually made by someone else. Very few factories, either foreign or American, used their own name on the lowest grade watches unless that was the only kind they made (like dollar watches). I have not included any English makers and not many antique watch makers because to do a complete listing would take a book in itself and they really don't show up that often as imports. Many of the old English watches that you see today have been brought over recently by antique dealers. A silver English watch of the common type is usually worth under $100.00 and most about $35 to $50. In my TRADEMARKS book there are many pages of trademarks that would help you identify many.

TYPICAL POCKET WATCH MAIL ORDER LIST

The following few pages is an actual copy of my January 1976 pocket watch mail order list. I have included this to give you some idea of how a watch actually sounds when offered for sale by mail. Please do not order any watches from this list because by the time you read this they will have long been sold. If you wish to buy watches by mail send your name and address with a self-addressed, stamped envelope and I will send you a copy of my next list. If you have one or a number of watches that you wish to offer me for sale, sit down and write out a description along with the price you want. I do not make offers because unless you know what you want for your watch I can't buy it anyway and we'll just be wasting your time and mine. I usually do not pay current retail price for watches and I'm sure you realize why. I must have a little room when I re-sell them, just as any other watch dealer would. If you know of anyone else who has a fair size collection of watches for sale, say $3,000.00 and up, and you think they are priced fairly and you do not wish to buy them yourself, I would appreciate a collect call giving me the information.

* *

Dear Friends,

You haven't missed any watch lists - I just haven't issued any for the past few months. I just bought a large collection (most of which are included here) and decided that I ought to send one out. Up to now, since my last list, I have sold practically every watch that amounted to anything to old customers who just call me on the phone and ask what I have. I do appreciate your business and confidence and since this list is going out to a lot of new folks who requested the list sometime ago, I hope you will see something here that you would like to have in your collection. It's hard for me to get together enough watches to put out a list so if you don't hear from me in a month or so, give me a call and we'll discuss the watches I have available. I keep a few close by the phone but the majority of my collection is kept at the bank down the street from my home.

Use the same rules as on previous lists with the 816-761-0080 phone number for night and 816-761-0064 for day. I would rather have phone calls than letters because most of the time if you wait long enough to send a letter the watches are gone and this involves me returning your money order. You may send a check but you will have to allow time for a call to your bank or the check to clear before receiving the watches. Postal Money Orders are preferred or cash sent by Registered Mail. This is the quickest and fastest way to do business.

You may have the watch in your possession two days and then return it if you are not satisfied. I would appreciate a call if the watch is not acceptable so I can sell it to someone else. I will stay by the phone this weekend to accept your calls and you may call me up until 12:00 Midnight CST. Watch this California! Phone rates are now very inexpensive before 8:00 in the morning and after 11:00 P.M. Attention investment and volume buyers! If you buy $1,000.00 worth of watches from this list I will throw in a watch of your choice worth up to $100.00 chosen from this list or will give you $100.00 credit on the next watch purchased.

I have tried to describe these watches as closely as I can by actually taking off the backs and covers and reading the condition directly to my secretary. As you know, these watches come from many different sources and I am not a watchmaker and if it isn't visible to the naked eye I won't know about it. Some of the watches I'm sure have been cleaned but if you plan to carry one I would suggest you take it to your jeweler and have it inspected. A watch can damage itself if the oil has dried out and it is very dirty. I do not check them to see if they are keeping railroad time but if something is seriously wrong with your watch that doesn't show up for a few days after the inspection period I will try to help you locate parts or whatever needs to be done to correct it.

A friend of mine is having Star Watch Case Company use their old dies and make some 16 Size railroad cases. I have a few of his first case. It looks like the center case on top of Page 44, Book 2. It is 10Kt yellow gold filled with a plain polished back instead of the Butler finish like Hamilton had them made. It is this exact case except Hamilton does not appear on the case and the lever slot is cut from 6 to 8 minutes to accept the majority of lever set movements. If you have some favorite watches in your collection that are poorly cased, these are just the ticket. Your cost delivered is $60.00 each. These are beautiful cases made in the old style and high quality workmanship and are also 10Kt yellow gold filled and will not show wear easily.

ROY EHRHARDT

3501 ILLINOIS 18S 24J BUNN SPECIAL. Mint Mvt. 1,382,425 except pointer on regulator missing (1-58-2). 20 YGF Fahys all-over decorated HC. Extremely fine with no brass showing. Mint Antique ART DS porcelain dial with small nick at 5. A fine looking very scarce watch. $400.00

3502 ILLINOIS 18S Ruby Jewel BUNN SPECIAL. Mint OF Mvt. 1,605,962 (1-58-2). Near mint 20 SB&B RR case. Mint antique bold ART DS porcelain dial. $400.00

3503 ILLINOIS 18S 23J BUNN SPECIAL. Mint OF Mvt. 2,312,633 (2-61-2), 6P. Near mint Dueber 20 YGF hinged ET OF RR case. $300.00

3504 ILLINOIS 18S 17J BUNN. Mint Mvt. 1,351,881 (Like 2-57-2 except not Chalmers). Near mint PP 20 SB&B OF RR case. Mint bold ART OP dial, one minor hairline. $150.00

3505 WALTHAM 16S 21J RIVERSIDE MAXIMUS Model 88. Mint Mvt. 7,000,287. Trace of discoloration on large winding wheel. (2-152-2). Mint 25 Yr. J. Boss hinged HC. Stag on back with floral decoration. No initial in shield. Mint Maximus DS Arabic dial with one minor hairline. $450.00

3506 WALTHAM 16S 23J RIVERSIDE MAXIMUS. Mint HC Mvt. 12,046,814, 99 Model (7-155-2). Beautiful factory new Phila. 20 YGF all-over decorated with ET and floral decoration. Case must be seen - can't describe it. Mint SS Waltham decorated dial with gold inlay. This is probably the finest specimen short of solid gold you could have for your collection. $550.00

3507 WALTHAM 16S 23J RIVERSIDE MAXIMUS, 6P Lossier Interterminal hairspring. Mint Mvt. 15,062,155 (7-155-2). Mint plus 20 Yr. Phila. SB&B OF all-over decorated, no initial case. Mint DS Maximus ART dial with two very minor hairlines. $400.00

3508 WALTHAM 16S UP-DOWN INDICATOR 23J Lossier 6P VANGUARD. Mint Mvt. 25,895,445 (9-155-2). Mint Waltham SB&B OF 14KWGF RR case. Mint DS bold RR dial marked "Vanguard 23 Jewels". $300.00

3509 WALTHAM 16S UP-DOWN INDICATOR 23J VANGUARD. Mint 5P Mvt. 16,029,962 (7-155-2). Factory new J. Boss 10K YGF SB&B OF RR case. Mint old style TS OP dial with two minor hairlines. $300.00

3510 ELGIN UP-DOWN INDICATOR 16S 23J B. W. RAYMOND Mint 6P Mvt. 34,900,945. Mint Elgin B.W. Raymond model, J. Boss 10KYGF SB&B OF RR case. Mint DS bold old style OP dial. $300.00

3511 ELGIN UP-DOWN INDICATOR 16S BU. AERO U.S. NAVY. 23J B.W. Raymond. Mint 6P Mvt. 34,900,724. Near mint Keystone white base metal case. Near mint, black with white numerals, white hands, metal DS dial marked "Bu. Aero U.S. Navy GCT Elgin". $400.00

3512 WALTHAM UP-DOWN INDICATOR 16S 23J U.S. ARMY AC. Mint 6P VANGUARD Mvt. 27,443,669. Very fine original Keystone white base metal case with Army nomenclature on back of case. Mint DS, black with white numbers and black hands, metal dial. $400.00

3513 ELGIN 16S 21J BRIDGE MODEL "GRADE 162". Mint Mvt. 6,469,825. A beauty! (1-84-2). Mint Keystone 10KYGF J. Boss SB&B OF case. Mint DS ART script dial. One faint hairline. $225.00

3514 ELGIN 16S VERITAS 23J. Mint Mvt. 23,634,796 (2-90-2). near mint 14KYGF Dueber SB&B case. Mint bold DS OP dial. $230.00

3515 ILLINOIS 16S 23J SANGAMO SPECIAL. Complete near mint watch. 14KWGF hinged case (like 1,2,3-69-2). "Illinois Watch Company Sangamo Special" written in a circle on the inner lid. Like Howards. Mint dial. $350.00

3516 ILLINOIS. Same as 15 except YGF. $350.00

3517 ILLINOIS SANGAMO SPECIAL 16S 23J. Near mint Mvt. 4,644,807 (3-69-2). 14KWGF Sangamo Special SB&B OF case (like 1-70-2). Mint DS RR dial. $250.00

3518 ILLINOIS 16S 23J SANGAMO SPECIAL. Mint Mvt. 3,524,943 (3-69-2). Mint old style pointed bow Sangamo case before they were marked. Wadsworth 14KYGF 25 Yr. SB hinged front. Mint DS RR dial. $200.00

3519 BALL 16S 23J ILLINOIS BALL. Near mint Mvt. B800,488. 14KWGF Ball case, decorated back, no initial, near mint. Mint Ball dial with original hands. $325.00

3520 ILLINOIS 16S 23J SANGAMO SPECIAL, square pattern damaskeening (1-62-2). Mint Mvt. 2,868,651. Jewelled barrel, 6P. A beauty and scarce! Mint ET Illinois 20 YGF SB&B OF case. Mint DS OP dial except faint hairline. $350.00

3521 ILLINOIS 16S 60 HOUR 12J BUNN SPECIAL (5-69-2). Mint plus Mvt. 5,180,991, 6P. Mint case marked "Bunn Special", SB&B Model 28 (4-69-2). Mint DS OP dial with "Illinois Bunn Special 23 Jewel 60 Hour" written on it. $300.00

3522 ILLINOIS 16S 60 HOUR 21J BUNN SPECIAL. Mint plus Mvt. 5,132,164. Near mint Bunn Special 14KWGF SB&B RR case (1-70-2). Mint DS OP RR case. $185.00

3523 ILLINOIS 16S BUNN SPECIAL. Mint motor barrel 6P Mvt. 3,604,730. Near mint SB&B 20 YGF ET OF case with minor brass showing. Mint DS OP MRR dial. $200.00

3524 ILLINOIS 16S 21J (161A) 60 HOUR. Motor barrel 6P mint Mvt. 5,511,791. Near mint GBSBDC Illinois case. Mint MRR DS OP dial. $200.00

3525 CASE ONLY 16S ILLINOIS BUNN SPECIAL MODEL 181. Brand factory new. Fancy 14KWGF Fahys SB&B OF case. Never had a watch in it. $125.00

3526 ILLINOIS 16S 23J Illinois Watch Company single ratchet Mvt. 2,232,991 (damaskeened like 6-59-2). First one I have ever seen. Mint ART OP dial. Fine Dueber 20 YGF SB&B OF case with a flying eagle and flag engraved on back with very minor brass showing on high places. $225.00

3527 ILLINOIS 16S 19J "60 HOUR BUNN". Near mint Mvt. 4,780,291. Near mint GBSBDC Illinois case. Mint SS RR dial and hands with two very minor hairlines. $200.00

3528 ILLINOIS 16S 23J SANGAMO SPECIAL. 6P, Mint Mvt. 2,430,702 (like (1-59-2). Near mint SB&B YGF Wadsworth PP OF case with huge initials on back - can't read them. Mint antique ART DS OP dial and hands. $200.00

3529 ILLINOIS 16S "GRADE 174" 17J. LS mint Mvt. 2,231,712 (6-59-2). Near mint 20 YGF HB&B ET and floral decorated, no initial, OF case. Beautiful mint "FERGUSON RR DIAL". $125.00

3530 ILLINOIS 16S 21J BUNN SPECIAL. Mint Mvt. 3,871,068 except trace of unremoved dust on large barrel wheel (like 5-69-2). 20 YGF PP SB&B OF case. Beautiful mint "FERGUSON RR DIAL". $165.00

3531 ILLINOIS 18S 21J BUNN SPECIAL. Mint Mvt. 1,664,991 (2-58-2). Near mint 20 YGF Keystone PP, SB&B OF RR case. Minor brass showing. Beautiful "FERGUSON RR DIAL" (1-191-2). $175.00

3532 ILLINOIS 18S 21J Illinois Watch Company. Adj. 3P, 2-tone cross hatched damaskeened patterned (like 6-61-2). All gilt screws 7 regulator. Near mint Mvt. 2,317,253. Factory new SB&B glass back display case. Beautiful "FERGUSON RR DIAL". $175.00

3533 ILLINOIS 18S BUNN SPECIAL 21 Ruby Jewel, 2-tone circular pattern damaskeened. Near mint Mvt. 1,524,826. Near mint 20 Yr. J. Boss SRC PP case in mint bold DS OP ART dial and hands. Minor hairline at 4. $135.00

3534 ILLINOIS 16S 17J ILLINOIS CENTRAL. Beautiful 2-tone mint Mvt. 3,117,859 marked both dial & mvt. "Illinois Central". Near mint 20 YGF SB&B OF RR PP case. Mint DS OP dial & hands. $125.00

3535 BURLINGTON 16S 19J. Complete watch is mint. Case is 14KWGF Wadsworth with a stirrup bow and decorated edges. Dial is the finest MRR DS OP I have ever seen. This is the best example of a Burlington RR watch I have seen. $150.00

3536 BURLINGTON 16S 19J. Mint Mvt. Near mint 20 YGF SB&B OF case. Shows some wear but no brass. Beautiful mint MRR dial. $120.00

3537 SETH THOMAS 18S 12J, 2-tone gold and nickel damaskeened mint Mvt. 790,545 marked "EDGEMERE CHICAGO, ILL." Crescent silveroid SRC case (like 13-12-2). Mint SS RBT OP dial marked "EDGEMERE" (Sears & Roebuck). $100.00

3538 ELGIN 18S HC 15J. Mint Mvt. 7,685,989, cleaned & oiled. Near mint 25 Yr. 14KYGF all-over decorated HC with house, forest and floral motif. $125.00

3539 WALTHAM 18S Keywind WM ELLERY. Mint gilded Mvt. 726,016. Extremely fine 18K ETHC. Shows some wear but extremely solid case. Mint flat hand-lettered Roman dial with original hands. Complete watch is original. $300.00

3540 WALTHAM 14S 16J MODEL 74. Complete watch is mint to factory new. Highest grade 84 Model. Mint Mvt. 1,144,138. In original 18K Waltham ET heavy HC. Roman dial is mint. This watch is definitely a keeper. $600.00

3541 NEW YORK STANDARD 16S. Convertible (Hunting or OF) mint gilded Mvt. 602,651 (9-47-2). Mint original pilot YGF all-over decorated with floral motif HC. Mint RRT dial with original hands. This watch is very rare, mint, complete & original. $350.00

3542 WALTHAM 16S 68 Model KW and KS from back. Looks to be 15J. Mint gilded Mvt. 190,006 in original Robbins & Appleton case No. 6003. Mint Roman SS hand-lettered dial with original hands. This is a complete and original watch in near mint condition. This is a real collector's piece. $400.00

3543 HOWARD 16S 19J SERIES 5. Mint Mvt. 1,143,894 (6-175-2). Near mint Howard 25 YGF HB&B PP OF case. Mint bold DS OP RR dial. One faint hairline. $175.00

3544 HOWARD 16S 19J. Near mint Mvt. 1,094,485 (8-175-2) in a Howard 14K solid YG HB&B PP OF Jurgenson lip case. Has small dings around edge. Mint ART dial and hands. $200.00

3545 HOWARD 16S 17J SERIES 9. Mint cross hatched damaskeened Mvt. 974,485 (11-175-2). Near mint 25 Yr. Crescent SRC case with Howard name in a ring. Mint MRR DS OP dial and hands. This is an un-marked 5P RR watch. $125.00

3546 HOWARD 16S 21J SERIES 10. Mint Mvt. 1,170,193 (3-175-2). Near mint SRC PP Howard case. Mint DS OP bold RR dial with one hairline. $175.00

3547 HOWARD 16S 17J MODEL 5. Mint Mvt. 1,145,175. PS, cross hatched damaskeened (11-175-2). Extremely fine, near mint ET SB&B OF RR case with minor brass showing on high edge. Mint ABT DS OP dial. $100.00

3548 COLUMBUS 16S 16J. Near mint Mvt. 128,072 (like 3-108-2). Very early 16S RR watch that is scarce. Fine 20 YGF HB&B OF case. Minor brass showing. Mint DS RRT OP dial and hands with four minor hairlines. $150.00

3549 BALL 16S 23J HAMILTON BALL. Mint Mvt. B607,658, 5P gold seal motor barrel in a Ball model 20 YGF SB&B OF reeded edge RR case. Mint SS Ball dial and hands. $300.00

3550 BALL 16S 17J COMMERCIAL STANDARD WALTHAM. Mint Mvt. B244,109. Near Mint NAWCO RR Model 10KYGF decorated edge case with extra dust cover and very heavy stem and bow. Mint SS Ball dial. $100.00

3551 BALL 18S 17J HAMILTON. Mint Mvt. 488,460, "999". Mint Hamilton GBSBDC case. Mint Ball dial with 8 minor hairlines. $120.00

3552 BALL 18S "333" Elgin made 17J. Near mint Mvt. 12,279,708. Solid SB&B OF Monitor case marked "25 Year". Original gold plated, now completely brass but solid. Ball dial has 3 minor hairlines. $150.00

3553 ELGIN OPERA WATCH' Mint OS Mvt. in about a very thin 12S Dueber 25 YGF case. Beautiful ET with a spiral effect both front and back. Dial is gold colored metal with decorated center. This is a very pretty mint watch suitable for a gift. $150.00

3554 NORTH AMERICAN RAILWAY 18S 21J HAMPDEN. Near mint Mvt. 1,839,523. Fine Hamilton GBSBDC case. Mint DS OP ART dial and hands. $150.00

3555 SETH THOMAS 18S 17J. 2-tone gold damaskeened Mvt. 788,288 marked "EDGEMERE, CHICAGO, ILLINOIS" (similar to 13-12-2). Good solid 20 YGF SB&B OF case with brass showing all over. Mint SS RRT dial with repair at 2:30, marked "EDGEMERE" (Sears & Roebuck). $75.00

3556 WALTHAM 14S SWEEP SECOND. Mint frosted 17J or better Mvt. 3,126,830. Mint Crescent HB&B YGF ET OF case. Mint OP dial and hands. Running good. $150.00

3557 HAMILTON 16S 22J SWEEP SECOND MODEL 4992B. Mint Mvt. in original Keystone base metal case with Army writing on back. Mint original black face, 24-hour white hands. $75.00

3558 ELGIN 16S 21J B.W. RAYMOND SWEEP SECOND MODEL. Near mint Mvt. 41,756,870. Original base metal Keystone case made for the Army by Elgin with lettering on back of case. Mint black face 24 Hr. GCT dial. White hands have been re-touched. $85.00

3559 ROCKFORD 16S old model. Mint 17J 2-tone cross hatched damaskeened Mvt. 385,966. GRADE 103 (3-138-2). Winding is stiff. Probably needs oiling. Mint 20 YGF all-over decorated HC. Cliff house & boat scene with ET and floral decoration. No initial in shield, mint DS RRT dial with original hands. This complete watch is like new and original. $250.00

3560 ROCKFORD 18S 17J. Mint striped 2-tone gold damaskeened Mvt. 800,062. Mint Phila. silveroid all-over decorated SB&B OF RR case. Perfect, beautiful "FERGUSON DIAL". A very scarce combination! $175.00

3561 ROCKFORD 16S 17J. Mint Mvt. 552,037. Near mint Star Stellar white SB&B OF RR case. Perfect "FERGUSON DIAL". $140.00

3562 ROCKFORD 16S 17J WINNEBAGO. Mint Mvt. 674,387. Mint Hamilton GBSBDC case. Mint DS OP ART dial and hands, with 2 minor hairlines. $160.00

3563 WALTHAM 14S 13J gilded RIVERSIDE. OF Mvt. Model 74 (4-142-W). This is very unusual watch because it is completely original in original Waltham 14K solid gold HC but the second bit pinion has been cut off of this OF movement and installed in a HC. Case has Jurgenson lips and a very long antique type stem and bow with a genuine box hinge on the side instead of at the bottom. Very hard to explain. PP back and very large old English initials on front—can't make them out. Maybe "EIMIF". Mvt. and dial and inside of case looks brand new. Outside shows slight wear. $450.00

3564 WALTHAM 6S. Mint 15J Mvt. Mint 25 Yr. Keystone YGF all-over decorated, no initial HC. $100.00

3565 WALTHAM 16S 21J VANGUARD' Mint Mvt. 18,024,927, 5P. Mint Star white base metal SB&B OF RR case. Mint DS OP ART RR dial and hands. A very scarce watch! $225.00

3566 WALTHAM 16S 17J AWW CO. (6-156-2). PS, near mint 25 Yr. Crescent YGF SB&B PP OF RR case. "FERGUSON DIAL" with few hairlines but no parts missing. $85.00

3567 WALTHAM 16S 16J 1872 MODEL. Beautiful mint Mvt. 2,020,060 (3-16-W). Hint of rust on winding wheel not noticable. Original coin silver ET OF case. Mint SS Roman dial &hands. This watch is very collectible and all original. $160.00

3568 WALTHAM 18S 21J VANGUARD. Near mint Mvt. 10,069,489. Ticks but won't run. Near mint base metal SB&B OF case. Near mint DS ART dial and hands. Two minor hairlines. $75.00

3569 WALTHAM 18S 21J "845". Near mint Mvt. 12,653,170. Factory new Defiance chrome SB&B OF case with double track steam engine on back. Mint DS OP dial and hands. $85.00

3570 WALTHAM 16S 23J VANGUARD. Mint Mvt. 22,052,806 in a factory new Defiance chrome SB&B OF RR case with a double track diesel on back. Mint DS bold OP RR dial and hands. Two invisible hairlines. $110.00

3571 HAMPDEN 16S 23J GRADE 104. Mint Mvt. 3,322,142 (plates like 4-24-2). Fine Supreme yellow SB&B OF RR case. Mint DS OP old ART dial.

3572 HAMPDEN 16S 23J SPECIAL RAILWAY. Mint plus Mvt. 3,327,232 (plates shaped like 4-24-2) with raised gold cups and rayed damaskeening. OF case is Dueber 20 YGF all-over decorated with fine ET and hand-engraving. Mint DS OP RR dial and hands. This watch is completely mint throughout. $225.00

3573 HAMPDEN 16S 23J SPECIAL RAILWAY, 2-tone and nickel damaskeening. Mint Mvt. 1,899,054 (plates like 1-24-2). Near mint SRC case. Mint DS OP ART dial. This is a HC Mvt. in an OF case. $175.00

3574 HAMPDEN 16S 21J GRADE 105. Mint Mvt. 3,396,644. Fine snap back and front Keystone case. Mint DS OP bold ART RR dial. $100.00

3575 ELGIN 16S 21J GRADE 360 VERITAS. Scarce if not rare! Near mint Mvt. 13,482,280. Less than 1,000 made. 10KYGF SRC PP OF RR case. Original mint DS porcelain dial. ART with minor hairlines. $200.00

3576 ELGIN 16S 17J GRADE 280. Mint Mvt. 10,127,683 RR watch. Factory new Spartan white SB&B OF RR case. Mint DS OP ART dial, minor repair at 7. $150.00

3577 ELGIN 16S 19J B.W. RAYMOND. Mint Mvt. 17,403,883. Extremely fine 20 YGF PP SB&B OF RR case. Mint DS OP bold RR dial. Minor brass showing. $100.00

3578 ELGIN 18S 19J B. W. RAYMOND. Near mint Mvt. 13,358,933. 20 YGF SB&B OF RR case. Minor brass showing but good and solid. Factory new "FERGUSON DIAL". Looks same as watch on back cover of Book 2. $150.00

3579 ELGIN 12S 19J LORD ELGIN. Mint Mvt. 27,591,568. 8 Adj., stream line damaskeened. Original 14K solid WG Elgin HB&B case with dust cover. Mint frosted silver colored dial with white raised numbers and hands. Egg-shaped bow. A dandy little hi-grade watch—very collectibe. $150.00

3580 ELGIN 16S 15J GRADE 50 convertible. Near mint Mvt. 3,507,359. Original pilot YGF ET edge-decorated HC. Mint SS Roman dial and hands. An over-all fine watch. $125.00

3581 ELGIN 16S 17J B.W. RAYMOND 3/4 PLATE. Mint Mvt. 14,845,881, 5P, LS. Fine 20 YGF SB&B OF RR case. Mint DS bold OP dial. A scarce RR watch! $135.00

3582 AURORA 18S 15J. Adj., near mint gilded Mvt. "RR GRADE NO.6" Breguet hairspring. Pat. Reg., original 14KYGF Keystone case presented in 1893. Some brass showing. Mint DS OP RBT dial with original hands. $150.00

3583 SOUTH BEND 18S 17J "GRADE 341". Mint Mvt. 403,925. Fine solid 20 Yr. SB&B OF RR case. Minor brass showing. Mint DS OP ART dial and hands. Marked "Jeff B. James". Watch looks original $80.00

3584 HAMILTON 18S 23J GRADE 946. Mint Mvt., fine silveroid case. Mint MRR DS OP Dial. Nick at lever. $275.00

3585 HAMILTON 18S GRADE 938. Mint 17J gold cup Mvt. 44,066. Very, very scarce! Mint over-all decorated SB&B YGF OF case. Mint DS OP ART dial and hands with one hairline. Marked jewelers' name. $250.00

3586 HAMILTON 18S GRADE 929. Near mint 15J Mvt. 27,601. Jewelers' name "M.F. Plambeck, Denver, Colorado" on Mvt. and dial. Fine silveroid OF case. Original dial with four hairlines. $150.00

3587 HAMILTON 18S "RR GRADE 937". 17J, mint Mvt. 15,507 marked "J. Vander Fanden Special". Cased in a YGF loose fit but complete HC with brass showing. Mint DS RRT dial with same name on dial. $160.00

160

ANNOUNCING A NEW BOOK

CLOCK
IDENTIFICATION AND PRICE GUIDE
198, 8½X11 Pages, Plastic Bound to lay flat.
By: Roy Ehrhardt & Malvern "Red" Rabeneck — 1977

THIS BOOK CONTAINS

—4,000 CLOCKS PICTURED OR DESCRIBED—

—MOST OF THE CLOCKS YOU SEE EVERYDAY—

—IDENTIFICATION AND DATING OF 150 OF THE MOST
IMPORTANT CLOCK MAKERS SHOWN IN CHART FORM.
BEGINNING WITH THOMAS HARLAND IN 1773 DOWN
TO THE PRESENT TIME.—

—BEAUTIFUL COLOR COVERS—

—BY THE PICTURES IS YOUR CLOCK ORIGINAL—

—THE ONLY BOOK OF THIS KIND EVER PUBLISHED.
TWO YEARS IN PREPARATION.—

Price $15.00

This book contains carefully selected actual pages from original factory sales catalogs, factory advertisements, supply house catalogs, and sales brochures. It covers American and imported clocks from 1850 to the 1940's. The following information is given for each clock:

—THE YEAR IT WAS OFFERED FOR SALE—

—THE FACTORY DESCRIPTION—

—THE PRICE IT SOLD FOR ORIGINALLY—

—THE PRESENT RETAIL VALUE—

Over 95% of all clocks manufactured or sold in the United States since 1850 can be identified and a reasonably close retail value arrived at by comparing your clock with a picture of it or a similar one in the book.

This is a very unique book. The original antique and historic material has not been altered. Long after the current retail prices no longer apply to the clocks shown herein, it will still be very valuable to anyone interested in clocks for research and identification purposes.

This is a book about the clocks you see every day and were sold commercially throughout the world since 1850. You can apply the information contained within to clocks that you see and wonder about, and to those that are offered for sale either by a dealer, trader or collector on a day-to-day basis.

No other collectible that is as readily available to collectors and investors has the potential to increase in value over the next few years as do old clocks. This book tells you why. The actual index is shown on the back of this page.

If you have any interest in clocks, you can't afford not to have a copy.

Additional Copies of this Book may be Ordered from the
Author-Publisher:

ROY EHRHARDT
P. O. Box 9808
Kansas City, Missouri 64134

Send $15.00 plus 50 cents postage and handling—U.S. and Canada. Foreign Countries—Check with your Post Office for rate, your choice, Air or Sea Mail, Book Rate. Book and carton weigh 1 lb. 12 oz.

INDEX

FOR PRICE REVISIONS, SEE ERRATA PAGE 189

3588 HAMILTON 18S 16J GRADE 930. Mint Mvt. 35,516 marked "J. C. Gray Special, Cortland, New York". Good solid OF YGF case with some brass showing. Mint DS ART dial. $150.00

3589 HAMILTON 18S 15J GRADE 928. Mint Mvt. 108,112. Solid SB&B YGF case with brass showing over all. Mint SS Roman dial. $150.00

3590 HAMILTON 18S 17J GRADE 936. Mint Mvt. 114,705. "Willis A. Cates, Portland, Maine" on Mvt. and dial. Solid YGF case with brass showing. OP DS dial with repair and few hairlines. $65.00

3591 HAMILTON 18S 17J RR GRADE 937. Near mint Mvt. 111,412 marked "Thomas Fitzgerald". Mint Hamilton GBSBDC case. Mint DS OP ART dial. $135.00

3592 HAMILTON 16S 23J GRADE 950B. Mint Mvt. 2-15329. Near mint original Hamilton 10KYGF case. Original Hamilton dial and hands marked "23 Jewel Railway Special." $200.00

3593 HAMILTON 16S 21J GRADE 992 ELINVAR with gold center wheel and touch of rust on one winding wheel (like case 4-44-2). Original Wadsworth 10KYGF bar style case. Mint DS porcelain bold RR dial. $150.00

3594 HAMILTON 16S 21J GRADE 992B. Complete watch is mint in a factory new case like 4-44-2. $160.00

3595   RARE—WALTHAM   CRYSTAL   PLATE
Four size Rock Crystal Plate, 16 ruby jewels in gold settings. Gold train, exposed pallets, compensation balance, adjusted to temperature isochronism and position, Breguet hairspring, crystal top plate. Watch No. 42. Full picture and factory description can be found at Watch No. 1, Page 166 of my new WALTHAM BOOK. This watch is cased in an 18K solid gold, plain polish, exhibition back case. It is open face with a mint dial except a tiny nick under the bezel at 1:30. You must push the pendant to open the movement which is under glass. There is slight damage around the top balance jewel which has been repaired by adding a small piece of metal to strengthen it. To the untrained eye this appears to be part of the original watch so I don't consider the damage to be of much significance. It has been reported, although nothing reliable that I have seen, that Waltham might have made as many as 80 crystal plate watches of all sizes. To my knowledge I know of only 5 or 6 and at least three of those are damaged to the point of not being collectible. $2,400.00   P.S. This watch is completely original and in otherwise mint condition.

3596 THE PRESIDENT. 18S U.S. WATCH COMPANY, WALTHAM, MASS. Adj, Serial 150,276, all appears on the plates. This is a beautiful 2-tone, nickel movement and is exactly as appears as Watch No. 9, Page 101 of my Book 2. The case is an open face, all-over decorated, no initial in shield, apparently gold filled, screw back & bezel, open face case marked only with the word "President and No. 86738". The condition is mint. The dial is a perfect double sunk Arabic red track, original porcelain dial marked "The President". $1,500.00

3597 ROCKFORD PROTOTYPE. Back plates are made of aluminum with four gold cups showing and is apparently 15J. Only the letters "R. W. Company, Rockford, Illinois" appears on the barrel bridge. All of the parts are stamped "No. 13" on the unfinished side. The watch has a regulator like 13-136-2. The plates look exactly like Watch No. 7-137-2 except no serial numbers or decoration on the balance cock. The dial is a single sunk, Roman red track, original porcelain mint. The case is a screw back and bezel, open face display case. The movement is hunting. Complete watch is mint. $2,500.00

3598 CAPTAIN'S WATCH. Double train, mint, light gilt frosted movement. Probably about 32 jewels. About 16S. No numbers or writing on movement. Inside dust cover has a dedication to "Luther C. Clark, 18 Gramercy Park, New York, K18, No. 9362". Outside dust cover "William F. Ladd's Improved Patent, Quarter or seconds timing Watch No. 9369, Manufactured by Delachaux Freres Lochle". Inside back cover again has the name of the factory and K18 and the serial number. The outside case is near mint, engine turned, perfectly solid, and would be considered mint except shows slight wear on the engine turning on the edge of the case. The dial is mint with a full outside chapter ring marked in quarter seconds with a small chapter ring at the top and one quarter jump second hand marked "William F. Ladd, New York". This is Keywind, Keyset from the back with stop mechanism slide actuated. Firm price. . . $1,000.00

3599 ELGIN 16S 23J B.W. RAYMOND UP-DOWN INDICATOR. Mint Mvt. 33,595,155. GRADE 494. Factory new Elgin J. Boss 10KYGF SB&B RR case. Similar to 5-75-2. Mint bold DS OP RR dial. $400.00

3600 ELGIN 21J 16S B.W. RAYMOND UP-DOWN INDICATOR' Mint Mvt. 29,484,242. Near mint cased and timed at the factory, B. W. Raymond Model, J. Boss, 10KYGF SB&B RR case (like 1-75-2). Mint Montgomery DS original porcelain RR dial with one almost invisible hairline. $330.00

3602 WALTHAM 16S 23J VANGUARD UP-DOWN INDICATOR, 6P, with Lossier Interterminal hairspring. Mint Mvt. 25,402,730 Mint Waltham J. Boss 10K YGF SB&B RR case (like 1-75-2). Mint SS RR dial with 24 hour figures on the inside track. $250.00

3603 CHESHIRE 18S 7J. Mint gilded Mvt. 59,319. Page 188-2. In a mint original gold plated, engine turned, no initial HC. Mint Cheshire dial as shown on page 88. Watch appears to be original.$125.00

3604 WALTHAM 16S MODEL 1860 (KW-16). Beautiful bright gilded 15J Mvt. 250,678 marked "Appleton Tracy & Company" in a near mint ET, KW, KS from the back, HC. Mint hand lettered dial, dedication inside front cover "December 25, 1876". This is a very scarce, originally cased pocket watch. $450.00

3605 ELGIN 16S 21J GRADE 72. Near mint Mvt. 607,161. (Same as 72-82-2). Mint SS Roman dial in a GBSBDC case. $240.00

3606 WALTHAM 16S 23J RIVERSIDE MAXIMUS. Mint Mvt. 10,530,257. Near mint 25 Yr. J. Boss, DB OF, case. Mint depressed center ART dial. $330.00

3607 WALTHAM 12S 21J RIVERSIDE MAXIMUS. Mvt. 10,508,091. In a near mint DB 14K medium weight Wadsworth case. Large initials covers almost entire back of case, reeded edges but has couple of small dings. Mint DS Maximus ART dial. $250.00

3608 ILLINOIS 16S 23J. Mint Mvt. 2,357,722 marked "23 diamond ruby and sapphire jewels, adj. 6 positions, Illinois Watch Company, Springfield". The mvt. looks like 3-69-2 but has in addition gold train, gold cups and screws and gold outriggers on two of the bridges. It also has a four piece bridge instead of the usual three as on the Sangamo Special. The information on the Illinois Serial Number List on this movement is sketchy but indicates it is one of 19 produced in this run and as of yet I have not been able to find any more on the list. The grade is indicated as No. 310. This watch is PS and has a mint DS OP dial and hands with one faint hairline. You may buy the movement only—$600.00—and/or I have a near mint PP OF hinged 14K solid gold case for another $150.00. Very little is known about this watch at the present time. I have seen one other and it could have been this watch.

3609 MANHATTAN 18S. Mint gilded Mvt. 86,088 that looks exactly like the one on top of Page 185-2. Mint Fahys No. 1 YGF all-over decorated, extra thick case and dial made especially for this watch. Dial is flat, RBT. An excellent example of this early watch. Supposedly made only 9 years. $135.00

3610 AUBURNDALE 18S, 1/8TH JUMP SECOND TIMER. Looks exactly like 188-2. Completely all-original and running. Serial No. 2326. $350.00

3611 WALTHAM 12S 21J BRIDGE MODEL. Mint Mvt. 8,774,792. Beautiful hi-grade gold train, raised gold cups with American Watch Company written in script on the Mvt. Mint perfect DS OP dial. In a fine CWC Co. ET, no brass showing, case. $400.00
I have a brand new 14K ET Solidarity case that I would include for $110.00

3612 ILLINOIS WATCH COMPANY 18S COLUMBIA (6-53-2). Mint gilt Mvt. 461,746. Extra fine 4 oz. coin silver hinged case with gold hinges—some worn decoration but a very heavy and solid case. Mint SS Roman dial. $90.00

3613 ILLINOIS 16S 17J BUNN, OF. Mint Mvt. 3,330,094. YGF PP case in extra fine condition. Mint bold DS RR dial. $100.00

3614 WALTHAM 12S 19J RIVERSIDE. Mint Mvt. 23,064,187. Near mint DB hinged 14K solid YG Colonial case with "Waltham Watch Company" in a circle on the dust cover. Beautiful silver dial with raised gold numbers. $120.00
3615 SEARS ROEBUCK & CO. 16S 17J GRADE 174 (like 6-59-2) with "Sears Roebuck Company, Chicago, USA Special" on both the Mvt. and the mint DS HC dial. Case is silveroid. $100.00

3616 RAILROAD KING 18S 17J. Beautiful 2-tone cross-hatched damaskeened Mvt. 290,793. "Railroad King" in gilt lettering on the barrel bridge. Case is all-over decorated, near mint, hinged, OF. Dial is beautiful antique ART DS OP with original hands. This is a fine, very scarce watch for the railroad collector! $250.00

* *

ABBREVIATIONS

MOVEMENT	DIAL	CASE
16S= 16 Size, etc.	DS= Double Sunk	ET= Engine Turned
J= Jewels	SS= Single Sunk	SB&B= Snap back & bezel
Mvt.= Movement	TS= Triple Sunk	DB= Double back
OF= Open Face	IDS= Imitation Double Sunk	HB&B= Hinged back & bezel
LS= Lever Set	OP= Original Porcelain or glass	SRC= Swing ring cup
PS= Pendant Set	MRR= Montgomery Railroad	HC= Hunting case
KW= Keywind	RBT= Roman Black Track	OF= Open Face
KS= Keyset	RRT= Roman Red Track	PP= Plain polish or Bassine
DR= Double Roller	ART= Arabic Red Track	GBSBDC= Glass back snap bezel
P= Position (5P,etc.)	RR= Railroad	display case with stem/crown
		KYGF=Karat yellow gold filled
		KWGF= Karat white gold filled

The name TIFFANY AND CO. on any watch seems to make it more desirable to collectors. As you can see by this advertisement and the one on page 186 in Book 2, they offered a very large and varied line of both high and medium grade watches. A number of companies made watches for Tiffany and are now selling from around $100.00 for a small 12S gold Longines up to thousands of dollars for the top gold complicated watches. Any attempt here to value them would be meaningless. I would say—compare it to a similar watch in this book and then add some or ask someone you could trust.

TIFFANY WATCHES.

PATENT REGULATOR.

10, 12, 13, 14, 15 and 16 Lines, for Ladies.

17, 18, 19 & 20 Lines for Gentlemen.

1877 THE JEWELERS' CIRCULAR AND HOROLOGICAL REVIEW

PLAIN REGULATO

TIFFANY & CO.

MAKERS OF

Fine & Complicated Watches,

WORKS AT GENEVA, SWITZERLAND.

Office (Wholesale only),

No. 14 JOHN STREET, NEW YORK.

GEO. R. COLLIS, Manager.

Movements, after being cased, are submitted to severe adjustment tests in temperature and positions for at least 30 days, and when shipped from this office, guaranteed to be as fine timekeepers to carry as are made.

If desired, dealers can have their own names (with or without ours) engraved on the movements, which we furnish in cases of 18kt. gold, red or yellow, in from 3 to 30 days after receipt of order.

Repeaters ! Chronographs ! Split Seconds ! Quarter Seconds ! Fifth Seconds ! Calendars !

And all other styles of Complicated Watches in great variety.

☞ *An elegant assortment of Ladies' Watches, artistically cased in 18kt. gold, or movements cased to order.*

18 and 19 Line Patent Escapement, Bridge Movements, finely adjusted, especially for railroad use, in Open Face and Hunting Sterling Silver Case.

☞ *Also, General Agents for Messrs. PATEK, PHILLIPE & CO., Geneva, Switzerland, a full line of whose watches will always be found at our office.*

1884 ADVERTISMENT

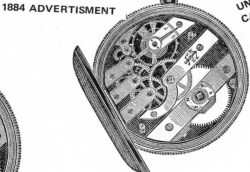

No. 20. Melville Lever, Key W. 15 Jewels. Sil. Case.

No. 30. Lever. Stem W. Nickeled. Full Jeweled. Nickel Case.

No. 25. Melville Lever, Key W. 15 Jewels. Sil. Case.

TRADE MARK. REGISTERED.
M.&S.
IN HOC SIGNO VINCES.

ESTABLISHED 1854.

HENRY MAY,

Wholesale Dealer in

WATCHES, DIAMONDS,

AND

JEWELRY,

No. 19 JOHN STREET,

P. O. Box 3685.   New York.

SEND FOR PRICE-LIST.

No. 35. Brighton. 8 Size, Nickeled. 15 Jewels. For Elg. Case.

No. 40. Melville, 8 Size, Gilded 15 Jewels. For Elg. Case.

No. 10. Melville Lever. Stem W. 15 Jewels. Sil. Case.

No. 15. Melville Lever. Stem W. 15 Jewels. Sil. Case.

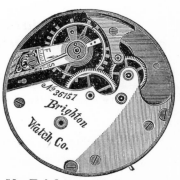

No. 45. Brighton, 18 Size, Key W. Nickel. 11 Jewels.

No. 50. Brighton. 18 Size. Stem W. Nickeled or Gilded. 15 Jewels. For Elg. Case.

164

No. 3.

No. 4

THE FEW EXAMPLES OF THESE WATCHES I HAVE SEEN ALL APPEARED TO BE HIGH GRADE.

NICOUD WATCHES,

STEM WINDING,—HUNTING AND OPEN FACE,

GENTS' AND LADIES' SIZES.

No. 5 A.

NICOUD & HOWARD,

SOLE IMPORTERS,

14 MAIDEN LANE,

P. O. BOX 2269.   NEW YORK.

No. 5 B

SMALL STEM-WINDERS A SPECIALTY.

☞ Prices sent upon application accompanied by business cards. ☜

No. 7.

No. 8.

LADY RACINE,
Open Back.

REGISTERED

1879
ADVERTISEMENT

RAILROAD REGULATOR.

LADY RACINE,
Open Face.

REGISTERED

CONTINENTAL.

CONTINENTAL.

LADY RACINE.

RAILROAD REGULATOR

J.G.

TRADE MARK
REGISTERED

LADY RACINE.

167

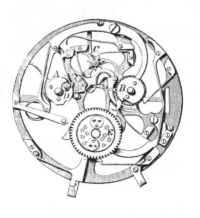
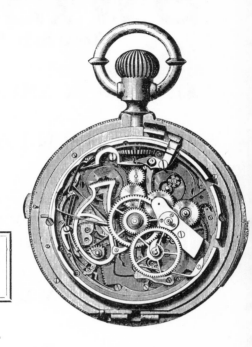
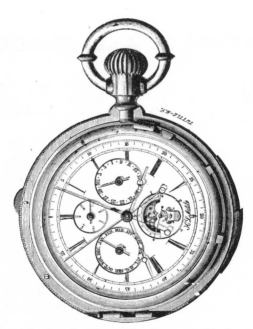

1884

LONGINES
THE LEADING LOW PRICED WATCH.

OPEN FACE
AND
HUNTING MOVEMENTS,

IN VARIOUS SIZES

In Nickel, Silver and Gold Cases.

WARRANTED.

Nickel, O. F. S. W., 20 lines.

FULL JEWELLED

WARRANTED.

Fits 18 Size S. W. Open Face and Hunting Cases. Exp. Balance, 15 Jewels.

AGASSIZ MOVEMENTS,

6, 8 & 16 SIZE S. W. MOVEMENTS

TO FIT OPEN FACE AND HUNTING AMERICAN CASES.

FINISHED IN THREE GRADES.

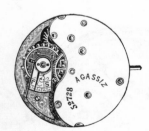

The First Quality, although of a medium price, is *adjusted to Heat, Cold and Positions.*

Fits 8 Size Cases.

Fits 16 Size Cases.

Observatory Certificates furnished when desired. These Movements have achieved a high reputation, which has induced unscrupulous parties to *imitate them.* The Trade is therefore cautioned against *spurious goods* made with intent to deceive. *Finished Watch Material and Duplicate Parts* for all Longines and Agassiz movements can be obtained from the Jobbers and Material Dealers throughout the country.

ASK FOR DETAILED MATERIAL CATALOGUE.
THE ABOVE GOODS FOR SALE BY THE LEADING JOBBERS.

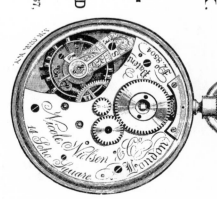

171

ADOLPH GOLDSMITH,

SOLE AGENT FOR THE

RELIANCE ✦ WATCH ✦ COMPANY,

38 MAIDEN LANE,   NEW YORK.

FULL LINE OF

Gold and Plated Jewelry.

EVERY DESCRIPTION OF

Swiss Watches

A SPECIALTY.

"RELIANCE,"
18 Size, to Fit Waltham Cases.

"RELIANCE,"
Nickel Stem Winder in all Sizes.

"RELIANCE,"
Ladies' 8 Size, to Fit Waltham Cases.

SALTZMAN & CO.,
Importers.

Fine Swiss Watches a Specialty.

SOLE IMPORTERS
OF THE

AUGUSTE SALTZMAN
V. VUILLAUME   **WATCHES.**
ALBERT VUILLE

Special Notice. { The Trade is respectfully notified to beware of imitations of the name of Saltzman, marked on Watches of an ferior grade, and purporting to be the genuine Saltzman.

GOODS SENT FOR SELECTION ON APPROVED REFERENCE.

Factory, Chaux de Fonds, Switzerland.   Salesroom, No. 15 MAIDEN LANE, New Yor

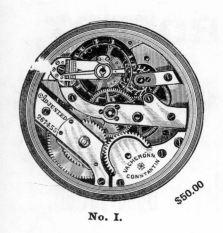

$50.00

No. I.

ESTABLISHED 1810.

1884 ADVERTISEMENT

$50.00

No. VIII.

WATCH MANUFACTORY

OF

VACHERON & CONSTANTIN,

GENEVA.

TRADE MARK.

VACHERON &
CONSTANTIN

TRADE MARK.

VACHERON &
CONSTANTIN

All these Celebrated Movements are made interchangeable, and to fit 14 and 18 Size Waltham and 16, 18 and 6 Size Elgin Cases.

Also a Complete Assortment of Ladies' 12, 13 and 14 line Open Face and Hunting Watches.

Chronographs, Split Seconds, Minute and Five Minute Repeaters, in stock and made to order.

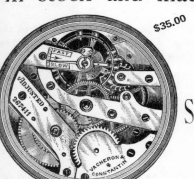

$35.00

No. IX.

$35.00

CHAS. LEO ABRY,

Sole Agent for United States and Canada,

63 Nassau St., New York.

P. O. Box 611.

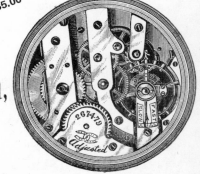

HORSE SHOE.

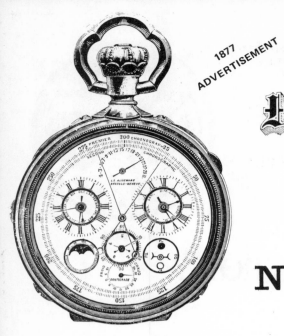

J. EUGENE ROBERT,

Importer of Watches

—AND—

Watch Movements of Every Description,

No. 30 Maiden Lane, New York

Would respectfully direct the attention of the Trade to LOUIS AUDEMARS' CELEBRATED WATCHES, universally acknowledged to be the FINEST FINISHED, and the most perfect time-keeper made. The manufacturer has achieved a world-wide reputation for the excellence of his watches, and for which he has received numerous gold medals from the prominent Expositions of the world.

The above wood cut represents the prize watch, now at the Paris Exposition—*a marvel of horology.* It is a clock striking watch: striking hours and quarters in passing, minute repeating at will, double chronograph, acting independently, double time, perpetual calendar, showing the phases of the moon, metalic thermometer, lever escapement, cylindrical hairspring, compensated to temperature and positions, 45 ruby jewels, triple stem-winder and double hair setting attachment.

☞ In addition to the above we have a full line of the most desirable mercantile Watches to be found anywhere

---

MATHEY BROS., MATHEZ & CO.

WATCHES DEMAGNETIZED.

BRASSUS, SWITZERLAND.
21 AND 23 MAIDEN LANE, NEW YORK.

WATCHES OF PRECISION.

MANUFACTURERS AND
IMPORTERS OF

PLAIN AND COMPLI-CATED WATCHES

American Sizes.	Swiss Sizes.
16 Size.	18 Lignes.
12 "	17 "
0 "	10 "
	8 "

10 SIZE SPLITS.

12 SIZE MOVEMENTS.

SPLITS AND REPEATERS

A SPECIALTY.

SOLE AGENTS FOR
CHAS. H. MEYLAN.

FINE ENAMELED
AND JEWELED
WATCHES.

AGENTS FOR THE
NEW OMEGA WATCH.

SOLE AGENTS FOR THE CELEBRATED LE COULTRE RAZORS.

Waltham Dial Co.

Waltham, Mass.

ANYTHING IN

DIALS

DANIEL O'HARA.

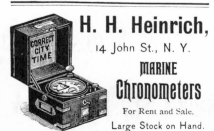

H. H. Heinrich,

14 John St., N. Y.

MARINE Chronometers

For Rent and Sale.
Large Stock on Hand.
Springing, Readjusting and Repairing for the Trade

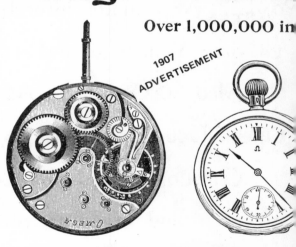

Omega Watch

Over 1,000,000 in

The "Omega" are pendant-set, fit 0 and 16 size Waltham cases, and are made in 5 different grades as follows:

7 Jewels, Expansion Balance, Double Roller, Nickelized.
15 Jewels, Expansion Balance, Double Roller, Nickelized.
15 Jewels, Expansion Balance, Double Roller, Nickel, Pat. R
17 Jewels, Expansion Balance, Double Roller, Nickel, Pat. adjusted.
17 Jewels, Expansion Balance, Double Roller, Nickel, adjust 5 positions.

WARRANTED FINE TIMEPIECES.

ALL PARTS INTERCHANGEABL

Above made to order with dealer's name if des